FRENCH NOVELISTS
From the Revolution to Proust

FRENCH NOVELISTS

From the Revolution to Proust

FREDERICK C. GREEN

Professor Emeritus of French Literature
University of Edinburgh

FREDERICK UNGAR PUBLISHING CO.
NEW YORK

Republished 1964
with some changes by the author

By arrangement with J. M. Dent & Sons Ltd.

First published 1931

Printed in the United States of America

Library of Congress Catalog Card No. 64-21611

FOREWORD

In the following critical account of the growth of the French novel from the Revolution to the present day I have tried not to make my history too selective. An age peopled solely by Balzacs, Stendhals, and Flauberts would be magnificent but incredible: somehow the presence of a Ducray-Duminil, a D'Arlincourt, or a Champfleury humanizes the situation, and bridges the gulf between legend and historical fact. My aim, then, is a twofold one. It is, on the one hand, to discover anew why the great masters are a source of such perennial delight; on the other, to explain the extraordinary vogue enjoyed by writers whose works now moulder dustily in the Bibliothèque Nationale.

There are many omissions in this study. Of that I am very sensible, but those who are familiar with the vast output of fiction in the period will understand why. In a study devoted to tendencies it is impossible to linger too long over individual works or authors without compromising the unity of the general scheme, the purpose of which is to trace the evolution of that most active and living organism—the French novel.

I gladly seize this opportunity to thank the American Council of Learned Societies for financial help in amassing material for the present work. My gratitude to the Council is enhanced by the fact that its generosity has been extended to one who is not an American citizen.

F. C. G.

1931.

CONTENTS

CHAPTER I

REVOLUTIONARY FICTION

SUCH a mass of writings has crystallised round the French Revolution that a sort of cabbalistic quality is associated in our minds with the date 1789. It has become a commonplace with historians to regard this year as the end of an old order of things and the beginning of a new. Writers of every political colour, though of course from different motives, share the opinion that 1789 marks the dawn of a new era in the political, social and literary life of France. Few indeed will dispute that in politics and in the social order the Revolution introduced sweeping changes. It would be impossible, for instance, to point to a more striking contrast than that offered by the government of the old regime and the *Convention* of 1792. In society, too, a complete upheaval took place when the proletariat usurped the position formerly held by the nobility and higher bourgeoisie, though it cannot be said that a corresponding transformation was effected in political and public morals, since the moral tone of the new governing classes was even lower than that of their predecessors. Corruption, gambling, prostitution, speculation, in short all the vices which had characterised the social life of the old regime, flourished with unabated vigour under the Revolution.

When we consider the influence of the Revolution upon literature, the situation is more complex. What strikes one most forcibly is the miserable quality of imaginative writing during the whole Revolutionary period, i.e. from 1789 to 1800. One peers in vain through the reek of gunpowder for a glimpse of those sunlit fields once strewn with the petals of careless Fancy; or of those classic groves once haunted by brooding Thought and white-lipped Tragedy. Did the clank of the guillotine, one wonders, drown the sweet, pleading accents of a Manon Lescaut? Was the passionate, tortured voice of another Phèdre lost in the hoarse bellowings of the beast-like mob? Only one form of literature, and that a bastard one, flourishes in the political eloquence of Citizens Danton, Saint-Just and Robespierre, those convincing and spirited ambassadors of the goddess of Reason. The steady exodus of *émigrés* continues, leaving behind it magnificent libraries to supply pipe-spills and butter wrappers for the *sans-culottes*, for what is the use of books now to gentlemen engaged in the more serious business of keeping a steady head upon their shoulders? The *salons*, and this is a point emphasised by all French historians of literature, the *salons*, nurseries of wit and learning in which so many of the great *literati* of the old regime received their baptism of fame, are one by one shut up and deserted. "The Revolution," says M. Lanson, "closed the *salons*. By suspending fashionable life for ten or twelve years it withdrew literature from the conventions of thought and the elegancies of diction imposed by the latter." In other words, and he but echoes the general view, the Revolution checked the normal evolution of literature, an interesting if disturbing suggestion which must be as gratifying to the politician as it is intolerable to the man of letters. Apparently, then, the only salvation for art and literature lies with the supporters of the new regime, but they, it seems, are so engrossed with their guillotine, their speeches and their pillage as to have no time to devote to the futile pleasures of the imagination. The printing-presses are busy vomiting forth streams of political pamphlets and newspapers. What room is there for trumpery productions like poems and plays and novels?

This general picture of literary conditions at the Revolution is impressive, but it would be unwise to accept it *en bloc* without subjecting the details to closer scrutiny. As usual, we speedily discover that we are confronted by one of those half-truths which emerge from careless generalisation to stick like burrs to the skirts of history. As our business here is with the destinies of only one branch of literature, the novel, it will be enough to examine the influence of the Revolution on that genre, though most of the following observations are equally applicable to drama.

During the thirty years preceding 1789 the French novel lapsed into a state of exhaustion. Its two great mines of inspiration, the ideal and the real, jealously guarded their treasures against the feeble scratchings of mediocrity, ready, however, at any moment to surrender them to the masterful onslaught of genius. Rousseau's brilliant and suggestive *Nouvelle Héloïse* initiated a period of fumbling and groping. Novelists found their view of life obscured by a mist of nebulous and Utopian ideas on morality, politics and religion, or else, in the rare cases where they contrived to escape from this clinging and mephitic atmosphere, they saw humanity through the distorting glass of a cold and cynical egotism. To the majority man appeared as a creature naturally good, but in whom contact with society had poisoned the wells of sensibility. Such novelists, therefore, yearned and slobbered over him in turn, weeping over his misfortunes, exalting his altruism, singing pæans in praise of an impossible Platonic relationship between the sexes and, in the main, presenting a picture of French *mœurs* which is ludicrously untrue if applied to society as a whole, but faithfully portrays the spiritual leanings of that minority of sensitive souls who sought a refuge from chill reality in such perverted idealism. In thirty years this school produced only one work of artistic merit, Bernardin de Saint-Pierre's *Paul et Virginie*, and that has survived, not because of the exaggerated sentimentality which endeared it to the public of 1787, but because of its realistic and beautiful picture of exotic nature and because of its admirable sincerity. There were other novelists, descendants of the *libertins* of the bad old days of the Regency, who regarded mankind as an amusing colony of warring organisms, each bent on procuring the maximum of material pleasure at the expense of his neighbour. Their disillusioned realism reached its climax in Laclos's *Liaisons dangereuses*, which offers as false an interpretation of life as *Paul et Virginie*, and launched the novel on an incline that carried it swiftly and fatally to the horrible productions of the novelist who gave his name to a new vice, the infamous marquis de Sade, one of the "victims" who would doubtless have been rescued from the Bastille on the glorious fourteenth of July had he not been transferred to the madhouse at Charenton. Rétif de la Bretonne, the only novelist whose work even suggests that rhythmic balance of the ideal and the real which is the hall-mark of the classic novel, was a sex-ridden maniac who exhausted himself in a vain effort to follow the hundred Utopian will-o'-the-wisps that flashed backwards and forwards across his imagination. He is a good example of the truism that a hair's breadth separates madness from genius, but he lacked the "little more" that might have made him a Balzac.

There was, then, no particular reason why the fall of the Bastille should have suddenly produced a renascence in the novel. Nor can we consider the Revolution responsible for its temporary eclipse. In one sense, of course, it is true that the Revolution led to the decay of fiction, yet it was not the political disturbance of 1789 but the moral and intellectual revolution of the whole preceding century, the so-called *philosophie* of Voltaire and of Rousseau, which checked the natural development of this genre, the object of which is to interpret life as it is and not to picture it as it ought to be lived. In 1789, then, the novel was in a sorry pass. Is it true, as some maintain, that the events of the Revolution rendered its situation still more hopeless? Or on the other hand was not some struggling young genius now presented with a Heaven-sent opportunity for astonishing the world with a masterpiece of fiction?

The closing of the *salons* could have little influence on the development of the novel. The majority of the novelists who were writing prior to 1789 had never set foot in a *salon*, and the fact that they had written novels would certainly not have entitled them to do so. The habitués of the famous *salons* of the last half of the eighteenth century, the people who met at D'Holbach's, Necker's or at Mme Geoffrin's, would have considered it a waste of time to discuss novels. Rousseau's *Nouvelle Héloïse* is an exception, but Rousseau was a notorious character and had already achieved a reputation by his other works. Novelists well known to the general reader of the age of Louis XVI. continued to write during the Revolution, unperturbed by the disappearance of the *salons*. That insufferable blue-stocking, Mme de Genlis, who escaped the guillotine, went on spinning her wearisome yarns, the popularity of which is one of the gravest indictments of the intelligence of the French nation. That idol of the scullery-wench, Ducray-Duménil, followed up his *Alexis* (1788) with his four-volume *Victor ou l'Enfant de la Forêt* (1796), in which by a veritable *tour de force* he manages to compress the worst features of every French novelist who preceded him. To make matters worse he invents for his incidents a nightmarish German setting—Ducray-Duménil, whose knowledge of Anglo-German fiction can be gauged by the following introduction to Volume III. of *Victor*: "O you! Celebrated German and English novelists! Eloquent songsters of the passions: Werther, Goéther, Schiller . . ." Here, I think, one may leave this French apostle of those great and influential German novelists, Herren Werther und Goéther, to the indefatigable researchers in comparative literature who are ever on the watch for new evidence of Franco-German literary interaction.

In 1790 Bernardin de Saint-Pierre published his *Chaumière indienne*, a poor work from the artistic point of view, but interesting because it reflects the social obsessions of the time. It harps on the familiar theme of inequality, attempts to reconcile Revolutionary ideals with orthodox Christianity and to combat the teachings of philosophers like Condillac, who trace all conduct to sensation. Rétif de la Bretonne in his *Nuits de Paris* (1788–94), as if unaffected by current events, continued to portray the various classes of society, interspersing his really interesting observations on life with his queer Utopian dreams and his shameless and revolting sexual reminiscences. Louvet de Coudray, the author of that most popular and licentious work, *Les Aventures du Chevalier de Faublas*, had already published several parts of it before 1789. He produced the remainder under the *Constituante*, making no attempt to change the tenor of the novel. It is not easy, unfortunately, to obtain details of the novels which charmed the leisure of the public during the Terror, for, though owing to the removal of the censorship there was a plethora of periodicals, nearly all of these journals confine their attention wholly to politics. It is clear, however, from a journal called *La Décade philosophique* that, if anything, the number of French novels has decreased, though translations of English authors, already much in demand before 1789, were still eagerly sought after because of the democratic sentiments which they expressed. In a laudatory review of Charlotte Smith's *Célestine* (1794) we find an interesting exposé of the reasons for which good *sans-culottes* should read novels in preference even to histories. The author prudently warns his reader that he is speaking of novels of merit and not the *ci-devant* lucubrations turned out for the *classe nobiliaire*, novels which did not analyse the passions but wasted their readers' time with ludicrous descriptions of society. Comparing fiction with history he writes: "A novel is more within the scope of us common people and it is also bound to interest us more. In it we discover our own hearts, our passions, our very selves. Everyday morality is shown in action; the novelist reveals to us our maladies and indicates the remedies." Robert Bage, the delightfully sardonic author of *Barham Downs* and the *Fair Syrian*, had many French admirers, who found in him all the attractions of Richardson flavoured with an original and astringent humour; exciting and harrowing tales of virtuous females seduced and persecuted by lords, who, one is sorry to say, were abetted by clerical gentlemen. *Caleb Williams* by William Godwin was immediately translated into French and, as might have been expected, Godwin's bold and subversive doctrines, which were those of the founders of the Revolution, woven into the fabric of a pathetic tale of virtue persecuted by aristocratic tyranny, endeared him to the readers of the *Décade philosophique*, which gravely opined that *Caleb Williams* should be placed in the hands of all administrators and judges. It is interesting to observe the change in the opinion of this paper with the establishment of the *Directoire*, for, commenting on Mrs. Inchbald's *Nature and Art* (1796), the reviewer inserts a note of warning. The moving narrative of the misfortunes of Agnes, seduced and afterwards sentenced to death by her judge and erstwhile lover, William, was, of course, too savoury a morsel not to appeal to the public appetite for melodrama. Mrs. Inchbald's reflections on society, however, were too communistic for the taste of the *Décade*, which considered her attacks on the vices of the rich somewhat overdrawn, whilst her observations on the inequality of fortunes really alarmed the reviewer. "The consequences of these declamations," he said, "might lead far, as we have already learned in France by the excesses of our extravagant levellers."

Though the number of purely French novels published during the Revolution was small, one cannot really attribute this decline to political unrest. It would be natural to assume, no doubt, that the public was so obsessed by current events as to have no time for imaginative literature, were it not for the fact that, as we have seen, foreign novels were much in demand. *Tom Jones* was reprinted in 1796; *Robinson Crusoe* in 1797; the *Vicar of Wakefield* was translated in 1797 and again in

1799; while Sterne's *Sentimental Journey* reappeared in 1799. Again, from 1790 to 1793 over thirty new theatres were opened in Paris alone. It is true that in most of these the repertoire consisted largely of plays written to stimulate the patriotic zeal of the audience. It is, however, remarkable that this period did not give rise to a similar flood of popular works in fiction, yet if we except the novels of Pigault-Lebrun, whose *Enfant du Carnaval* (1792) and picaresque *Barons de Felsheim* (1798) are joyous, coarse novels of adventure in the manner of Smollett and therefore not revolutionary in colour, there are no novels which echo the spirit of the stage at this time. It was not until 1797 that the French nation discovered a type of novel exactly suited to its taste, and this, as we shall see, was again to come from England.

That native novelists were becoming more active in 1795 is evident from the following comment in the *Décade*: "The Revolution has not been disastrous to novels. New ones are appearing every day, certain proof that they still find a great number of readers. It seems that in the midst of political troubles the mind needs more than ever to occupy itself with chimeras, to get outside itself and to wander in another universe." The final words are prophetic, for they indicate precisely the type of novel now destined to enjoy a startling vogue, the *roman noir*, introduced by "Monk" Lewis and Ann Radcliffe, a species of fiction as divorced from reality as it could well be and picturing indeed "another universe."

Ann Radcliffe's *Mysteries of Udolpho*, her *Italian*

and Lewis's *The Monk* were first known to the French through translations in 1797. Their effect was electric. The public feverishly absorbed these tales of mysterious, lonely castles perched on beetling, romantic cliffs. It thrilled deliciously at the descriptions of convents haunted by bleeding nuns, of subterranean passages shadowy with horror, and, with starting eyes, devoured the recital of the crimes of Ambrosio, the diabolic monk who sells his soul to the Evil One. Ann Radcliffe, unlike Lewis, usually provided a rational explanation for her exciting and improbable situations, but Lewis was not the man to pander to such miserable weakness. Amidst lightning flashes and dreadful thunderclaps his hero, shrieking horribly, is borne aloft by Satan only to be dashed remorselessly hundreds of feet below on to the jagged rocks. The *roman noir*, as it was christened, found many imitators in France. M. Lebreton, in his excellent *Balzac*, explains this mania for the melodramatic and supernatural novel as follows: "The national stock of imagination was, even at its maddest, no longer sufficient for the needs of a generation emerging from the Revolutionary torment and one which had grown up to the sound of the tocsin and the cannon under the perpetual menace of death. In the way of emotions it had the right to be blasé and to show itself exacting; it had to have super atrocities." This is very logical, and it would be a most satisfactory explanation if it showed why the English who had not been brought up to the tolling of the tocsin had already evinced the same curious taste in fiction, nay, had initiated the vogue. The

Décade reviewer is nearer the truth in his diagnosis of the contemporary state of mind: the public wanted to escape from drab reality into the realms of the imagination. But the spiritual lassitude of 1797 was but the aggravation of a similar psychological condition which we find prior to the Revolution. It was, indeed, the very spirit which sought a desperate remedy for its anguish in the political excesses of 1789. The public of the old regime found a temporary outlet for its vague idealistic longings in the sentimental vapourings of Rousseau's imitators: the public of 1797, which was a more popular one, required images of a more vivid and tangible sort to satisfy its emotions. All through the eighteenth century there had been readers for highly coloured and melodramatic novels. Prévost's abound in gloomy situations, rooms draped in black, coffins, mysterious burials at dead of night and meetings in underground passages. That very popular novelist, the chevalier de Mouhy, catered to the same taste for the *macabre* in his *Mémoires du comte de D. B.* (1735), and before the vogue of Radcliffe hundreds devoured Ducray-Duménil's *Victor* and gloated over the adventures of the mad nuns in the vaults of the convent. The interest in Young's *Night Thoughts*, in *Ossian* and in the gloomier plays of Shakespeare, so clearly reflected in French literature from 1760 to 1789, all point to that forthcoming revolution in literary taste which is called Romanticism. The political and social upheaval of the fourteenth of July cast off the shackles which, so to speak, fettered the nation's body, but its spiritual enfranchisement was necessarily a slower process. The imagination of the French novelist was starved and had been for many a long year, but then so was the imagination of novelists all over Europe. The first stirrings, the first definite promise of a new and more vigorous literature, came from the northern countries, and the vogue for the romantic *roman noir* was but one of the flashes that announced the coming storm.

There is another reason why the Radcliffian school of novelists appealed so strongly to the French public of the *Directoire*. Whilst to Protestants of a certain class the convent has always been associated with something infernal, mysterious, and sinister, the French, on the other hand, until about the middle of the eighteenth century, were disposed on the whole to regard conventual life as a subject for bawdy and Rabelaisian jesting. The *philosophes*, of course, encouraged this tendency, but gradually enunciated another and more serious point of view. Working on the theme of the enforced profession, they spread harrowing tales of young girls browbeaten into taking the veil and undergoing unnamable tortures in the underground cells of these secret and mysterious institutions. Except for the fact that Diderot was too much of a rationalist to resort to the miraculous even in fiction, the picture which he unfolds in his *Religieuse* contains sinister elements that remind one most forcibly of the atmosphere enveloping the terrifying *romans noirs*. His novel, though it circulated in manuscript in 1760, was not published until 1796, but it reflects the popular beliefs of the last forty years of the eighteenth century. It was the same spirit of hatred for oppression and persecution which ensured the success of *Clarissa Harlowe* with the French of the seventeen-sixties, and naturally enough the public of the Revolution was saturated with the same hysteria.

Yet literary tradition dies hard, and there were many who remembered Boileau's contemptuous remarks about the use of the supernatural in literature:

> Une merveille absurde est pour moi sans appas;
> L'esprit n'est point ému de ce qu'il ne croit pas.

The *Journal des Arts* for 1798 identified itself with those "men of taste, moralists and politicians" who attacked the new novels of the "Monk" school, and cries imploringly: "No more devils, spectres, ghosts or brigands!" The *Décade* for 1798, welcoming with unfeigned relief Mrs. Bennett's pathetic *Rosa, or the Beggar Girl*, pointed out that the prevailing French conception of the English manner in fiction was quite erroneous. It reminded its subscribers that the Radcliffian novels, whose chief characteristics are the sombre and the horrible, were not typical English novels. To discover the *manière anglaise* one must go back to Fielding, Goldsmith, Swift and Sterne. What constitutes the true English style, it said, is "a great variety of tones, things, circumstances, verdicts and characters. It is a very happy combination, when governed by good taste, of the pathetic and the comic; of pictures of nature and of society; of the descriptive and the dramatic. It consists in a very marked intention, in a minute and often scrupulous effort to present moral and physical truths." It is different from that of the typical French novel, which is much simpler and where the writer takes up less space and has a much more limited scope. "All the affections of the soul have found their historians with us," continues the *Décade*, "but we are less apt to assemble them in one and the same composition and we touch upon fewer at one time. We subordinate them all more to love, to which, in our manner, we relate everything. It absorbs everything else." All sorts of ideas enter into the cadre of the English novel, but French novels, though more polished, are merely good novels, whereas the English ones are nearly always good books.

Many other French critics warned their compatriots against the *romans qui font peur*, and pointed the way to sanity and better art. At the beginning of the Consulate, indeed, there were indications that the novel of horror was losing ground, but, as we shall see, this was but a temporary eclipse. The *Décade* notes with satisfaction a falling-off in the number of translations of English novels, but says that the Radcliffian novel has left its mark on the style of French novelists, whose predilection for "descriptions of the sun and moon, for romantic sites and *romanesque* episodes shows all too plainly that they have naturalised what the French call *le spleen anglais*."

A counter-current was now evident which later merged with the stream of *romans noirs*. I refer to the historical novel, examples of which were now beginning to filter into France from Germany. Just before the Revolution the French themselves, who, of course, had always cultivated the love novel with an historical though conventional setting, had begun to evolve a species of fiction in which there was an obvious attempt to reconstruct the picture of manners of the Middle Ages. As early as 1765 De Sauvigny published his *Histoire amoureuse de Pierre le Long et de Blanche Bazu*, in which he tried to reproduce not only the manners but the idiom of medieval times. De Meyer, that enthusiast whose cult for the olden days was such that he urged a revival of jousts and tourneys, was one of many idealists for whom the past was an era of simplicity and goodness. He tried, like De Sauvigny, to recapture the spirit of the Middle Ages in his *Geneviève de Cornouailles* (1784) and in his *Amours de Bayard* (1787), but his picture of manners was pitifully inadequate and, moreover, it was submerged in a flood of nostalgic and sentimental twaddle. Exactly the same defects were reproduced by his successors of 1800, who, as the *Décade* cruelly expressed it, wrote novels "which really resemble nothing at all. Sometimes they make their imaginary heroes travel amongst peoples who do not exist; or else they depict manners which have no relationship to those of the places they describe, or again they exaggerate to an emphatic degree and fall into the trivial and commonplace instead of remaining simple and naïve."

One of the most vigorous opponents of the *roman noir*, Belin de la Liborlière, was an historical novelist. Belin in 1799 wrote an amusing skit on the English "diabolical" novel which was much appreciated by the *Décade*. The hero, M. Dabaud, is a fanatical admirer of the *Monk*, the *Italian* and the *Mysteries of Udolpho*, so his friends, to cure him of this unholy passion, carry him, drugged, to an old abbey which has been fitted up in the approved Radcliffe manner. Here the poor wretch is forced to witness all the horrors of a *dénouement à la Monk Lewis*; spectres, clanking chains, dragging bodies and skeletons emerging from coffins. As a climax the devil appears in person and compels the now gibbering Dabaud to sign a pact that in future he will mend his ways and read no English novels save those of Richardson, Fielding, and—only a devil would have thought of this torture—Mrs. Bennett!

Having, as he thought, disposed of the *roman noir*, Belin published his *Anne Grenvill* (1800), which he no doubt confidently imagined would herald a new era in fiction. In this absurd work nothing is interesting except the preface, where Belin exposes his theory of the historical novel. "What is the use," he asks, "of racking your brains to invent interesting situations when history offers a thousand events full of interest? . . . But it is easier to caricature what is going on round about us than to trace faithfully the manners and usages of a distant century; to let the imagination wander at will over the vast field that we create for it than to enclose it within the severe limits of dates and of real distances." (It is easier) "to accumulate at will circumstances that can be manipulated without our having to render an account to the reader than to restrict ourselves exactly to the course of events whose place is fixed by the pen of the historian; to draw characters to which we are free to add whatever shades and tints we choose than to reproduce those celebrated men to whom we may lend no other virtues and vices than those they actually possess." The great advantage of the historical novel, according to Belin, is that the lover of history will no longer have to delve amongst dusty archives for facts concerning his heroes. "He will have the joy of reading what they have done cleverly interwoven with what they might have said or done. He will experience a real pleasure at seeing a clever and thorough analysis of character which the historian for reasons of brevity could only roughly outline; he will feel a sort of gratitude towards the author when he sees the latter impute to the events dryly consecrated by tradition, causes and effects which he knows are not true but which appear possible and probable." All this is very illuminating because it reveals, I think, the inherent defect of so many French historical novels which were about to appear. This kind of tale, if Belin's method were followed, was bound to become, not a novel at all, but a sort of elaborate biographical and historical study in the manner of M. Maurois and his school, but not of course so vivid or so convincing, since at this stage the psycho-analytic method of interpreting character was unknown. Belin's geometric system effectively laces up the novelist in a strait-waistcoat of fact and prescribes definite limits to the flight of his imagination, whilst in all good historical novels the writer, in his characterisation, gives fact as wide a berth as possible since, being a novelist, he is primarily concerned not with facts but with probabilities. Belin's error lay in the illusion that well-known historical characters can easily be transformed into powerful novel heroes, whereas in reality nothing is more difficult, because the average reader knows so much about them that he violently resents any attempt to tamper with his conception of these historical figures. That is why all the great historical novelists either concentrate upon little-known characters, or when they introduce Cromwells, Napoleons or Richelieus, relegate them to a secondary rôle. For the same reason, too, when they do put great men in the limelight they select them from a period in history remote from the reader and therefore so unfamiliar to him as to allow full play to the author's imagination.

At this stage circumstances were not favourable to the development of the historical novel. This was not, as one might be tempted to think, because of the unpopularity of the old regime, since amongst the inferior historical tales which appeared from 1800 to the Restoration we find novels dealing with every century in French history. Millevoye, the poet, in his *Satire des Romans du Jour* (1804), does not in the least exaggerate in his description of such fictions:

> Plus funestes encor, des écrits méprisables,
> Bizarre accouplement de l'histoire et des fables,
> Portant à l'avenir des traits défigurés,
> Flétrissant sans pudeur les noms les plus sacrés;
> Plus de freins, plus de lois: leurs lignes mensongères
> Dénaturent les lieux, les temps, les caractères,
> Cachent la vérité sous de vains ornements,
> Des âges confondus tronquent les monuments

Et du siècle écoulé compromettent la gloire. . . .
Eh! n'est-ce point assez des fautes de l'histoire
Sans que d'autres romans, avec impunité
Aillent mentir pour elle à la postérité?

Though the historical novel dealing with the Revolution was not to become popular until 1812 a few colourless works like the *Amants vendéens* by Gosse (1801), the *Petits Émigrés* (1795) by Mme de Genlis and Mme Toulongeon's *Lettres de la Vendée* (1801) revealed a fumbling appreciation of the dramatic possibilities of this theme. The real reason for the inferiority of the historical novel in the early years of the new century was, however, that no genius, no Walter Scott, had yet appeared to reveal the riches hidden in this new lode. Meanwhile, too, the novel was developing with great vigour in another direction.

CHAPTER II

THE INDIVIDUAL AND SOCIETY

THE real French Revolution was not that reshuffling of classes which followed the events of 1789, but the great moral change preceding it. The triumph of the intellectuals of the eighteenth century was the victory won by rationalism over religion and the substitution of a lay morality, based on the so-called natural laws, for the orthodox morality of the Church which claimed to interpret the divine will. And this new rationalistic outlook was shared by many who detested Voltaire and the Encyclopædists, by people who preferred to work out their own moral problems without any help from their confessors, by men who would rather order their conduct by the light of their own reason or, as they called it, by their common sense without having resource to cut and dry formulæ. A morality of this kind was bound to become a purely social morality. We find it reflected thus in nearly all the novels of the latter half of the eighteenth century, which are intensely preoccupied with the problem of the individual and his relation toward society. The theme was destined then to become a fruitful one for writers of fiction, and when the old clear-cut class boundaries began to disappear the question of what individual conduct should be in certain circumstances acquired a fresh and vital interest.

It was precisely because this new spirit was abroad that Rousseau's *Nouvelle Héloïse* aroused so much discussion. His bold and suggestive treatment of the theme eventually produced, as we shall see, an important school of novelists who subordinated society absolutely to the individual. But Jean-Jacques, it will be remembered, flinched before that issue and gave his novel an orthodox "moral" ending, whereby the fallen woman was gloriously rehabilitated, and indeed emerged as a pattern of all the virtues. This dénouement, however, attracted the censure of the Church and its lay adherents, who considered it immoral that a woman who had broken two of the Ten Commandments should be allowed to die in a strong odour of sanctity. Others, perhaps the majority, failed to see why a woman who had broken a social law should appear as the incarnation of all the social virtues. These lay moralists cared not a straw for the personal and spiritual aspect of Julie's lapse, but Rousseau's attitude seemed to them socially dangerous, for it attacked one of the foundations of society—the family. Such was the point of view of rationalists like Diderot and D'Holbach, for whom morality consisted, indeed, in the satisfaction of individual desires, but only to the point where this can be done without disturbing the social organism. Rousseau had, however, hundreds of admirers who were so blinded by the poetry and the idealism of his pictures of domesticity as to ignore the moral question raised by Julie's lapse. It was enough for them that Julie should figure as the priestess of the new religion of sensibility, for that in their eyes was the great spiritual force governing human relationships. Rationalists and sentimentalists alike dreamed of a society based on the angelic principles of perfect friendship, charity, tolerance, and humanity. After the Revolution, France with her new-born liberty, her equality and above all her fraternity was to light the avenue leading to a universal brotherhood of man. Such were the ideas which at the close of the eighteenth century found eloquent expression in every form of art and particularly in the novel. It is not strange then that novelists tended more and more to lose all touch with life's realities, for, as we have observed, it was this spirit which temporarily paralysed fiction. Still, there were several writers, even in the ranks of the *âmes sensibles*, who were unconsciously impelled to examine the new social doctrine of altruism in its actual relationship to the individual, and it is this common curiosity which, I think, links together writers otherwise so very dissimilar as Mme de Souza, Mme Cottin, Mme de Krüdener, Mme de Staël and Mme de Duras.

These ladies have other traits in common. You will search in vain in their novels for a vivid picture of the social conditions and exciting events of the Revolution, and, after all, that is but normal. How could they write of horrors so recent as to be fresh in the minds of all; of experiences so ghastly in their monotonous repetition as to be devoid of all savour of romance to those who were trying to forget them? What does surprise one at first is, that though nearly all these writers resided abroad during some part of the revolutionary period, there is little in their novels, if we except Mme de Staël's, to show that they were greatly influenced by foreign literature or ideas. This is very typical of the eighteenth-century spirit, for despite the great curiosity of the age of Louis XVI. regarding foreign *mœurs*, this interest was essentially of a literary sort. There was a stereotyped and legendary England, which was as much a literary tradition as the legendary Mauritius of *Paul et Virginie*; and besides, is not the result of travel usually to confirm ancient prejudices rather then to correct them? So we find in these novels, as indeed in most of the writings of the *émigrés*, a bland indifference to the reality of experience and a quiet refusal to break with tradition.

Mme de Souza, whose first husband, M. de Flahaut, was guillotined in a gallant effort to save a friend, escaped to England and afterwards lived in Switzerland and North Germany. Yet in her novel, *Adèle de Sénange*, there is no echo of her terrible experiences. Here we have the spirit of all that was good in the education of the old regime, where it was considered almost indecent to make the public the confidant of one's intimate emotions. Even that intelligent ferret, Sainte-Beuve, nuzzles in vain amongst the literary remains of Mme de Souza for personal revelations. *Adèle de Sénange* might have been written in 1770, for though the hero, Lord Sydenham, is an Englishman, he has in reality no nationality; he is simply an *honnête homme* who falls in love with Adèle, the wife of the elderly M. de Sénange and is too much a man of honour to disturb the peace of one who has befriended him. Mme de Souza describes her own manner admirably in these words: "I want to show in life something that no one ever looks at, and to describe the ordinary emotions which make up the history of our everyday existence . . . the fugitive details that fill the gaps between the big events of life." So there are no *cris de cœur*, no passionate conflicts "nothing to moan or knock the breast," no lyrical descriptions of nature, only a quiet tale, gently told, of a wise old man who knows that his wife is unconsciously in love with a young man for whom he, Sénange, has a paternal affection. The charm of *Adèle de Sénange* lies in what the author suggests but does not tell. Few novelists have this elusive trick of creating atmosphere by the suppression of the obvious, and above all by artistic selectiveness in expression. The note of the novel is restraint, and in the characterisation of Sénange this restraint acquires the beauty of stoic dignity, for though painfully aware of Adèle's unconscious preference for Sydenham, the old man suffers but does not revolt. It would be interesting, by the way, to trace the evolution of the husband in French fiction from the jealous and ludicrous old men of the seventeenth-century *romans comiques* to the type portrayed by Mme de Souza, who tacitly accepts the institution called *un mariage de raison* with all its possible dangers, and shows how these dangers may be overcome by the exercise of common sense and by the cultivation of true sensibility. When she explains that Sénange married Adèle to take her from the convent, it would be wrong to conclude that Mme de Souza is indulging in insidious anti-clerical propaganda. On the contrary, Adèle's happiest years were spent in this institution, but Sénange realised that she was not temperamentally suited to the vocation towards which she was drifting, since she is an eminently social type.

It is hard to see why Sainte-Beuve, and, more recently, Professor Baldensperger, talk of the influence of Fanny Burney on Mme de Souza, unless it be that in *Charles et Marie* (1802) she attempts to lend the atmosphere of an English country-house to a very sentimental and tenuous love story about a Cinderella daughter, a blue-stocking sister, a despotic father and a patient invalid mother. There is absolutely no comparison between the boisterous raciness of Fanny Burney and the quiet but penetrating psychology of the French novelist.

Eugène de Rothelin (1808) is a domestic novel of native strain, in which Mme de Souza suggests a technique later elaborated and brought to perfection by Balzac. She reveals how a single situation viewed from different angles and through different temperaments can lead to the complete disruption of a society and menace the happiness of a second generation. A young girl, Amélie, the niece of the tyrannous and ambitious M. d'Estouteville, is given in marriage to the father of the hero, Eugène de Rothelin. The husband learns after a year of marriage that his wife has long been in love with her cousin, Alfred d'Estouteville. Amélie dies, and old De Rothelin conceives an inveterate hatred for the D'Estoutevilles, in particular for the sole survivor of the family, Mme d'Estouteville. But his son Eugène is in love with the latter's granddaughter, Athénaïs, and has, moreover, a warm affection for the old lady whose *salon* is a school of manners for young men about to enter society.

Eugène hears his father's version of the Amélie tragedy and tells it to Athénaïs. The result is a painful tangle of passions and emotions: Eugène's affection for his father who has sacrificed a brilliant career to bring up his boy; the love of Athénaïs for Eugène; her shaken faith in her grandmother, and the old lady's sentiment of family honour which for a time keeps her from presenting her side of the story. Finally she reveals the facts: the despotism and materialism of her husband, the self-abnegation of Alfred, who went into the Order of Malta to save Amélie from the convent, and the self-sacrifice of the latter, who married so that Alfred could return from Malta to his mother. And, even when M. de Rothelin is aware of the truth, Mme de Souza is too good a psychologist to suppose a swift revolution of feeling. It is only after a long process of mental adjustment that the old man finally eradicates his old conception of Mme d'Estouteville and consents to his son's marriage. The whole novel is a criticism of the rigid family code of the old regime; a wise and discreet plea for a different relationship between parent and child, in which love and a respect for the wishes of the individual might be substituted for severity, or what is worse, that eternal moral blackmail which is too often levied in the name of filial gratitude.

If Sainte-Beuve was ever disconcerted, in his eternal rummaging for "confessions" in literature, it was when he found himself faced by the contrast between Mme Cottin the bourgeoise and Mme Cottin, the fiery author of *Claire d'Albe* (1799), *Malvina* (1801) and *Amélie Mansfield* (1803). To do him justice he unearthed two lovers, but apparently they sighed in vain, so Mme Cottin did not obtain a place in the immortal gallery of the *Portraits de Femmes*. The probability is that this cosy little Protestant widow, whose domestic virtues were a byword amongst her friends, protected herself against the thunderbolts of passion by using literature as a lightning-conductor. Here is an extract from one of her love-letters: "You fill my heart, my imagination, the Universe, Space. I see nothing save through your thoughts. I love nothing save after having loved you. I experience no sentiment which is not linked with you . . . In a word, I live all in you to the point where sometimes I imagine that there is as much of you in Paris as in the Pyrenees where you are. Ah! my friend, how dangerous such a love would be if you were not its object!" But for the last sentence these lines might have been written by one of Mme Cottin's heroines, who were solely created, it would almost seem, to complete in the world of make-believe the emotional life which the author interrupted to devote herself to her domestic duties. Of her three most interesting heroines, Claire, Malvina and Amélie, one is a married woman and the other two are widows, for it is obvious that Mme Cottin dislikes unmarried girls. Indeed they seldom figure in her work, or if they do it is as colourless nonentities or as selfish and brazen hussies. Her heroines, who have a strong family likeness, have no defects of character: all are generous, talented ladies, full of restrained sensibility which at the crucial moment flares up into passionate love. Yet even in the throes of passion they are haunted by remorse. Claire d'Albe cannot forget her conjugal obligations, Malvina is tortured by a promise made to a dead woman, whilst Amélie's consciousness of guilt brings her to sorrow and death. Few of Mme Cottin's heroes or heroines survive the last chapter: indeed, no French author save Prévost is so much at home with Death. She is a specialist in death-bed scenes, and, incredible as it sounds, even after our Samuel Richardson she contrives to extract fresh pathos from this much-abused but convenient device for bringing a novel to a close. But at least she is merciful and spares us the stabbings and poisonings of the old tragic novel of the Spanish school: we realise with Mme Cottin that we are on the threshold of the Romantic age, and that henceforth grief and internal hæmorrhages are to be the main causes of mortality in fiction.

Had Mme Cottin only dared to forget her Calvinistic upbringing she would have been a thorough Romantic. She is a curious product of two schools of fiction, that of Richardson, which is reflected in her melodramatic love of the persecution theme, and that of Rousseau, as revealed in her embarrassment when she deals with the problem of the individual and his duty to society. *Malvina* is simply a re-cast of *Clarissa Harlowe* based on the *romanesque* fallacy that good women are fatally attracted by libertines. Sir Edmond, the Lovelace in this case, has an imposing catalogue of crimes to his credit, including, for instance, the seduction of a girl of sixteen whom he marries off to an unsuspecting elderly peer. Malvina's reception of this information is typical. "You were strangely guilty, Edmond," she remarks quietly, "but such as you are, my destiny it is henceforth to cherish you." As in nearly all the novels of the Richardson brood, a pathetic fatalism takes the place of the tragic conflict which one finds in the purely French novel of passion. From the first it is clear that Malvina, like Clarissa Harlowe, is a predestined victim of love. She will be virtuous, of course, but she will die killed by too much sensibility and too little common sense.

The dishevelled philosophy of Jean-Jacques Rousseau is perceptible in *Claire d'Albe*, which hinges on the following situation. The heroine is married to an elderly manufacturer whom she admires for his philanthropy, but though she has borne him two children, Claire has the uneasy feeling that her "destiny is not fulfilled." Destiny duly arrives in the person of Frédéric, an authentic *Naturmensch* reared in the mountains, and full of that uncouth frankness which insensitives would dismiss as ordinary bad manners and lack of education, but which a Rousseauist would have no difficulty in recognising as the hall-mark of the *âme d'élite*; for Mme Cottin obviously shares Jean-Jacques's view that the nearer one approaches to the primitive the more chance one has of finding virtue in its pristine splendour. Half amused, half piqued at first by Frédéric's indifference, Claire is soon alarmed, for this child of nature moves swiftly from indifference to Platonic adoration and then to a passion which terrifies her by its violence. Frédéric, who venerates his benefactor, D'Albe, resolves to go away, but Claire points out that his departure would reveal the truth to her husband and cause him needless pain. Frédéric must therefore stay, and if he can, dissimulate. He can. A fierce emotional duel is now engaged, and Claire's last illusion disappears when she realises that she is hopelessly in love. An intolerable situation arises, for D'Albe is at first unconscious of the change in his wife and protégé. Claire now decides that her lover must go, but Frédéric, "devoured by love and desire," threatens suicide. It becomes clear now to the wife that her husband suspects her, and summoning up all her courage, she insists on Frédéric leaving, on the pretext that the affairs of her friend and confidante, Élise, need his supervision.

Here the novel might have ended, for Claire is prepared to sacrifice her love to her conjugal duty. But Mme Cottin's exuberant imagination will not be denied. D'Albe the philanthropist suddenly develops a vindictive jealousy, and aided by Élise of all people, concocts an elaborate and absurd plot to convince his wife that Frédéric is inconstant and insincere. The result is, of course, to revive her passion. In the words of Élise, who tries to oppose

D'Albe's foolish scheme, "If you make her doubt Frédéric she will doubt everything. Beware lest, by persuading her that her love was an illusion, you make her wonder whether virtue is not an illusion too." This is precisely what happens. Claire, as all the countryside knows, is dying of grief. The news reaches Frédéric, who had been told that she was well and had apparently forgotten him. In a frenzy he rushes to her house and finds her in the garden bending over her father's tomb. With a strange disregard for probability and good taste, Mme Cottin selects this as the site for her critical scene in which the lovers consummate their passion. Claire dies shortly after, but not before confessing to her husband and begging him to pardon and help Frédéric. A mysterious cloaked figure follows the funeral, and, as the last sod is laid on the grave, rushes away crying exaltedly: "Now I am free. You will not be long alone!"

This dénouement reveals the suppressed Romantic in Madame Cottin and explains the sudden and improbable change in the characters of D'Albe and Élise. The husband, up to a certain point, was portrayed as a model of generosity, and whilst he remained so, the lovers could not satisfy their desire without degrading themselves in the mind of the reader. But the Romantic in Mme Cottin urged her to make a sacrifice to the doctrine of the "rights of passion," so she sacrificed the husband by presenting him in the unsympathetic rôle of an unreasonable and crafty persecutor. Claire's fatal illness is the result of his diabolical scheming, and her death thus becomes in reality a vindication of the Romantic creed, which as expressed in Frédéric's exalted language runs: "Friendship, faith, honour, all is false in the world. There is nothing true but love, nothing real but that powerful and indestructible sentiment which attaches me to your being." Mme Cottin, the Protestant, fights a losing battle with her other Romantic self, for all her sympathy is obviously with the lovers. As for M. d'Albe, the protagonist of the institution of marriage, the author would agree with Élise that he gets what he deserves: "You ought to have remembered that any force employed in combating nature will sooner or later succumb." In plain language, if society opposes the passion of the individual, society must be prepared to take the consequences.

Mme de Krüdener, though not French—she was born in Riga—enriched French literature by a novel which is almost a masterpiece of its kind. This strange woman, who has left the imprint of her Slavonic mind on the history of Europe, lived for a time in Paris, where her husband was Russian ambassador. We are not concerned here with her amours, but in her love as in everything she was extremely passionate. One day suddenly touched by grace, Mme de Krüdener said her "mea culpa," and henceforth devoted to religion the ardour which she had hitherto squandered upon ungrateful men. In Germany she attached herself to Jung Stilling, the head of a mystic sect, but abandoned Stilling for the man whom she called the Saviour or the White Angel, the Emperor Alexander III. of Russia. The Black Angel was, of course, Napoleon. Wandering up and down Germany and Switzerland Mme de Krüdener preached the gospel of universal brotherhood and love, prophesying the coming of that *annus mirabilis* when the White Angel should finally overthrow the Lucifer of Corsica. And when 1815 came with a victorious allied army in Paris, the White Angel might have been observed, with a Bible under his arm, slinking from a side door at the Tuileries to the lodgings of Mme de Krüdener, with whom he spent hours in mystic communion. Alas! angels, like men, are inconstant, and Alexander was afterwards to renounce his spiritual doctor, who died in the Crimea in 1824, whilst a bewildered Europe wondered whether it had witnessed the passing of a great saint or a consummate charlatan.

This was the woman who in 1803 created a sensation by publishing her novel, *Valérie*. Cynical contemporaries of hers assure us that it was a sensation carefully stage-managed, and the author herself is said to have declared that she wrote the book merely to be even with that insufferable school-ma'am, Mme de Genlis, who wrote novels and played the harp with equal success. Mme de Krüdener is reported to have said: "Of the two kinds of folly by which Mme de Genlis has attained celebrity I have chosen the easier: I have written a book. It remains to be seen whether I have achieved the same end." But this flippancy was for the *salon*. Secretly she was still tormented by those mystic longings which drove her as a girl from the society of the Paris intellectuals back to the solitudes of Courland plains. This mystic religious malaise found an immediate outlet in *Valérie*, and later in the strange vocation of which we have spoken.

This novel, one of the most beautiful prose-poems in French, relates the hopeless passion of Gustave Linar, a young Swedish nobleman, for the Countess Valérie, wife of his greatest friend. Valérie is a woman such as Heine might have suggested in one of his lyrics, capricious as a child, spiritually perfect, "delicate and slender as a thought." The three travel together through Italy, for Mme de Krüdener is the first French novelist to institute the practice of "touring" her chief characters. Others, like Mme de Staël in *Corinne*, imitated her but not with happy results, for they produced bad novels and indifferent Baedekers. However, Mme de Krüdener uses her discovery to create atmosphere, and in this she succeeds admirably.

The count, who is thirty-eight, is a mature man compared to the dreamy, sensitive lad of twenty-two. Somewhere in the novel you will light upon these words which so fittingly describe Gustave: "I am like those hidden, subterranean springs whose waters quench the thirst of none and will yield naught but melancholy. I bear within myself an element which devours me; yet people pass me by and do not understand." This secret, devouring element is the poet's insatiable craving for an ideal, unattainable beauty. It is fated, then, that this ardent and artistic soul will fall in love with the woman who for him is the incarnation of that ideal beauty, fleeting glimpses of which he has already caught in the majestic and sombre natural setting of his boyhood years. So, in his letters to his *fidus Achates*, Ernest, we witness the slow unfolding of his love and its remorseless swelling and surging into an obsessing and terrible passion. But by a happy inspiration Mme de Krüdener treats the familiar theme in an original and interesting way. Gustave fights alone, with no ally but his sense of honour, for he does not tell Valérie of his love. During the whole moral conflict he has no confidant but Ernest, who is merely a device necessary to the letter-form in which the novel is composed. During the greater part of the narrative the latter remains in the background, and only at the close does he intervene in the action. Mme de Krüdener thus set herself a difficult task, since the novel becomes necessarily the description of a state of mind. The physical action is of the slightest, yet the suspense is retained until the end.

Italy, with her grave, antique beauty, her light, her music and the perfume of her flowers, holds a fatal and voluptuous charm for the dreamy and melancholy Northerner. More and more Valérie becomes identified in his imagination with the ideal beauty of which he has always dreamed. "I have changed my sky," he tells Ernest, "but I have carried with me my fanciful dreams and my immoderate desires." In Italy all nature veils a secret voluptuousness. As the reality of his love dawns upon him in all its terrible significance he tries to cast it aside, horrified at the thought that he, Gustave, could even meditate such treachery towards a dear friend. He seeks relief in solitude till his companions become concerned at his *sauvagerie*. In reply to Valérie's gentle rebukes he tells her that he is in love with a married woman in Stockholm. Some instinct prompts Valérie not to tell her husband. She pities Gustave and makes him promise to master his criminal passion.

There are great artistic possibilities in the situation imagined by Mme de Krüdener, and she exploits them superbly. Ironically the count sees Gustave as a young man lacking in sensibility, for so he interprets the latter's brooding desire for solitude. Gustave now passes through a calmer phase, beautifully symbolised by Mme de Krüdener in that scene in the churchyard beside the tumbling Adige, where Valérie recalls her childhood spent beside a far northern lake with its floating pine-cones and fringe of scarlet rowan trees. As he sees her standing with spring blossoms drifting down upon her, Gustave enjoys the brief illusion that he loves her as a brother loves his sister. But back in Padua, seated beside Valérie at the opera, abandoning himself to sweet, sensuous music that speaks of passionate love, he awakes to the despairing reality. Ernest, echoing the voice of conscience, urges him to go; and his letter wafts a chill wind from the north to the warm scented Italian garden where the nightingale sobs out her liquid and voluptuous notes.

Valérie falls ill in giving birth to a child, which dies, and Gustave's anguish almost deprives him of his reason. Now there is no respite from the tortures of his passion. Valérie and her husband leave for a visit to Florence, and the lover is left with his sombre reveries. His soul is as if a hurricane had swept across it, leaving a desert in its wake. Valérie sends her portrait, and Gustave places it in a room which becomes for him a shrine. He makes the acquaintance of a girl, Bianca, who strangely resembles Valérie, and with pathetic naïveté buys her clothes like Valérie's, seeking an illusory happiness in her society. But Bianca falls in love with him, and his sense of honour will not allow him to go on with this strange masquerade.

With the return of the count and Valérie the suspense becomes intolerable. It is here that one realises Mme de Krüdener's genius in breaking away from the more usual situation where two members at least of the triangle participate in the moral conflict. The tragedy is intensified by being concentrated in one individual, and the struggle becomes a purely spiritual one. In novels like *La Nouvelle Héloïse*, for example, individual desire clashes with social conventions, and our knowledge that the two lovers share each other's sorrows makes their situation seem pathetic rather than tragic. But the spectacle of a lonely man battling with his soul fills us with awe. In Gustave's case every avenue of escape is closed. He is on the point of yielding to the count's urgent pleadings for complete confidence, but when the latter suggests that it might make it easier for Gustave if he first opened his heart to Valérie, we realise, like the hero, that he cannot endure the torture of a long explanation to a husband who has not the slightest inkling of the truth. Gustave, on the eve of leaving for ever, loses his self-control, and in a tense and convincing scene he nearly tells Valérie, who forms a suspicion of the truth, but such is her innocence that it is only a suspicion.

Gustave seeks quiet in a lonely village in the Appenines, intending at first to go into a monastery, but a chance encounter with a Carthusian monk who has vainly sought escape in this way convinces the hero that there is no refuge in religion. For a time Nature offers some solace, and he seems to find a sympathetic echo in the silence of the mountains and in the ceaseless rush of their torrents; but Gustave is not at heart a true Romantic. True, the blindness of society irritates him sometimes, and he becomes impatient at man's inability to distinguish between the sordid, little passions and the great spiritual conflagrations which reflect the white light of eternity. Yet he is not like Rousseau, a misanthrope, so that the melancholy voluptuousness which the Romantic derives from natural beauty fades away, leaving him once more alone with passion. Now his letters show a man slowly burnt up by a great love which consumes him all the more swiftly because it has no outlet. Ernest at last tells the count, who learns from Valérie that she has suspected the truth.

The dénouement is the inevitable one. Before his death Gustave is relieved of his intolerable pain, for he knows that Valérie and the count are informed of his secret. In her description of Gustave's last hours Mme de Krüdener almost attains the beautiful simplicity of Prévost in *Manon*. Almost, for one flaw mars the crystal. There is an echo of the theatricality of Saint-Pierre and Chateaubriand in the morbid episode of the plot of ground chosen by Gustave for his grave and the conventional tree on which he carves his *memento mori*. Yet the final scene redeems this. Gustave has now found perfect tranquillity of soul. No longer is he haunted by the terrible fear that he will die misunderstood and unremembered. So with gladness he welcomes the dawn of a day that ushers in the end of life and dies with his face turned to the rising sun as its light comes stealing down the mountain-side.

The epigraph to *Delphine* (1802), "Un homme doit savoir braver l'opinion, une femme s'y soumettre," is the bitter comment on life wrung from a woman whose experience is reflected in the prism of this novel. For *Delphine* is Mme de Staël, a woman of almost masculine power and sweep of intellect, yet intensely feminine in her craving for love, in her urgent need to surrender herself to a man worthy of such adoration. And here is precisely the source of the tragedy which darkened the life of Delphine as it did that of Mme de Staël. Germaine Necker, who afterwards contracted a loveless marriage with the Swedish ambassador to Paris, the baron de Staël, was reared in the intellectual forcing-house of a pre-Revolutionary *salon* where men like Grimm, Raynal and Morellet exposed their theories on literature, philosophy and politics. Encouraged by her parents' friends to write and to talk about her opinions, admired and petted by a father whom she idolised, Germaine was doomed to that bitter disillusionment which the larger world reserves for the clever child who steps outside the domestic circle. She was not a *bas-bleu*, though Talleyrand, who married the lovely and stupid Mme Grand, wickedly said that he had done so to rest himself after the learned and brilliant conversation of Mme de Staël. On the contrary she was a woman of great talent, almost of genius, very eager for fame but still more for love; generous to an imprudent degree, quick to make friends and painfully sensitive to rebuffs. Before the appearance of *Delphine* she was already a famous but not a happy woman. Fame without love is an empty thing, and her experience of love had been very bitter. Her marriage was a foregone failure and she had nothing in common with her husband. Her affair with Narbonne filled her with naïve wonder that "men can pass as good and yet have inflicted on a woman the most frightful pain which it is given to one mortal creature to produce in another." But the great tragedy of her life opened in 1794 when she fell in love with Benjamin Constant, that strange and disturbing man, half Lovelace and half Werther, who was to torture her during her whole life. If we cannot accept Léonce, the hero of *Delphine*, as a portrait of Constant, he has at least those ideal qualities which Mme de Staël still persuaded herself she saw in the future author of *Adolphe*. If we add to these experiences the consciousness that she was ostracised by a great section of Parisian society, and that she was an object of loathing to Bonaparte, we can imagine her state of soul when she composed *Delphine*. The novel was written in the year of her husband's death, at a moment when she was free to marry Constant but loved him too well to do so.

The letter-form of the story is a device which,

though it lends great vividness to the picture of passions and sentiments, has always the great drawback of lending an air of improbability to a novel; for certain incidents appear to have been artificially constructed and inserted to preserve continuity in the action. However, Mme de Staël displays great ingenuity in this regard. Her digressions are few and plausible, and the suspense is maintained to the end. Léonce de Mondoville, the son of an orthodox Spanish *grande dame*, is about to enter into an arranged marriage with Delphine's bigoted and devout cousin, Mathilde de Vernon. The marriage is only rendered possible by the great generosity of Delphine, who is a rich widow, for she had given Mathilde part of her fortune. The character of Mathilde is a simple one, but her bigotry is so monstrous as to make her almost interesting. Her mother, however, is a most intriguing woman, incarnating duplicity and cynicism. Too intelligent not to realise Mathilde's stupidity, she has deliberately educated her as a *dévote* in order to make social life possible for her. A false report arrives that Léonce has been murdered by brigands while crossing the Pyrenees, and it is typical of Mme de Vernon that she immediately makes plans for another match for Mathilde.

At first sight Delphine and Léonce fall in love. Delphine is much perturbed for Mathilde's sake, but resolves to lay the matter frankly before Mme de Vernon, whom she regards as a sincere and sympathetic friend. The latter cleverly avoids a meeting and secretly hurries on preparations for the wedding, though Léonce has made it clear that he is not interested in Mathilde and indeed is in negotiations with his mother, to whom Delphine has been represented by Mme de Vernon as a *femme forte*. Meanwhile a catastrophe occurs. A close friend of Delphine's, Thérèse d'Ervins, a weak and passionate woman married to a jealous and despotic husband, is madly in love with a M. Serbellane. The story of this illicit love affair, which is carried as a subsidiary plot, is used as a feeder to the main current of action and is frequently drawn on in order to complicate the relations between the two chief characters. Thérèse, nurtured on Saint Augustine and on romances, is an excellent foil to the enlightened and intelligent Delphine, who throughout the novel protects and dominates the weaker woman.

The latter's affair is discovered by the husband, who is killed in a duel by Serbellane, and as Delphine had generously allowed the lovers to meet in her house, scandal has it that she is Serbellane's mistress. Mme de Vernon, who offers to explain the situation to Léonce, perfidiously encourages his suspicions, and he marries Mathilde. The cloven hoof of Samuel Richardson is visible in the harrowing description of the wedding ceremony which Delphine secretly attends.

Too late, Léonce learns the truth, and a dramatic scene ensues in the death chamber of Mme de Vernon, a scene which Mme de Staël transforms into a bitter attack on religious bigotry. Mme de Vernon extorts a promise from Léonce that he will keep her crime a secret from his wife. Delphine stands firm against the passionate pleading and lyrical sophistry of Léonce. "The morality which forbids us ever to cause the unhappiness of another is above all the doubtings of the reason or the heart." She tries to go away, but Léonce stops her carriage and, overcome by his grief, she stays. Now the great moral conflict is engaged, the conflict between individual passion and the social laws. In Léonce's case it is a battle between his desire and public opinion: for Delphine, who is above all social conventions, it is a struggle between love and her moral instinct, since Mathilde, unpleasant and bigoted though she be, is innocent. Léonce spends most of his time at Bellerive, Delphine's country house, and the lovers exist for a time in the illusion that their ideal, Platonic relations can endure indefinitely. Society gossips, and Delphine's republican ideas, imprudently and frankly expressed, compromise her social position. Léonce, a strong Royalist, finds himself tacitly disapproving Delphine's championship of a Mme de Lebensee, a Protestant divorcée who has married a Revolutionary.

A further complication arises in the person of De Valorbe, an unbalanced Romantic whose disgust with life is chiefly due to the fact that the world will not share his own opinion of himself. The Thérèse-Serbellane episode having really closed with Thérèse's retirement to a convent, Mme de Staël is driven to invent another sub-plot in order to sustain the interest of the main action. This is a technical defect, since the only *raison d'être* for Valorbe is to persecute Delphine and make her once more the object of scandal. The cloven hoof again.

The divorce law of 1792 is about to pass, but despite Lebensee's eloquence, Delphine refuses to take advantage of it because of the injustice to Mathilde. There is a dramatic meeting between the two women, and Mathilde, who is *enceinte*, begs Delphine to go away, but makes her promise not to tell Léonce about the meeting. Neither of the two ladies, it will be observed, gives Léonce credit for possessing even ordinary perspicacity. De Valorbe is aided by Delphine to escape from the Revolutionaries, but is surprised entering her house by Léonce, who thrashes him. De Valorbe tries to make Delphine's consent to marriage a condition of his refraining from a duel with Léonce.

Events now move rapidly. To the despair of Léonce, Delphine disappears. De Valorbe, in a frenzy and dishonoured in the eyes of his regiment, follows her to Switzerland where Delphine takes refuge in a convent directed by an aunt of Léonce. De Valorbe lures Delphine into a trap, pretending that he is poverty-stricken and arrested for debt. In an access of madness he almost ravishes her, but is interrupted by the police. Once more Delphine is compromised, but her superior, who, on account of her resemblance to her nephew Léonce, has an extraordinary ascendancy over Delphine, persuades her to take the veil. Meanwhile her lover, having lost his wife and child, arrives in Switzerland to find that Delphine is a nun. Mme de Staël lifts this scene from the plane of melodrama into that of tragedy by the simplicity of her narrative. Léonce now sees only one escape—suicide, and Lebensee, who symbolises the Revolutionary ideal, urges Delphine to come to France, break her vows and marry Léonce. The latter consents, though it is evident that he is doing violence to his conscience. The two lovers proceed to Léonce's ancestral home in the Vendée, but they are not happy. At this point they realise for the first time that there is an obstacle due to a fundamental difference in their characters which not even love can bridge. Delphine with her positive mind defines their situation thus: "Whatever we do we cannot isolate ourselves from society, and the opinion of others is a sort of poison pervading the air we breathe."

Mme de Staël wrote two dénouements, retaining, I think, the better one, since it derives logically from her hypothesis. Léonce, back in the Vendée and exposed once more to the atmosphere in which he was brought up, is driven into a state bordering upon hysteria by the opposition of public opinion to his marriage with a renegade nun. Mme de Staël spares him the final ignominy of a break with Delphine because the heroine dies and Léonce finds a soldier's death in the Royalist army. In the other dénouement the hero, who is in the zone of the armies, saves the life of a relative and is condemned to be shot by the Republicans. There is a melodramatic interlude in prison, where Delphine takes poison and insists on accompanying the firing-squad. She falls dead and the soldiers are so touched that they refuse to fire till goaded by the insults of the frenzied Léonce. This ending is not merely melodramatic but also technically weak, since it leaves the real issue in the air. What interests us is the dénouement of the problem presented by the clash of two natures, or, to express it in more general terms, the clash of two ideals: that of the traditionalist Léonce and that of Delphine, the woman of the new age. According to Mme de Staël there is no happiness in the world for souls like these. In the words of Delphine: "Léonce, beings such as we are would always have been unhappy in the world. Our sensitive, proud natures are out of touch with destiny." And by destiny, she means Society which tolerates in the individual no rebellion against her inexorable laws. A great man might, perhaps, to quote her epigraph, "brave public opinion," but he must be a superman, superior intellectually even to Mme de Staël, generous enough to rise above petty considerations of amour-propre in the trying rôle of lover to a *femme supérieure.*

The bare résumé given above indicates the chief defects of *Delphine*, which is overloaded with incident. This is due to the author's anxiety to make her heroine not only the mouthpiece of all her own sentiments, passions and opinions, but also her advocate at the bar of public opinion. Delphine is constantly explaining herself, and nothing is more intolerable in a novel than a heroine who gives detailed reasons for her conduct. Mme de Staël was persecuted; she was ostracised by society; but that is no reason for persecuting her heroine. A novel is not, as someone said, "a mirror flashed along a highroad." It reflects life, but it also condenses life, for all interpretation implies synthesis. The woman in Mme de Staël is too apt to thrust aside the artist who is the medium between experience and the work of art. Strictly speaking, no good novel is a pure confession. All great art postulates choice and restraint, qualities which a subjective writer finds it difficult to exercise. He feels too keenly, and where his artistic sense prompts him to be brief, his amour-propre lures him into prolixity. Mme de Staël feels so intensely that she is often betrayed into a sentimentality which rings false and melodramatic, as for instance when the dying heroine passes away to the music of the march that haunted her on Léonce's wedding day. This is cheap and all the more unpardonable, because it is retained in the second dénouement which the author purged of other equally unartistic matter contained in her first version. One does not read Richardson with impunity, and Mme de Staël, adored *Clarissa Harlowe*.

Yet *Delphine* with all its defects is a fascinating novel. It is not a picture of Revolutionary manners—it was too early for that yet—but it throws into bold relief the ideals which dominated the two rival parties on the eve of the Terror. The keynote of *Delphine* is pity: it is a plea for mediation and for reconciliation where none was possible. Mme de Staël recognised this bitter truth and symbolised it in the hopeless ending that she gave to her novel.

In *Corinne* (1807), the subjective note already so evident in *Delphine* rises to a strident pitch. We become not merely the confidants of Mme de Staël's painful emotional experience, but also the students to whom she lectures on cosmopolitan art and literature. One has no quarrel with the lectures, for as such they are admirable, but the most docile novel reader becomes petulant when Lord Nelvil and Corinne interrupt a most passionate love passage and wander off arm in arm for a quiet intellectual chat on Roman remains or modern Italian poetry. One feels a dawning sympathy for Benjamin Constant as the character of Corinne unfolds revealing that complex and bizarre nature which was Mme de Staël's, a nature in which intellect rises to the intensity of a passion and where passion acquires a metallic and intellectual lustre. Here again we have the individual at grips with society; again the conflict between two codes, that of the traditionalist and that of the ideologist. Oswald, Lord Nelvil, is an Englishman, a passionate Tory with a natural inclination to melancholy, which is intensified by his extraordinary reverence for his father whose personality, reaching from beyond the tomb, has a powerful influence on the action of the story. Oswald has all the inhuman characteristics of the perfect prig. Corinne, on the other hand, though of English extraction, has all the impetuous passion, the poetry and the quick generosity of the southern Latin. Yet these emotional qualities are tempered by an intellectual power which enables her to argue brilliantly with any of the men in the admiring circle where she reigns as queen. Other women play practically no part in the novel if we except the shadowy, sentimental Lucile, who exists merely because Lord Nelvil's father chose her as his son's future wife. There is indeed no room for other women in Corinne's world; and how could there be? for Corinne is the greatest poetess in Italy, the "priestess of the muses." She is above jealousy and above the ordinary conventions. Before her the greatest men in Italy humbly bow the knee, offering wealth and lineage in homage to her genius.

Oswald, spiritually and physically shattered by an unfortunate love experience, which had caused his father's death from grief, sees Corinne first in unique circumstances, for he witnesses the ceremony of her apotheosis at the Capitol where amidst shouts of "Vive le génie! Vive la beauté!" she receives the crown of laurels never before accorded to a woman. Once Oswald's English prejudice against feminine geniuses and against Italians is overcome, he too yields to Corinne's charm and simplicity: his sombre memories vanish as imagination and sensibility are reawakened. Corinne is attracted by his nobility and by a certain austerity which arouses new and delicious emotions. At last she feels that she has met the ideal lover, the man who will adore in her not merely the great artist, but also the passionate woman. Oswald, initiated by her into a new world of æsthetic and intellectual beauty, falls in love. But all his social instincts rebel against the idea of marriage with this brilliant creature. Would his father have approved of Corinne? He tries to picture this exotic flower amongst the aspidistras of a Bloomsbury drawing-room, and his imagination cowers before the contrast. And, when the secret of her birth is revealed; when he learns that his father had actually seen Corinne and had refused to consider her as a possible daughter-in-law because she was too *vive*; when he learns, moreover, that Corinne had fled in horror from the chill social atmosphere of an English home to seek moral independence in Italy, Oswald is torn between his passion and his duty to society and tradition. Meanwhile Corinne suffers tortures at her lover's irresolution. She shudders at the thought of England; yet, despite the discordance in their views and tastes, Oswald and she are linked inseparably by "emotions drawn from a common source; by an indefinable, secret likeness which supposes a common nature." In short, they share the Romantic or Platonic illusion that some mysterious outside power has destined them for each other. Platonically, then, they go off together to Ancona and to Venice, and Oswald's gentlemanly fears as to Corinne's reputation are allayed by her airy explanation that, as strictly speaking there is no society in Italy, scandal and calumny do not exist. Besides, as she tells Oswald's French friend D'Erfeuil, in reply to his objections: "What you say is wise, very reasonable and very applicable to ordinary persons and to ordinary situations; yet, very innocently, you would be causing me frightful harm if you were to judge my character according to those great common categories for which there are ready-made maxims." Here Mme de Staël formulates the doctrine which was to be the very pivot of Romanticism: that great genius or great passions are laws unto themselves; in their case no petty considerations like social conventions must prevent the individual from expressing his ego.

But here Corinne and Mme de Staël part company. The two lovers do not sacrifice society to their passion. Oswald, who is an officer on leave, goes back to England and is once more enmeshed in the web of filial and social obligations. Corinne secretly follows him and in the approved *East Lynne* manner watches a melancholy Oswald open the cotillion with Lucile at a ball given by the latter's mother. All that is lacking to complete the melodrama is the traditional child, the fluttering rags and drifting snowflakes. Oswald marries Lucile, and Corinne, her faith in love destroyed, sadly returns to Italy. For a moment it seems as if the novel were about to enter on a new phase, since Lucile is jealous of Corinne, and Oswald, who cannot forget her, insists on taking his wife and child to Italy. But there are no further complications. Lucile, subjugated by Corinne's charm and sensibility, models herself upon her rival, so that, as the author naïvely puts it: "Lord Nelvil's curiosity increased daily as he remarked new graces in Lucile. He very quickly guessed that she had seen Corinne." Husbands have been murdered for less!

The novel opened with the apotheosis of Corinne at the Capitol; it closes on a similar note, with Corinne improvising her swan-song in one of the rooms of the Academy of Florence amidst the respectful and subdued applause of a public which knows that its great idol is dying. That incorrigible love of the limelight which was Mme de Staël's weakness explains but does not excuse the defects of *Corinne*. Not only does it produce the melodramatic situations into which she projects her heroine, and those complications which a word could have prevented, but it throws the whole novel out of focus. Corinne is so perfect that all interest in her as a human begin dissolves; she inspires admiration and interest of a kind, but it is the interest one feels in a public monument. And as a result Oswald, who is overshadowed by her personality, becomes quite improbable, since neither he nor any other man born of woman could fill the rôle for which he is intended by the author. Nor can one sympathise with Mme de Staël's criticism as echoed in Corinne's letter: "He has sullied the object of my cult . . . he is not the man I thought he was." The irresistible comment arises: "No, poor devil; how could he be?"

Mme de Duras did not begin her career as a novelist until 1824, yet so closely is she related by temperament to the ladies whose works we have been discussing that one must ignore the interval of seventeen years which separates her *Ourika* from *Corinne*. A child of ten when the Revolution killed her father, driving her first to Martinique and later, in 1797, to England, Mme de Duras, by the liberalism of her thought, and in particular by the restrained ardour of her style, reflects ideals which were obscured by the smoky fanaticism of both Republicans and Royalists. The artist in her visualised the possibilities latent in a theme that Bernardin de Saint-Pierre had already treated in his *Chaumière indienne*, but in his sentimental theorisings Bernardin failed to exploit the dramatic interest which stands out so clearly in Mme de Duras's novel on the colour question.

Physically Ourika is a negress, but all her education has been received in France, thanks to her benefactress, Mme de B., an aristocratic lady who treats Ourika as her daughter. Two great psychological crises are presented, the first of which occurs when Ourika, overhearing a chance conversation, realises that she is a negress, and that unless some man can be bribed to marry her she can never share the destiny of other girls of her intelligence and upbringing. From this moment Ourika's spiritual life changes. To quote Mme de Duras: "There are illusions which are like the light of day; when we lose them everything else disappears with them." Out of a chaos of emotions—self-loathing, terror of the unknown future and shattered pride—there emerges one which dominates all others—the consciousness of isolation. Ourika's despairing cry: "Seule, pour toujours seule!" has the authentic ring of tragedy, for she is no moody Romantic brooding on Society's unwillingness to adapt itself to her ego. All her aspirations, on the contrary, have their root in a normal and reasonable desire for happy intercourse with her fellow-creatures. We have here the modern counterpart of the Greek conception of fate which now appears as the social order. The sentimental Mme de B. hopes that Ourika may surmount her destiny by force of character, but her friend the marquise, who voices the opinion of society, disillusions her: "Ourika has not fulfilled her destiny; she has placed herself in society without its permission and society will avenge itself."

The Revolution comes, with its *Société des Amis des Noirs*, and the hope dawns in Ourika's mind, as it did in the minds of many, that now all the old social prejudices will disappear. Yet she realises sadly that salvation, if it came, would be procured at the expense of a caste to which her benefactress belongs and to which she herself owes all the happiness she ever enjoyed. She is quickly disillusioned as she realises the bogus philanthropy that underlies the pompous *Fraternité et Égalité* of the demagogues. And further, any sympathy she had felt for the down-trodden members of her own race vanishes at the news of the bloody massacres of San Domingo. During the Terror she devotes herself to Mme de B., and for a time forgets her own tragedy in the joy of sharing the dangers and sufferings of the Royalists.

But on the death of Robespierre the dreadful consciousness of isolation returns; for Mme de B. once more reorganises the circle of her friends who regard Ourika with veiled amusement and contempt. Her sunny, confiding nature changes since, where formerly her life had been largely one of feeling, it is now passed in a critical examination of her situation. She has, however, a great source of happiness in her friendship with Mme de B.'s grandson, Charles, who makes her his confidante. Unconsciously Ourika falls in love; she wears gloves and veils in a pathetic effort to forget her colour, and lavishes all the resources of her wit and grace on Charles, who becomes secretly engaged to a French girl. Ourika has now to suffer the torture of listening to the daily confidences of the lovers, for they come to her for advice and encouragement. The second crisis comes when the marquise, irritated at Ourika's reluctance to confess the reasons for her melancholy, brutally tells her that she is in love and is, moreover, committing a sin in not fighting against her passion. The realisation that her affection for Charles is love, that it is no longer a secret, and the conviction that she is guilty of a moral crime overwhelm Ourika, benumbing all her faculties. In her anguish she turns for relief to the Church, and a wise priest reassures her as to the purity of her heart. He tells her that the solution of her troubles lies not in a vain effort to overcome social prejudice but in devoting herself to the service of God, in whose eyes alone negroes and whites are equal.

In *Édouard* (1825) Mme de Duras approaches the question of social inequality from another angle, and imparts fresh interest to the old theme of caste prejudice. The originality of *Édouard* comes from the fact that the author approaches the problem, not from the outside as Rousseau did, but from inside. Édouard's father is a bourgeois and the lifelong friend of the marquis d'Olonne, whose family honour and fortunes he once saved. Édouard, on his father's death, is practically adopted by D'Olonne, and in the family circle is treated as a son. He shares the exile of the marquis and falls in love with the latter's daughter, Natalie. But as in *Ourika* this intimacy serves but to accentuate the social gulf, for on the family's return to Paris Édouard sees that D'Olonne's affection for him is purely a personal matter and that outside the home he has no intention of forgetting caste distinctions. Yet we gather that even a D'Olonne might relent, and Natalie pleads with Édouard to elope with her to Holland. The real obstacle, however, is the hero's pride and his sense of honour, for even if the father forgave him his position in the eyes of society would be intolerable. And when, for example, the cynical duc de L. repeats the slander that Natalie is Édouard's mistress, the social code denies the latter the right to avenge the insult by a duel. His own class, represented by his parvenu uncle, regards him as a clever intriguer who is using Natalie's love as a stepping-stone to a career; the Faubourg Saint-Germain, like the duc de L., is cynically amused, but though it tolerates the bourgeois as a lover it would ostracise Édouard and Natalie if they married. The hopelessness of the situation is quietly and powerfully expressed in D'Olonne's interview with Édouard, on the eve of the latter's departure for Lafayette's army. The old man is left torn between his sense of duty to his caste and his love for the young man who has refused all offers of service from his second father. Nothing, as Mme de Duras knew, is more truly pathetic than such a moral impasse, where each recognises the justice of the other's attitude but bows to a higher external authority. The novel ends in this spirit of fatalism, and any other conclusion would have been false and inartistic. Happy endings in novels are too often obtained at the cost of improbability. Mme de Duras belongs to the small number of novelists who, having formed a definite opinion on life, have the courage to express it in their work with courage and vigour.

All these writers, we have observed, discuss some aspect of that most absorbing problem that is now to lend vitality to the novel: the clash between the individual and his social environment. In none, however, do we find that spirit of open revolt against tradition which, after a long period of silent and active preparation was even now invading French thought and literature under the banner of Romanticism. One cannot but observe, however, in the novels of these five ladies, that though their general attitude is one of tragic acquiescence towards life, the characters express their emotions with a poignancy and absence of restraint unknown to a Mme de Clèves or a Manon Lescaut. In Mme de Krüdener and in Mme Cottin there are echoes of Rousseau's naturism. In Mme de Staël's passionate appreciation of lyricism as an art form, as well as in her subjective manner as a novelist, there are signs, too, of the great and impending revolution in literature. By some strange alchemy of light that alabaster *Temple du Goût* of the seventeenth century, silhouetted now against a stormy sunrise, seems to exchange its classic contours for the sinister and beetling turrets of a mediaeval Rhenish castle.

CHAPTER III

ENNUI

At a time when all France and the more civilised part of Europe rang with the praises of Bernardin de Saint-Pierre, when hundreds of tiny, freshly baptised Pauls and Virginias were enrolled protesting in the phalanx of the worshippers of his exotic *Paul et Virginie*, a young Breton nobleman, François de Chateaubriand, could have been discovered closeted with M. de Malesherbes, that most upright and faithful minister to Louis XVI. This lad of nineteen, his imagination fired with visions of far-off unexplored countries, was pleading to be allowed to conduct an expedition of discovery to the North-West Passage. But the Revolution frustrated all his plans, and when, in 1791, he did finally set sail for the New World, it was not as the leader of a voyage of discovery but as one of a party of emigrants seeking a new home in Ohio. Yet this sojourn, brief though it was—for Chateaubriand hurried back to France at the news of the king's arrest—proved indeed to be a "glorious summer" for French literature. If Mauritius gave us *Paul et Virginie*, America inspired the poem-novel *Atala*, which appeared in 1801. So a night brought fame to this ruined gentleman, the gallant ex-officer who had starved on the benches of Kensington Gardens poring over a tattered manuscript for which a bibliophile today would give a ransom. Who was this Atala who has inspired dramatist, painter, poet, and novelist, and plastered all Europe with those ghastly German lithographs that pursued the author himself many years after in his travels through Carinthia?

Chateaubriand, who after all is the best judge in this matter, describes *Atala* as "the epic of the natural man." His idea, he tells us, was to portray the manners and customs of the North American Indian by incorporating his picture in the setting of some well-known historical event. And indeed *Atala*, though later fused into the *Génie du Christianisme*, was originally a fragment from that mine of American impressions from which he extracted also *Les Natchez*, *Le Voyage en Amérique* and to some extent the novel *René*. *Atala* is a "sort of poem, half-descriptive and half-dramatic. Everything consists in the portrayal of two lovers who walk and talk in the solitude in the midst of the stillness of the desert." One understands why Chateaubriand's friends called him the *enchanteur*, for only an enchanter could initiate his reader with such nonchalance into the fairy cave of *Atala*.

This is the tale of the love of Chactas, a young Indian of the Natchez tribe, for Atala, a daughter of the Seminoles. Yet Chactas is not a pure savage, since he was, till the age of seventeen, brought up by a Spaniard called Lopez, whilst Atala, we discover later, is Lopez's daughter and a Christian, though she has lived all her life with her tribe. The story, which is related by Chactas when he is very old, has the indefinable sadness of an old man's tale, that sadness which is always latent in the contrast between what is and what used to be, between the hot passion of seventeen and the wintry stillness of seventy. The young Chactas, responding to the call of his blood, leaves Lopez and wanders into the hands of Atala's people, who prepare to burn him at the stake. Atala pleads with him to escape, but when he sees her he forgets death and torture and thinks only of love. They walk away from the camp lost in the wonder of each other, and Chactas is recaptured. Now Atala realises that she cannot live if he is dead, so she drugs his guards, cuts her lover's bonds and flees with him to the forest. They move ever northwards, their passion increasing the deeper they plunge into that uninhabited land of unspeakable beauty, where the primitive call of Nature almost stills the warning voice of religion. At the moment when Atala, faint with love and weary of the spiritual conflict, is about to give herself to Chactas, a mighty storm sweeps over the forest and lightning blasts the tree beneath which the lovers are sheltering. They hear the tolling of a church bell, that of a mission kept by a venerable priest, Father Aubry, who gives them refuge. Now we learn the real cause of Atala's torment — a vow extorted from her by a fanatical mother, who on her deathbed made her daughter promise to take the veil. The old priest tells her that the vow is not binding but it is too late. In the forest, Atala, knowing that she had reached the end of her endurance, took poison. "I was about to violate my vow," she says, "I was about to plunge my mother into the flames of the abyss: already her curse was upon me: already I lied to the God who saved my life. When you kissed my trembling lips you did not know that you were embracing only death."

The story is very simple, but, told by Chateaubriand, it becomes a thing of sensuous beauty glowing with the fire of genius. In language that recaptures the imagery of the Song of Songs, the author retraces the life of a vanished race, a race of fierce warriors and swift hunters, ruthless in battle, stoical and contemptuous in the face of death. In words blazing with colour and vitality he describes the primitive beauty of their ceremonial, the noble grandeur of their songs of mourning and of love; of the strange spirit worship which they have preserved unchanged since the childhood of the world. The song of Atala which begins: "Heureux ceux qui n'ont point vu la fumée des festins de l'étranger . . ." is justly famous, for not only does it reflect the poignancy of the author's own experience but recaptures the very spirit of exile. Rarely, too, has the passion of love found more beautiful and more unrestrained expression than in Atala's speech: "O my young lover! I love you like the shadow of the woods at noonday. You are beautiful as the desert with all its flowers and all its breezes. If I lean over you I shudder: if my hand falls on yours it seems to me as if I were about to die. The other day the wind blew your hair across my face as you rested on my bosom and I thought I felt the light touch of the invisible Spirits. . . ."

No artist can set himself a more difficult task than to recall the spirit of antique beauty, yet Chateaubriand has succeeded because he is a great poet. Yet his greatest achievement is his picture of Nature, a veritable pageant of delight. Alas! Here, as was to be feared, the sexton beetles of literature have been busy. One does not know whether to weep or roar with laughter at the spectacle of those industrious critics who have solemnly filed down the Mississippi valley on the heels of Chateaubriand, verifying the "accuracy" of his descriptions, casting grave doubts on the authenticity of his zoology and botany, and, in a word, prostituting the whole craft of criticism by reducing it to the dimensions of an algebraic equation. When a man writes lines like these: "Often, in the great heat of the day we sought a refuge under the mosses of the cedars. Almost all the trees of Florida, in particular the cedar and the green oak, are covered with a white moss which descends from their branches to the ground. When at night in the moonlight you perceive on the naked savannah a solitary yew clad in this drapery you would think you saw a phantom trailing its long veils behind it. The scene is no less picturesque in broad daylight, for a host of butterflies, of brilliant insects, of humming-birds, of green parakeets and azure jays, clings to these mosses, producing then the effect of a tapestry on white wool on which the European craftsman has embroidered dazzling insects and birds . . ." we should, it seems to me, thank the Lord that we did not die before 1801 and protect such imagery from the trampling hooves of the pseudo-scientific critic.

Those who know the incredibly gorgeous tints of Nature's palette in the New World—and in Chateaubriand we realise it is indeed a New World—salute in the author of *Atala* one of the great painters in literature. But he has done more than paint Nature; he has, like W. H. Hudson, interpreted Nature's inner substance, for even in the great solitudes he knows she is never silent. So for him her forests are "laughing hostelries" or cathedrals whose naves whisper a thousand sighs. Here is one of his nocturnes: "The night was delicious. The genie of the air shook out her blue tresses fragrant with the perfume of the pines, and one caught the faint amber odour of the crocodiles lying under the river tamarisks. The moon shone in the midst of a stainless azure and the pearl-grey light flooded the vague crests of the forests. Not a sound could be heard save I know not what distant harmony that reigned in the depths of the woods. It seemed as if the soul of solitude sighed over the whole expanse of the desert."

When a great poet writes a novel there is always a danger that he may prove lacking in those qualities which we associate peculiarly with the novelist. In *Atala*, happily, such is not the case. The action marches powerfully to a dénouement which, if we remember the primitive and unsophisticated character of the heroine, is highly probable. With great artistic skill Chateaubriand, all through his novel, fuses the emotional life of his lovers with the elemental forces of nature, and the storm, so wonderfully depicted, synchronises with the spiritual crisis of the heroine, and this without leaving the slightest suggestion of theatrical effect. A modern writer perhaps would have dispensed with the moralisings of Father Aubry, but then we might have missed the magnificent description of Atala's death and burial, where for the first time in French fiction the poetry of Christianity finds adequate and noble expression. One must not forget either that *Atala* formed part of *Le Génie du Christianisme*, the object of which was to revive the old religious spirit which the Revolution suppressed but could not, of course, kill.

The originality of *Atala* does not lie in its psychology, though in his pictures of Indian life the author reacted vigorously against the legend of the "good savage" which had become firmly rooted in French literature. "I am not," he explained, "like Rousseau, an enthusiast for savages, and though I have perhaps as much reason to complain of society as that philosopher had to thank it, I do not believe that *pure nature* is the most beautiful thing in the world." True, Chateaubriand had seen the savage outside the covers of books, but so had Saint-Pierre, yet nothing could be more literary and less *vécu* than the picture of the savage mind in *Paul et Virginie*. Without sacrificing truth or probability to the prevailing cult of sensibility, Chateaubriand, who was a superb artist, has struck that happy mean which lies between the extremes of idealism and of realism, so that in *Atala* he has presented a picture of savage *mœurs* wherein reality and poetry are finely harmonised. However, his real contribution to literature and the quality which distinguishes him so sharply from all his predecessors is his richly coloured style.

Already Saint-Pierre had foreshadowed the great revolution in expression of which Chateaubriand is the undisputed leader. He smashed the cast-iron casing, the so-called *style noble* which for generations had strangled the imagination of novelist, poet and dramatist, and, though in *Atala* this revolt against Neo-Classic tradition is confined as yet to form, in his next novel, *René*, Chateaubriand appears not merely as a Romantic in expression but in his whole outlook on life.

It would be difficult to overrate the historical importance of *René* (1802), for its influence can be traced not only in the novelists of the Romantic school, but also in the poetry of Lamartine, Hugo and their followers. Interesting parallels, too, have been drawn between Chateaubriand and Byron, whilst *René* has also often been compared to Goethe's *Werther*, with which Chateaubriand, like all other French men of letters of the *Directoire*, was of course very familiar. Yet the upshot of all such discussions on influences, interesting though they are, is simply that in the transition years which lie between the closing eighteenth and the dawning nineteenth century, a spiritual malady, a *mal du siècle* as it has been called, swept over Western Europe. This strange distemper of the human soul, which, in obedience to the peculiar genius of writers of diverse nationalities, manifested itself in many and various forms, did, however, produce a distinctive literary type, the Romantic, possessing certain fundamental traits common to all countries. Many volumes have been written in the attempt to define the Romantic malady and to trace its symptoms in the literature of the nineteenth and twentieth centuries. So French Romanticism has been defined as a revolt against the Neo-Classicism of the old regime, as the expresssion of an inexplicable *tædium vitæ*, as the struggle of the individual to liberate his ego from the shackles of social laws, as a subjective attitude towards life by which the universe appears as the reflection of the soul of the Romantic. All this is true. All these elements and many more enter into the composition of this complex psychological state, which we shall now examine in so far as it is reflected in the French Romantic novel, and that, properly speaking, derives immediately from Chateaubriand's *René*.

The tragedies which complicated and saddened the lives of the characters portrayed in French fiction prior to this stage in its development, all result from problems which are very clearly defined. The sorrows of a Mme de Clèves, of a Des Grieux, or even of a Saint-Preux, can all be traced to causes which, though they constitute insuperable obstacles to happiness, are easily described. Mme de Clèves, conscience-stricken because she is convinced she is guilty of her husband's death, sacrifices her love to remorse. Des Grieux's passion for a prostitute altered his whole life, but could not obliterate the effect of his early education, whilst Saint-Preux saw in himself the victim of caste prejudice which prevented his marriage with Julie. But the sufferings of a René, his profound and poignant pessimism, can be attributed only to the fact that he exists. Chateaubriand has tried to describe his hero's state of soul in the following lines taken from *Le Génie du Christianisme*: "It is that [state of soul] which precedes the development of the great passions when all the faculties, young, active, complete but imprisoned, have found no object for their activity save themselves. The farther nations advance in civilisation, the more this drifting state of the passions increases: for then a very sad thing occurs. The great number of examples which we have before our eyes, the multitude of books which treat of mankind and of his sentiments, give to us ability without experience. We are disillusioned without having known joy: we still possess desires but no more illusions. The imagination is rich, abundant, marvellous: existence is poor, withered and disenchanted. With a full heart we inhabit an empty world, and without ever having experienced anything we are disabused in regard to everything.

"The bitterness which this state of soul sheds on life is incredible; the heart turns and tortures itself in a hundred directions in order to use the forces which, it feels, are useless to it."

It is clear from the remainder of this preface that Chateaubriand realised the originality of his creation, and he was not in error, since with René a new type enters the French novel. René's psychological condition, which as the author tells us elsewhere, is "a defect peculiar to the young men of the century, the defect which leads to suicide," is one from which Chateaubriand himself suffered. This Romantic complex, this *mal du siècle*, is attributed by Chateaubriand to the influence of Rousseau, "who first introduced amongst us these reveries which are so disastrous and so culpable. By isolating himself from men, by abandoning himself to his dreams, he made a large number of young men believe that it is a fine thing to cast themselves adrift on the sea of life. Since then the novel, *Werther*, has developed the poisonous germ." Needless to say, these belated lines full of post-factum contrition, were dictated by the exigencies of Chateaubriand's later plan of incorporating *René* in the great work of religious propaganda called *Le Génie du Christianisme*, where to say the least it is strangely out of place, as an examination of the novel will show.

René is in America, where he has sought a refuge from the tragedy which he now narrates to old Chactas and a Catholic priest, Father Souël. The external action of the novel can be told in a few words. René, whose early boyhood was passed amongst strangers, returns to his father's château in Brittany every autumn. There is no sympathy between father and son, so that all René's affection is lavished on his sister Amélie. On his father's death the boy, already a prey to his fatal *ennui*, travels all over Europe seeking some ideal object on which to expend the pent-up, mysterious, creative forces within him. Contact with society and even with nature serve but to convince him that he is out of tune with the universe. The consciousness that he is alone in a wilderness of men tortures his vivid imagination, and he resolves to take his life. Amélie's strange avoidance of René and her evident relief at his absence sharpen his grief; when he learns, moreover, that she is about to take the veil, his cup of bitterness overflows.

Enlightenment comes when at the solemn ceremony of the profession of vows he overhears her whispered prayer: "God of mercy, grant that I never rise from this funeral couch, and pour Thy goodness on a brother who does not share my criminal passion." In a blinding flash everything now becomes clear to René, and by a strange revolution his soul, now provided with a real and terrible object for its grief, is delivered of its mysterious *ennui*. All idea of suicide vanishes. "I no longer desired to die now that I was really unfortunate. My grief had become an occupation which filled every moment: my heart is by its nature so full of *ennui* and misery." He leaves for America nursing a sorrow which, awful as it is, he prefers to the old vague and formless sufferings that tortured him. The Romantic is now transformed into a hero of Classic tragedy, for by what seems at first a distortion of psychological truth René persuades himself that Amélie's incestuous love is a divine punishment for his guilty resolve to take his own life, a sort of Christian parallel to the Fate of the Ancients. But if Chateaubriand's object was to portray René as a tragic victim of fate he adopts a method which defeats its own purpose, for, as Aristotle would have told him, a misfortune out of proportion to the hero's fault must seem to the reader not tragic but revolting. And in René's case not only is there disproportion between Amélie's unchaste passion and René's criminal reveries, but there is, it would seem at first, actually no logical connection. Did Chateaubriand perhaps remember Diderot's pronouncement in the *Discours sur la Poésie dramatique* (VII. 329): "If there is one thing which is pathetic it is the spectacle of a man rendered culpable and unfortunate despite himself"? If we accept the Romantic malady as something over which the sufferer has no control—and in René's case this is true—then the situation of Chateaubriand's hero provides indeed "the spectacle of a man rendered culpable and unfortunate despite himself." For the question is not, "Is René responsible for Amélie's incestuous passion?" for obviously he is not; but, "Is it probable that René, constituted as he is, can convince himself that he is responsible?" Chateaubriand makes him say: "I had wanted to leave the earth before the order of the All-Powerful: it was a great crime. God had sent me Amélie at once to save me and to punish me." Before the catastrophe René described his attitude towards religion as follows: "My heart loved God, but my intelligence refused to acknowledge Him." There was no salvation for him, no contact with God, Nature or Society, so he saw no escape save by suicide. What Chateaubriand tried to portray was the conversion of René, that spiritual transformation produced by divine agency. He himself, it will be remembered, had experienced such a change of soul in 1798, on the death of his mother and brother. Picture him in 1797, this exile of twenty-six, friendless and poor in London, racked by sickness. The news comes that his brother and his sister-in-law have been guillotined. Like René he is conscious of his isolation; he is aware of his genius but convinced that it is doomed to wither in the bud. Like René, too, he has lost all faith either in God or man. Remember now what happened. He wrote his *Essai sur les Révolutions*, that desolate cry wrung from the heart of a Romantic, a book of doubt and pain, the book which hastened his mother's death. Then came the conversion. Two voices, the voices of his dead mother and brother, produced the great spiritual change. "I became a Christian," he writes, "I did not yield, I confess, to any great supernatural enlightenment. My conviction came from the heart. I wept and I believed."

Viewed then as a confession, and it is so, for the similarity between René's state of mind and that of the author is undeniable, the explanation of René's conversion is not so improbable. One need not be a mystic to see that, given a character like René's, the dénouement of this novel is not psychologically improbable. "Le cœur a des raisons que la raison ne connaît pas." Two types of critic have attacked Chateaubriand's novel: the Voltairian rationalist and the orthodox Christian. The mistake of the former is that he is not rational enough. His rationalism is too subjective, too intolerant to admit the probability that there are sensitive souls like René's which are capable of passing quite logically from a state of Romantic *ennui* to a sombre belief in the existence of God, as the result of a great spiritual shock. Yet the same critic would accept complacently a situation whereby a novel-hero, having lost his memory, regains it in a railway accident. The question which the critic must ask himself is, if I may again insist, not, "Would an ordinary man behave as René does?"

but, "Would René—who is not an ordinary man but a Romantic—experience the psychological change of which he tells us?" Surely the answer is in the affirmative. The theological critic falls into a similar error, and confuses the issue by explaining like Vinet that God is not so unreasonable as to make René responsible for his sister's crime. With all possible deference to Vinet and other writers who have doubtless good reasons for stating what would be the attitude of the Deity in this particular case, their arguments are beside the point, which is not, "What would Providence do?" but, "How would René think?" The answer is that he would quite probably think as Chateaubriand makes him think in his novel. Another objection, however, will occur to the alert reader. It is this: Whilst it is true that René's sudden conversion actually happened in real life, in fact to Chateaubriand himself, this is not a reason why it should appear in a novel. As Boileau said: "Le vrai peut quelquefois n'être pas vraisemblable." This opens up a very debatable question, not to be decided by any sweeping generalisation, and it is an objection that is peculiarly applicable to the subjective or Romantic type of novel. Everything depends, of course, on the nature of the real experience which the author attributes to his hero. If it is sufficiently representative of life, if it reflects a psychological condition like *le mal romantique* which was prevalent in Chateaubriand's youth, or a mysterious spiritual process like conversion, which is of all time, then it is not one of those improbable realities which destroy the artistic beauty of a novel. On the contrary it interprets, as here, the veiled significance of life, and surely that is the very *raison d'être* of the novelist. Would that all writers of subjective novels respected probability as Chateaubriand did in *René*.

What possessed Chateaubriand to introduce the incest theme into his book? Here there is naturally no question of subjectivism, and we can dismiss at once Sainte-Beuve's ignoble insinuation which is repeated by Anatole France, for even a perfunctory reading of Chateaubriand's correspondence with his sister Lucile will convince the most prejudiced of the monstrousness of these suggestions. The question of incestuous love, as M. Souriau points out in his *Histoire du Romantisme*, had interested the great foreign Romantics, Goethe, Schiller and Byron. But Chateaubriand, without going abroad, could have found the same theme discussed in at least two popular French novels of the eighteenth century, both by that precocious Romantic, the chevalier de Mouhy. They are: *Les Mémoires posthumes du comte de D. B. avant son retour à Dieu* (1735) and *Le Masque de Fer* (1750).

Now here indeed one can speak of improbability and bad art, for a passion which is probable though monstrous in a Phædra seems improbable and more monstrous in the sweet and gentle Amélie. Chateaubriand's Romantic imagination obscured his artistic instinct. No ordinary catastrophe, he felt, would meet the case of René, that *grande âme*, that passionate and elemental soul. Away then with the little misfortunes that complicate the lives of the bourgeois! Great misfortunes, like great passions, are meet only for great souls. So far, so good; but why attribute the incestuous love to Amélie, who is a sensitive but not a Romantic type—to Amélie, who finds peace and happiness in her religion? "When I hear the storms muttering," she writes from her convent by the sea, "when the sea-birds beat their wings against the window I, poor dove of heaven, think of the happiness I had in finding a refuge from the tempest. This is the holy mountain, the lofty peak from where one hears the last sounds of earth and the first strains from heaven. It is here that religion sweetly deceives the sensitive soul; for the most violent loves it substitutes a sort of burning chastity in which the lover and the virgin are united." This is the language of a *romanesque*, of an erotic mystic, if you like, but not of a Romantic. Amélie is capable of a deep and enduring normal love, but one cannot imagine her in the rôle in which she suddenly appears in *René*.

The great poet of *Atala* excels himself in the marvellous art with which in *René* he conjures up the atmosphere of hopelessness which is the aura of his hero's soul. The grandiose Romantic hallucination, the belief that nature is a reflection of the individual's ego, is expressed with a power of imagery unsurpassed even by Hugo. In a series of impressions, each one a perfect lyric in prose, we follow René in his quest of an ideal, a desolate figure moving pitifully along an avenue of illusions which, like stations of the Cross, stand out bleakly upon a road that has not even a Calvary to mark its ending.

The inevitable comparison has often been made between Goethe's *Werther*, first published in French in 1776, and Chateaubriand's *René*. Some writers, Mr. Hume-Brown for example, see in *René* a mere imitation of the great German novel; others, like Vinet (1844) and more recently Professor Baldensperger (1905), look upon Werther as an elder brother of René. And indeed the two novels have several common traits. Both are confessions, for both up to a certain point reflect a personal and spiritual phase of the author's life, a phase of intense sensibility and painful self-examination accompanied by a paralysis of the will power. But here, it seems to me, the resemblance stops. Werther is conscious of a lack of harmony with the world of action, but not with Nature, for he is a Pantheist. Like Rousseau he is happy in the society of humble simple souls. It is only when he abandons his rustic paradise for the *salon* that he becomes conscious of his social and intellectual inferiority. In Wahlheim, on the other hand, he basks in the glow of satisfied amour-propre, for in the eyes of the common people to whom unconsciously he condescends, Werther is a "grosser Mann," a little Dr. Faust who does not consider it beneath his dignity to leave his Homer to romp with children much to the scandal of the village doctor. The law of association is a wicked and an impish thing, and I sincerely wish that in picturing Werther I could get rid of Molière's line: "Il sait du grec, ma sœur!" However, there it is.

René is a different type, a genius, a poet haunted by an ideal beauty which, instinct tells him, exists somewhere, but, as reason warns him, is not attainable in this world. Like Proust he tortures himself in a vain and exhausting *Recherche du Temps perdu.* Werther, on the contrary, has at least one definite desire. It is for Charlotte, the wife of another man, and in what, stripped of its gorgeous poetic camouflage, is quite simply an access of despair due to sexual frustration he shoots himself.

Here one becomes conscious of a defect which *Werther* shares with *René.* Up to the dénouement the psychological picture of the heroes is almost perfect, that is, up to the point where both authors relate their personal experience in language vital, sincere and of incredible beauty. But when they cease to be subjective, when they try to weld to an actual experience an element which we feel instinctively will not fuse, there results a flaw that mars the perfection of the work. In the case of *René*, as we saw, the incest episode spoils the beauty of the novel. Here Chateaubriand's alternative was to adduce the real reason for his (or René's) conversion, and that was his mother's death and grief. This, of course, he could not do. Goethe has less excuse. It was not of course necessary that he should, like Werther, shoot himself in order to preserve the psychological unity of his chief character. That would indeed be a case of "trop de zèle." His error was in taking as his model for his final Werther a certain Herr Jerusalem who apparently did shoot himself for love. This item of police-court news which caused a noisy excitement at the time was largely responsible, says Heine, for the sensational success of *Werther.* To put it bluntly, then, a novel which would otherwise have been a masterpiece was spoilt by a cheap and melodramatic ending in which Goethe sacrificed the artistic wholeness of his character to a youthful desire for mob applause. Can we, however, see one link between the Werther-Goethe and the Werther of the final phase? The real Werther, one feels, could not have taken his life however great his desire, and in the sad description of the suicide where the hero's hand falters at the fatal moment, surely there is a symbol of the tragic irresolution of the true Werther, that creature of exquisite sensibility doomed always to recoil before the stern logic of life, which demands not feeling but doing in return for such niggard happiness as it reluctantly doles out to humanity.

Though Senancour's *Obermann* (1804) is scarcely a novel even if judged by elastic modern standards, but rather a series of psychological vignettes, this seems a fitting place in which to discuss it. For, whilst it made no impression on the public of its day, this book later exercised a certain influence on the Romantics of the thirties, chiefly owing to George Sand's penetrating study of Senancour which appeared in the *Revue des deux Mondes* for 1833. Even then, however, as M. Lanson has suggested, *Obermann* was too metaphysical to be easily assimilated by the Romantic School, though the latter caught an echo of its own language and longings in the despairing plaint of a man who knew that he was spiritually dead. More than any other French novel, *Obermann* emphasises that social vacuum which is the atmosphere of the true Romantic, that *ennui* or conviction of the uselessness of existence which is not as in normal men the result of some great and sudden grief, not a lesion which Time and sympathy will heal, but an aching and eternal hopelessness enduring as long as life, nay which is life itself.

It would be hard to find in all French literature a more poignant book than *Obermann*, a work of the imagination which reveals with more sincerity and less vanity the sufferings of a Romantic soul. It has no composition, it betrays no artistic effort to mould its impressions according to a preconceived plan. Reveries, descriptions of nature, meditations on life and death and society file past just as they arose in the author's mind, a desolate procession of hours, each wearing one of the many masks through which Despair stares at a frightened Humanity. We first encounter Obermann as a young man faced by the necessity of choosing a profession. This circumstance starts the train of reflections that compose this confession. Driven to analyse his soul, Obermann becomes aware for the first time of the complete impossibility of gaining any contact with society. As he broods over the great mystery of man and existence, it becomes clear to him that in each single moment of life that which really matters is the conservation of his ego. He cannot change things, but he can jealously guard his individuality against the impressions made upon it by outward events, since it is the nature and the recurrence of these impressions which make for happiness or misery in human existence. He goes therefore to the vast solitudes of the Alps, for, like Rousseau, he feels that if he is close to Nature he will discover that primitive harmony whose secret man has forgotten with the passing of centuries of civilisation. But Obermann cannot elude the problem, insoluble to the Romantic, of how to live amongst men and yet remain different from them This is the essence of the *mal romantique*, this impossible dream of keeping one's individuality intact in the midst of a world of men. Human life demands action, and Obermann, like most Romantics, is an irresolute and sensitive dreamer. There are some Romantics who, like René, derive some satisfaction from the consciousness of their genius: in their hearts they view mankind with a secret disdain. But Obermann is not a genius and he has no will. He has not even desires, not even the instinctive desire for an ideal love or unattainable beauty. Obermann's life is all feeling, all sensation. It consists not in the hope of a future happiness or in the memory of a happy past. It is rather a dreadful consciousness that time is moving past relentlessly and that as the hours glide by, every one is the inexorable symbol of an empty and wasted existence. It is what he calls the "regret des temps qui coulent inutiles," the regret which devours and yet sustains his life, for is there not "a sinister beauty" in the spectacle of this *sentiment universel*?

As always with the Romantic temperament, Nature brings Obermann at least a temporary oblivion, and the intolerable sentiment of the futility of existence is quieted by the exquisite beauty of his environment. To this phase we are indebted for some of the most lovely poetry ever expressed in prose, because in Obermann, as in Rousseau of the *Rêveries*, the perceptions of sound and colour are sensitive to a supreme degree. In these moments, like Marcel Proust whom he resembles as an artist, Obermann finds language of haunting beauty to express his sensations:

> When the October sun breaks through the mists over the yellowed woods, when a trickle of water glides and falls in a meadow girt with trees at moon-set: when, under a cloudless summer sky a woman's voice sings at four o'clock, a little way off amidst the walls and roofs of a great city . . .

But such moods are rare, and soon even Nature withdraws her charm, leaving him once more a prey to a kind of delirium, not a delirium of the passions, but a "désordre des ennuis," an awareness of the discordance between himself and external things. Then he is like a man afflicted by accidental deafness, who guesses at the sounds he loved and hears them not. There is no echo in his heart of the universal harmony, "the music of the spheres." He is, as he sorrowfully realises, "absent in the living world."

The French critic and novelist, Jules Janin, in an article to the London *Athenæum*, dated 6 March, 1837, wrote:

> The brilliant reputation of Benjamin Constant in the tribune must not make us lose sight of his glory and his influence as a writer. *Adolphe* is not merely a romance—it is the faithful and powerful history of an unhappiness less rare than is believed. Adolphe is truly the young man of our era. He is the victim at once of knowledge and of *ennui*—knowledge without a purpose and *ennui* without a cause. It is because of *ennui* and of idleness that he loves Ellénore and exacts from her the heavy sacrifices of her reputation, her family and her position in society.

Benjamin Constant in *Adolphe* (1816) has analysed with heroic minuteness the psychological experience of a man endowed with the complex and delicate qualities of the great lover, but whose tragedy it is never to encounter the mysterious and dynamic force of love. *Adolphe* is a heroic book because Constant, in the tragedy of Adolphe and Ellénore, has synthetised not merely his relations with Mme de Staël, but with all the women who in turn gave him the fleeting and illusory glimpse of a happiness which he was destined never to enjoy, chiefly because of his strange temperament, but also because of the ambiance in which he grew to manhood. The positive and analytic faculty that Constant employs in his description of the sufferings of Adolphe and Ellénore, the absence of that glowing lyricism which irradiates works like *La Nouvelle Héloïse* and *René*, have misled critics even of the calibre of M. Rudler into what I feel is an error of diagnosis. This talented biographer of Constant denies that Adolphe is a Romantic. "Far from belonging to Romanticism," says M. Rudler, in his preface to the definitive edition of *Adolphe*, "he belongs to the party of the French ideologists." But in the notes which Constant himself prepared for the English preface to the second edition of his novel, the author gives the following analysis of his hero's character:

> I wanted to portray in Adolphe one of the principal moral maladies of our century: that weariness, that uncertainty, that absence of strength, that perpetual analysis which places an *arrière-pensée* beside all the sentiments and thus corrupts them at the moment of their birth. Adolphe is intelligent, for to-day intelligence has come down within the grasp of every character: he is irritable because an obstacle is a sort of galvanism that lends a moment of life to death: but he is incapable of continuity, of sustained devotion, of calm generosity. Ever since his childhood he has fed on the arid lessons of

a *blasé* world. In place of gaiety he has adopted its sad irony: for rule he has adopted its egoism. By continually observing and describing himself he thought he would rise superior to himself but succeeded only in suppressing his good qualities. This malady of the soul is more common than is believed, and many young men betray its symptoms. The decrepitude of civilisation has seized them: thinking to enlighten themselves by the experience of their fathers they have inherited their satiety. So, whilst the novels of former times depicted passionate men and unyielding women, those of the present day are full of women who yield and men who leave them. Authors do not realise the cause of this change. But the most mediocre as well as the most distinguished instinctively obey a truth which they do not know.

Here, surely, is a forcible reminder of Chateaubriand's preface to *Atala* and *René*, part of which has already been quoted. Is not Adolphe, like René, a man inhabiting an "empty world," a man for whom existence is "poor, withered and disenchanted"? Worse still, he has not the resource of René's "rich, abundant and marvellous imagination."

The novel itself confirms and elaborates Constant's précis, but we discover also in it details of traits and tendencies which later Romantic writers seized upon and developed in their fictions. Indeed, it is only by remembering *Adolphe* that we shall be able to account for that perplexing blend of intellectualism and passionate feeling, of positivism and idealism, which distinguishes writers like Stendhal and Flaubert.

The dolorous probing of the ego, the consciousness that one's soul is a captive beating against the wall of the universe, the intolerable atavistic memory of a primitive golden age before civilisation atrophied man's spiritual faculties, an age when no society opposed an obstacle to the fulfilment of individual happiness—these are the sentiments and circumstances which drive the Romantic Adolphe into the arms of Ellénore. He does not love her, yet he sacrifices her at the command of his inner self in the vain, unreasoning pursuit of an ideal happiness. It is this urgent intimate call, and not mere youthful vanity, which impels Adolphe to make love to this woman ten years his senior, this *déclassée* who is the mistress of the comte de P., the mother of the latter's two children and his wife in all but name. For with Ellénore that Romantic figure *par excellence*, the sweet and pathetic Magdalene, enters the French novel. Even Rousseau, though he made a passionate plea for the fallen Julie, waited till she was married to Wolmar before rehabilitating her. But meanwhile a Revolution had come and gone, and the special indulgence which was once extended to the mistress of a king is now the appanage of an Ellénore. How well Constant understands the *déclassée*, with her meticulous observation of the conventions, her suspicious watchfulness when the conversation threatens to overstep the limits of a conventual propriety, her pathetic assiduity in the observance of her religious rites, the fits of moodiness alternating with moments of expansive happiness according to the vagaries of the social barometer!

With a demonic ardour Adolphe lays siege to the heart of this unhappy woman, who finally succumbs to his passionate tears and entreaties. "I hope for nothing, I ask for nothing. I want only to see you, but I must see you if I am to live." In his monstrous egoism Adolphe greedily savours every moment of his triumph. Till she met him Ellénore, so he thinks, had never known the true meaning of love. In his Romantic fervour he sees himself as another Saviour, the bearer of a new gospel of hope and redemption. "Ellénore," he says, "had raised herself in her own eyes by a love pure of all calculation and of all self-interest." But almost immediately his exaltation disappears and he falls back into his normal state of *ennui* and torturing self-analysis. Ellénore does not hide her remorse, and Adolphe enters upon that dreadful phase of irresolution and self-deception to which his temperament condemns him. The time for his departure approaches, but Ellénore beseeches him to postpone his going for six months. The count grows suspicious, and Adolphe begs Ellénore to let him visit her less often, advancing all the arguments which men in his situation bring forward when they are tired of love, and which they never fail to attribute to their solicitude for the woman. The inevitable scene occurs, and Adolphe is forbidden the house by the count. With a sophistry worthy of Rousseau in his most fertile vein Adolphe now passes in review all the moral reasons for leaving Ellénore. He has offended the count, abused his friendship; he has deceived his poor old father, jeopardised Ellénore's future and, as he reflects with a wave of self-pity, he has wasted a brilliant career.

The months hobble past, months of mutual recrimination and false reconciliations. Obviously if there is to be action it must come from the woman, and it does, for Ellénore leaves the count and her children to set up house by herself. In despair Adolphe sees the net now closing round him. His father insists on his return, and Ellénore reluctantly grants him two months: for this brief respite Adolphe is pathetically grateful. Now he tries to tell her by letter that she must not come to see him, alleging every reason but the true one. Ellénore's reply, of course, is to appear in the town where he is living and to overwhelm him with reproaches. In a long and terrible scene the lovers, goaded by their fury, say for the first time what is in their hearts. Unfortunately Adolphe's father chooses this moment to threaten to expel Ellénore from the neighbourhood. Adolphe, in an access of chivalrous exaltation, rushes to her, convinced once more that he is in love until Ellénore disillusions him. They go off and begin once more that wretched existence outside the pale of society, that *collage* or cohabitation without love compared to which the most unhappy marriage is paradise indeed. Ellénore is exhausted by the torturing knowledge that Adolphe does not love her and that she is a complete outcast. Yet when the count offers her half his fortune to leave her lover, even if she does not return to him, she rivets another link in Adolphe's chain by refusing. Meanwhile Adolphe writhes in the tangled web of his own irresolution.

His imagination conjures up visions of a happy domestic life with a dream woman, who is of course the antithesis of Ellénore. Now his past life, seen through the mirage of a Romantic temperament, seems indescribably beautiful and happy. But suddenly the reality of the present casts a shadow over these memories from which he recoils, for do they not belong to an order of things in which

Ellénore can have no place? He reflects bitterly upon his spiritual bondage, persuading himself that he is the innocent victim who has sacrificed youth, paternal love, ambition and honour to a woman's caprice. Twilight brings softer thoughts, however, and the wintry stillness of the countryside evokes the consoling reflection that life itself is but a brief interval between two eternities. Thanks to the baron de T., an old friend of his father's, Adolphe regains contact with society, which refuses, however, to receive his mistress. His friend urges him to break with Ellénore, and Adolphe writes that he has resolved to do so. This letter, which the baron sends to Ellénore, ends her sufferings, for in spite of Adolphe's protestations she knows his love is dead.

Every great novel is a synthesis of experience, and *Adolphe* is a very great novel. Constant was but telling the simple truth when he denied that the story of Adolphe and Ellénore was a transcript of his emotional adventures with Mme de Staël, for Ellénore personifies all the women who ever passed through the devouring flame of his insatiable passion for love. One has only to read the famous *Cahier rouge*, that cynical but sincere account of Constant's youth, to realise that no woman ever existed who could satisfy the demands of this monstrous egotist. Adolphe's situation, if considered as an isolated one, is not unusual; many have experienced it at least once in a lifetime. But when we reflect that it is a symbol, the microcosm as it were, of the many and varied emotional adventures of Constant, the character of Adolphe acquires a deeper significance. He is no longer an irresolute individual betrayed by a passing caprice into a labyrinth of moral sufferings; he is a type, the peculiar product of a phase in civilisation. In Adolphe (as in Constant) we have the impact of the two dynamic forces which traverse French thought in the eighteenth century: the analytic intellectualism of the Voltairians and the religion of feeling practised by Rousseau and his adepts. Some of the young men of Constant's generation were fortunate enough to inherit only one of these tendencies; the tragedy of Constant was that he inherited both. In his soul the flowers of a rare imagination were instantly killed by the icy breath of intellectualism, yet he clung to the illusion that some day he would experience the spiritual beauty which comes from true sensibility. It is this illusion which explains the torment and the frenzy of his life and lends a deeper significance to the character of Adolphe, who thus appears as a new type of Romantic —the *homme fatal* of the later novelists, the type incapable of constancy, who ruthlessly immolates all women to pacify the inner demon which possesses him. This is what Constant meant in his preface when he foretold that reversal of the rôles attributed by the old novelists to their heroes and heroines. No longer, as in the romances of D'Urfé and Scudéry, will woman dictate her law to a sighing and obedient lover. Henceforth woman must suffer while the man passes on despairingly to another victim, haunted by remorse but steadfast in his pursuit of the mirage which hangs like a yellow Romantic moon low on the horizon of existence.

CHAPTER IV

THE HISTORICAL NOVEL

IMAGINE a young man under the Empire, resplendent in his undress uniform of willow-green riding-coat, cossack vest and casimir breeches, stepping into Ladvocat's on the Boulevard des Italiens to purchase a few of the latest novels. Here, prominently displayed, are the works of M. de Chateaubriand, of Mme Cottin and Mme de Staël, but I doubt if these will be his final choice. War or no war, how can he resist Miss Edgeworth's entrancing tales of fashionable life or Lady Morgan's *The Missionary*, or again, Miss Burney's *Geraldine*?—for in spite of Napoleon's diligent anglophobe propaganda the novelists of "perfidious Albion" maintain their hold on the French imagination. True, "Monk" Lewis and Ann Radcliffe are no longer translated, but you can detect their grisly influence in the new historical novels like *Hermine et Saint-Alne* (1810) with its three deaths and the massacre of Saint-Bartholomew in the first twenty pages, or in Mme Barthélemy-Hadot's *Stanislas Zamoscki* (1811) and its equally atrocious and improbable situations.

In 1813, however, the critic of the *Journal des Arts*, a paper which had conducted a long campaign against the impossible horrors of the *roman noir*, welcomes Picard's *Aventures d'Eugène de Senneville* as the sign of a much desired and belated reaction against these products of English bizarrerie and their eternal ghosts, brigands and wailing victims. He applauds the failure of Durdent's *Alisbelle et Rosemonde* and in a burst of premature triumph exclaims: "Ann Radcliffe is no more: the old castles, the damp, underground passages, the masked brigands, the deserted chapels, the disguised hermits have lost the half of their reputation." It was this journal which in 1811 noted with some relief the steady rise of the historical novel, even then beginning to threaten the popularity of the Radcliffe school, yet it was careful to encourage, not the historical novel dealing with medieval times which was frequently more horrible than any *roman noir*, but the historical novel basing its incidents on the Revolution and emphasising character in preference to mere situation. However, the critic does not dictate a nation's literary taste: he follows and if possible controls it. And, under the Empire the historical novelist, reflecting the trend of the public mind, disdainfully ignored the First Republic and fixed his gaze on the distant Middle Ages. Here was mystery and romance; rich material for his eager imagination. Here he could give free rein to his sensibility and satisfy that nostalgia for an ideal beauty which turned away mournfully from the spectacle of the new Cæsarism with its pseudo-classic gilded eagles, its army orders and inhuman efficiency.

Napoleon's censorship, severe as it was, did not seriously affect the destiny of the French novel, but the atmosphere of the Empire was unfavourable to the expansion of the new type of literature, Romanticism, which was now in preparation. The spirit that the Empire sought to foster was one of intense nationalism, whereas cosmopolitanism was one of the leading characteristics of Romanticism. Their imagination already inflamed by English and German works which they knew through indifferent translations, their appetite whetted by the news of greater treasures which the *émigrés* brought back from the land of Ossian, Shakespeare, Young, or from that of Goethe, Klopstock and Schiller, the young Romantics of the Empire formed a small army of scattered units moving towards an unseen rallying point in obedience to a common impulse and in defence of a common cause—Romanticism.

Waterloo over, astonished Parisians saw their Champs-Élysées thronged with English, German and Russian soldiers. The Palais-Royal, the Boulevards and the theatres presented an unfamiliar and cosmopolitan appearance. Bewildered at first by the rapidity and strangeness of these events, the public received the intruders with mixed feelings, but soon curiosity got the upper hand, and fraternising was the order of the day. The Faubourg Saint-Germain, which rapturously welcomed Louis XVIII., threw open its *salons* to the officers of the Allied armies, not perhaps very widely to the Prussians, for Blücher by his senseless brutality had done his best to make his country's reputation stink in the nostrils of even the most enthusiastic Royalist. Fortunately, however, the French *literati* were already familiar enough with German literature and Germans of the better sort to make the necessary allowances, even for a Blücher. But the real *entente* was with England, and the social and intellectual commerce between the two nations sensibly increased from the Restoration onwards.

The English word *romantic*, in its French form, *romantique*, which had cropped up here and there in books during the early years of the century, now passed into the current language. Jouy, in his *Hermite de Guyane* (1813), a gossipy journal of Parisian actualities, refers to the word *romantique* as

> a term of sentimental jargon used by some writers to characterise a new school of Germanic literature. The first condition which it exacts from its pupils is that they recognise that our Molière, our Racine and our Voltaire are petty geniuses hampered by the rules and who could not rise to the heights of that ideal beauty, the pursuit of which is the object of the *genre romantique*. This word, this invader, was at first admitted only in connection with and in the sense of the word *pittoresque*, and with this one ought perhaps to have been content. But it has suddenly passed from the domain of description which was assigned to it, into the spacious realm of the imagination.
>
> With all possible seriousness, people talk to you of *romantic thoughts* and *romantic intentions*: they love to lose themselves in a romantic vagueness. *Romantic exaltation* leads you to *melancholy ecstasy* and from that you have only a step to go in order to arrive at the lunatic asylum.

Jouy reflects the general hostility of the average Frenchman of the early Restoration towards this new and ill-understood literary movement. The reference to Germanic literature is of course an echo of the annoyance aroused by Schlegel's *Lectures on Dramatic Literature* in which, aided by Sismondi, he attacked the conservatism of French drama with its veneration for the so-called unities of time, place and action. The *Diable boiteux* (1816), a vigorous periodical, replied sharply to their criticism, denied the insinuation that the French were blind to the beauties of foreign literature and defended Corneille and Racine against what it called the sophisms and the intolerance of the German. On 21 July, 1822, for the first time in the annals of the French stage a company of English actors, the Windsor and Brighton troupe, attempted to play *Othello* at the Théâtre de la Porte Saint-Martin. Partly on national grounds, but also to some extent in defence of French literary taste, says the *Réveil*, a riotous mob pelted the actors with squelchy missiles and rushed the stage. A second performance under police protection was received with cat-calls and shrieks of derision at the strange uncouth idiom. The word *Kou-ine* was seized on with delight and repeated with gusto till the curtain was rung down. Thus ended the first public attempt to present Shakespeare in the original to a Gallic audience.

Referring to the new crop of imitations of the *roman noir* which ushered in the year 1822, the *Réveil* asked: "What is the meaning of Classic and Romantic? Do the absurd works which we see produced daily belong to Romantic literature? If so, there is no longer room for hesitation, for we must conspue and ridicule these barbaric productions, the result of a depraved taste and false exaltation." In its December number this paper brackets the term *romantique* and the new political expression *libéral-isme* as words "which have not yet acquired in discussion a precise sense or certain definition."

The *Diable boiteux* for March 1824 jeered at the

Romantic young man, at his vague melancholy and his unhappiness without a cause, and parodying his language made him describe himself as follows: "My head is a bee-hive full of honey, the quintessence of my readings from Ossian, Goethe and Klopstock . . . inflamed with an inextinguishable fire I seek I know not what to complete my being . . . in moral suffering there is an indefinable enjoyment very difficult to express and even to feel, but in which distinguished beings swim with a secret voluptuousness." Continuing its attacks the *Diable boiteux* adapted Boileau's famous line and applied it as a device to the Romantics:

> Rien n'est beau que le faux, le faux seul est aimable,

and in criticising the *Damné* (1824), a popular Romantic novel of the day, predicted a dazzling success for this work because it contained all the elements now in vogue in the new fiction: "pathetic and terrible situations, frightful phantoms, caverns, inquisitions, demons, virgins and *grands seigneurs*." To portray the human heart, this critic pointed out, requires the classic genius of a Racine. The Romantics, as they have no genius, are forced to resort to their delirious and extravagant imagination. "For them a thing is beautiful as soon as it ceases to be true." With great satisfaction he then quotes Viennet's attack on Romantic art in the *Épitre aux Muses* (1824),

> C'est une vérité qui n'est point la nature;
> Un art qui n'est point l'art, de grands mots sans enflure;
> C'est la mélancolie et la mysticité,
> C'est l'affectation de la naïveté;
> C'est un monde idéal qu'on voit dans les nuages,
> Tout, jusqu'au sentiment, n'y parle qu'en images.

The man who did more than any other at this stage to assemble the scattered elements of Romanticism was Charles Nodier, a writer of many talents whose short stories retain a certain charm. A delightful personality, a Monarchist under the Consulate and a Republican under the Restoration, always an inveterate friend of the "under-dog," Nodier, in April 1824, opened his salon at the Arsénal, of which he was chief librarian, to the young stalwarts of the new school. The Romantics could have found no more sympathetic or more inspiring leader than this valetudinarian of thirty-eight whose work, according to his friends, but feebly reflects the glowing fire of his imagination. To read Nodier's stories beginning with the *Proscrits* (1802) and ending with *Inès de las Sierras* (1837) is to view, as in a panorama, the procession of all the tendencies which disputed for mastery in French fiction during that epoch. A passionate admirer of *Werther*, a copy of which he always carried bound in crape, an equally fanatical devotee of Schiller, Nodier has left in the *Proscrits* a faithful picture of the young Romantic of the *Directoire*. Goethe's "fatal" novel, Shakespeare, Klopstock and Richardson—such are the influences which gave birth to this exalted tale of suicide, adultery and death, and, as its title suggests, it is a Romantic protest against society, incorporated for the moment in the person of Napoleon. But Nodier's tales are by no means all Romantic. *Séraphine*, *Adèle* and *Amélie*, for instance, are wistful idylls of youth and love, of lyrical and poignant sadness. Nodier was haunted by the vision of premature death, and his heroines often symbolise this obsession; frail, ethereal, exquisite creatures who recall the heart-breaking loveliness of Malherbe's line:

> Rose, elle a vécu ce que vivent les roses,
> L'espace d'un matin.

Yet if you seek Romanticism of the authentic, full-bodied vintage Nodier can offer that too in *Jean Sbogar* (1816). Here he is Byronic before Byron was really known in France, and it is not surprising that later critics accused him of imitating the *Corsair*, though *Jean Sbogar* was conceived several years before Byron's poem appeared. Sbogar is a true Romantic hero; an outlaw, a rebel against society, an atheist who despairs because he cannot believe, a passionate lover who will not sully the purity of his Antonia by linking her life to his. Sbogar leads a double life. In Venice he is known as the seigneur Lothario, the mysterious and wealthy philanthropist, the virtuoso without a peer in all Italy. At the Château of Duino he is the terrible masked bandit, Jean Sbogar, the friend of the poor and oppressed, the ruthless scourge of the rich and highly-placed. In Antonia's drawing-room he is a truly Byronic figure. "The dishevelled hair of this mysterious young man, the gloomy fixity of his sad and severe gaze, the painful contemplation in which he appeared to be plunged, the convulsive movement of that strange and twisted frown which misfortune had doubtless graven on his brow, all combined to lend something terrifying to his appearance."

So far as I know, *Jean Sbogar* is the first attempt

in the French novel to glorify the criminal. Sbogar is convinced that at certain stages in civilisation when society, threatened with extinction, has fallen into the hands of unscrupulous charlatans, a strong man arises to save society against itself. But this man "will not flaunt the standard of ordinary society. Ordinary society would repulse him, for he speaks a language which it does not understand and which it is forbidden to understand. To serve society he must break away from it, and the war which he declares against the social order is the first guarantee of the independence which society will some day find under his auspices. . . . Then these miserable brigands, objects of the horror and disgust of nations, will become their arbiters, and their scaffolds will change into altars."

We meet Sbogar in various disguises in the novels of Hugo, Balzac and George Sand. Essentially, however, he remains a being fundamentally good though breaking all the social laws; misunderstood by ordinary men, who wrongly judge him by ordinary human standards, wrongly because like Sbogar he is possessed of superhuman and dæmonic force, a magnetic and compelling personality, a Colossus who towers above the common mortals of his time, disdainfully spurning their conventions and petty prejudices, yet attached to the world by a sentiment of overwhelming pity for the sufferings of the oppressed. Nodier, in an article to the *Revue de Paris* (October 1829), insisted on the debt which Romantic literature owes to Christianity, and in the Romantic apotheosis of the criminal, as of the Magdalene, one can glimpse a strange perversion of Christian ideals. What appealed to the Romantics in the story of the life of Jesus was the fact that he was "despised and rejected of men," a "grand incompris," a social outcast. So with the *simplisme* which is so typical of all emotional and imaginative minds they persuaded themselves that, conversely, the sentiment of social incompatibility was evidence of incipient divinity, or, in the realm of art, of genius. Father Souël's stern rebuke to René: "Sir, you are not a man of superior intellect because you perceive the world in a hateful light," fell on deaf ears. And so in the Romantic novel the legend of *le bon criminel* superseded that of *le bon sauvage* with momentous consequences to art and the social order.

Could you have asked a *boulevardier* of the late Restoration: "Who is the greatest living French novelist?" he would have answered without hesitation: "Monsieur le vicomte d'Arlincourt." Even as late as 1835, when the vogue for what Nodier called *la littérature frénétique* had declined, Frances Trollope heard the works of D'Arlincourt referred to in Parisian drawing-rooms not as the exaggeration of Romanticism but as its most perfect expression. In 1821 D'Arlincourt burst upon a delighted world with a novel called *Le Solitaire*, which in five years ran through eleven editions, was translated into fourteen languages, inspired several melodramas and at least one opera by Planard and Caraffa. Soon all France was humming the words of a ballad which, says Monselet, remained on the lips of a whole generation:

Qui traverse à la nage
Nos rapides torrents?
Qui sur un roc sauvage
Va défier les vents?
A l'ours dans sa tanière
Qui donne le trépas?
De la biche légère
Qui devance les pas?
Chut! C'est le Solitaire . . .!
Il fait tout
Il voit tout
Il sait tout
Il est partout.

Curiously enough, D'Arlincourt, who was an intransigent Royalist, always denied that he was a Romantic. "Any great work of the imagination," he wrote in his grand manner, "written with purity, which shocks neither taste nor reason, and which joins to great thoughts a lively and sustained interest, whatever be its author's plan or whatever irregularities he permits himself, would appear to me to belong to the Classic genre." But with all deference to the vicomte it would be hard to find a more classic example of Romanticism than the *Solitaire.* In a castle perched high up in the Alpine solitudes, Élodie, the "virgin of Underlach" and beautiful niece of the gloomy Baron Herstall, hears of a mysterious and apocalyptic figure who inhabits the mountain peaks. Sometimes, wrapped in the folds of his sable mantle, he descends into the valley to succour the poor and unfortunate. This is the Solitaire, who later turns out to be no less a person than Charles le Téméraire and the slayer of Élodie's father, Saint-Maur. The Solitaire falls in love with Élodie and purloins her blue ribbon, but, appearing mysteriously in the chapel of the castle at dead of night, returns it to her with the words: "Daughter of Underlach, pardon the man of adversity who, unable to master the movement of his heart, thought that a ribbon worn by innocence could, like a celestial talisman, purify his sombre dwelling and restore calm to his heart."

The Solitaire saves Élodie from her abductor, Ecbert, and, single-handed, holds the pass against a regiment. "His resplendent blade is like the flaming sword of the Archangel at the gates of Eden, and on his helmet a black plume flutters like funereal crape on a triumphal monument." After a passionate love scene our Solitaire carries Élodie off to the mountains, she protesting feebly that there is no minister to bless these strange nuptials. "There are altars in the desert," cries the Solitaire with the most passionate exaltation. "Everywhere the Eternal receives the vows of men; everywhere the torches of Love and Hymen can be lit. Dare to trust me, tender flower of the valley." However, the tender flower of the valley resists, and the Solitaire, his exaltation gone, becomes once more the grief-laden outcast of society. "Farewell," he exclaims. "Death, my only hope, will soon end my sufferings." But before he dies he once more comes to the rescue of Élodie, who is being forced into marriage with a certain Count Palzo. I cannot resist quoting this episode as typical of the spirit of the whole novel, which is an incredible potpourri of delirious extravagance and naïve ineptitude. Élodie, on the eve of her marriage, summons the Solitaire. "This chapel," said the orphan, "is adorned for the nuptials of Élodie and Palzo. . . . At this reply the warrior impetuously shakes his glaive: his uncontrollable fury gets the better of his reason . . . a sinister light flickers across his face. . . . "Still more blood!" he cries. "This steel then has not yet shed enough. Lead me to Palzo." "Great God!" said the virgin of Underlach, "What are you going to do?"

To this level, then, had the art of novel-writing sunk in France of 1821. We have it on the authority of the *Feuilleton mensuel* for 1841 that D'Arlincourt, whose later novels, *Le Rénégat* (1822), *Ipsiboë* (1823) and *Brasseur-roi* (1833), are even worse than *Le Solitaire*, was for ten years regarded as the chief novelist of the Romantic school. It may seem hard to find a work matching the *Solitaire* for sheer improbability, yet we have only to open Victor Hugo's *Han d'Islande* (1823) to discover our error. Someone said once of Pélisson that he abused the privilege of being ugly: Victor Hugo certainly abuses that of being young, for he was eighteen when he wrote *Han d'Islande*. Now at the worst D'Arlincourt only arouses laughter: the author of *Han d'Islande* revolts his reader, for he seems determined to justify the classic joke that for the Romantic "Rien n'est beau que le laid." It is a labour to wade through this tangled mass of episodes, each of which is more horrible than its predecessor. Occasionally a descriptive passage occurs which reveals some acquaintance with Norwegian social life at the end of the seventeenth century and faintly foreshadows the art of the novelist of *Notre Dame de Paris*. Immediately, however, one is plunged back into the revolting atmosphere of the charnel-house, which is the chief source of Hugo's inspiration. Han, the brigand hero, was vaguely meant as a type of social pariah. He emerges, however, as a human orang-outang, a creature who quaffs sea-water from human skulls and ambles about accompanied by a tame bear of unbelievable ferocity which comes to his rescue at crucial moments. *Bug-Jargal* (1826) reflects the same paradoxical and aggressive spirit of revolt against the classic ideal of beauty. It deals with the negro revolution in San Domingo, the horrors of which are bellowed at us through the monstrous amplifier of the Hugoesque imagination. Bug, the hero, is a Romantic and improbable combination of bestiality and nobility of soul.

It is instructive to observe this violent counter-swing of the pendulum in the art of this young and undisciplined writer, for, strange to say, it is the symptom of a Romantic desire to obtain contact with the reality of life. Much confusion has arisen from the erroneous contrast made by many critics between Romanticism and Realism in literature, yet the critical writers of the early Romantic period were not guilty of this mistake in perspective. In this connection J. M. V. Audin's essay, *Du Romantique* (1822), published as a preface to a tenth-rate novel called *Florence ou la Religieuse*, is most illuminating and ought to be better known than it is. Audin writes of poetry, but his remarks are equally applicable to the art of the novelist. "The Classic poet," he writes, "seeking a beauty which cannot fall within the scope of the senses, eternal and immutable, takes as his criterion an immortal substance, the intelligence, and not perishable organs such as the eye or the ear. So all his marvels are spiritual. He scarcely ever traces other than moral griefs; rarely do you see him display physical suffering before your eyes." Audin, of course, has in mind French Neo-Classic art which he knows, and not true Classic art with which he is unfamiliar, as one can see from his embarrassment in finding examples in Homer to support his thesis. What interests us here, however, is his conception of Romantic art, whose ideal for him is "the exact representation of nature." Romanticism, in Audin's opinion, appeals primarily to the senses and not to the intellect, but it has also a spiritual element which he describes as "a certain mysticity, the object of which is to detach man from the earth and to put him into communication with the Divinity. Their (the Romantic) poetic exaltation seeks in the arts of the imagination and in religion, realities which of course they will never find there." What Audin has grasped clearly and what we have noted in the novels of the Romantics is their insistence on the universality of art; the right of the artist to juxtapose the real and the ideal; the spiritual and the material; the beautiful and the ugly; the natural and the supernatural. "Sometimes indeed," pursues Audin, "the poet lets you stray in a world whose existence, laws, and ensemble are of his own creation; the imaginary beings of which, not connected by any perceptible tie, are not within the scope of the senses. They can only be conceived by the intelligence which produced them. Sometimes he introduces you to a material world where your eye seizes all the resemblances of its creatures with those who live around you; where everything participates in the movement and feels, acts and thinks. . . . But," continues Audin, "whether the Romantic is concerned with the ideal or the real his expression will always contain an element of materialism. It is one of the sad necessities of Romanticism that, since it constantly appeals to the eye in its paintings, its images are perpetually drawn from an order of visible things." Another critic, E. Celnart, in an article to *La France littéraire* (1832), contrasts the Classic ideal of *Le Beau* with the Romantic ideal of *Le Vrai*. The world of the Classics is an ideal world: that of the Romantics is the real world in its entirety with all its dissonances and contrasts. And indeed the Classic hero is a generality, a symbol, the personification of a passion whose material environment has no artistic value. The Romantic, on the other hand, is essentially an individual, a passionate being too, but what interests his artistic creator is not the eternal, universal significance of these passions, but the relationship between the passions of that particular individual and his environment. The Romantic hero may feel a despairing sense of incompatibility with his natural environment, but he is nevertheless intensely interested in humanity and nature, and this intense interest is expressed in an acute sensitiveness to the reality which surrounds him. So, when he can forget the despair in his heart, the feeling of spiritual segregation and of disaccord with his human environment, that is to say, when he ceases to be purely subjective or lyrical, his powers of observation and analysis are focused on the external world, which he explores with a curiosity embracing the whole gamut of humanity and describes with a sense of colour and detail characteristic of all the Romantic novelists even in their wildest extravagances. Again, even when the Romantic is most Romantic, when he is most preoccupied with his ego, he often analyses the changing and subtle spectacle of his passions and emotions with a fidelity to truth and to detail which can only be called realistic. The absurdity, therefore, of attempting to contrast Romanticism and Realism becomes evident, for every Romantic is a potential Realist if *we speak in terms of art and not of morality.*

Romanticism is a consciousness of the limitations which the real world sets to the flight of the individual spirit upwards toward an ideal world that it instinctively perceives but cannot formulate. Yet this attitude of mind does not preclude a knowledge of the real world. It led to a revolt against the social order from which the Romantic recoiled with mingled feelings of hopelessness or impotent fury according to his mood. But he did not reach this stage without having explored all the intricacies of society, its complexity and its infinite variety. The conviction that the world was an empty place in comparison to the rich and coloured existence of which he dreamed was a state of soul which he arrived at later. The prisoner learned the geography of his prison before he escaped from it. Some novelists, like the devotees of the *roman noir*, lived for a time in a universe of ghosts and goblins; others sought in the distant past or in far-off lands a reflection of their world of dreams. Some, like Nodier, D'Arlincourt and Hugo, imagined men, symbols of their own inner revolt, who made glorious havoc with all the conventions and prohibitions that trammel the ordinary mortal. But not even a Romantic can escape for ever from the insistent reminder of the reality that surrounds him. Nodier escaped altogether into a wistful land of faëry. Hugo, on the other hand, swerved round like an animal at bay, and in his *Dernier Jour d'un Condamné* (1829) grappled with the grimmest of all realities—death. In a series of pictures which sear the mind he reproduced with awful probability the thoughts which pass through the brain of a criminal under trial for his life. Exercising with marvellous force his genius for contrast and imagery he describes the scene in the assize court at eight o'clock on a glorious August morning, the open window with its flowering plants, the vital joyous hum of workaday Paris, the cry of the street-vendors, the golden sunlight with its floating specks of dust—movement, colour, warmth, everything that we associate with life. The prisoner smiles. He looks at the jury, sleepy, yawning, good-natured bourgeois, with nothing in their faces to suggest that they have just arrived at a verdict of death. The fatal sentence is pronounced and the prisoner is led out stumbling like a drunken man. "Until the sentence of death, I felt myself breathing, palpitating, living in the same milieu as other men; now I distinguished clearly a sort of barrier between the world and myself. Nothing appeared now under the same aspect as before.

Those wide, luminous windows, that pure sky, that pretty flower—all was white and pale like the colour of a shroud. Those men, those women and children who pressed round me as I passed looked, I thought, like phantoms." Is this Romanticism or Realism? It is both. It is the language of a great and sensitive artist inspired with a profound moral and—if you like—Romantic horror of the social institution of capital punishment. This is a magnificent but terrible book, a book, as Jules Janin truly said, "No man can read a second time, but which, once read, no man ever forgets."

On the whole, from the Revolution to the Restoration the French novel was out of contact with real life, and an impartial observer writing in the *Quinzaine* in 1817 could say without exaggeration:

> For the last twenty years we have had in turn *Ossianic novels* which might have made one think that there was nothing in France but bards, heather, clouds and delirium; then the novels about troubadours whose Gothic descriptions represented all our roads as covered with knights, pilgrims and jongleurs; finally, for the list would be a long one, the historical novels of certain ladies who have long led one to believe . . . that they had burned all our old chronicles to read only *contes des ruelles* and the love declarations of our great men from Charlemagne to Louis XIII. and his son. Those are the vogues, but they pass, and we hermits still prefer an outline of our century to such fantastic conceptions, where each writer manufactures a borrowed truth and an imaginary nature. It is time that this genre became like dramatic poetry, the *image of society.*

And this was the unconscious desire of all novelists, Romantic and traditionalist. The novel had to be restored to its proper function, which is to interpret the reality of life, or else perish as did Neo-Classic tragedy. The subjective novel of psychological analysis, so magnificently exemplified in *René* and *Adolphe*, was by its nature esoteric and therefore developed slowly. But luckily subjectivism was not the only article in the creed of the Romantic school. That cult for mediaeval art and literature to which we have already referred had not abated: on the contrary the writings of the troubadours and *trouvères* seemed to the young reactionaries to be suffused with colour and glamour. Saint-Pierre and Chateaubriand with their chromatic style had revealed undreamed-of treasures in the French language, treasures which their disciples were eager to exploit. But Saint-Pierre and Chateaubriand had gone to exotic nature for their inspiration. Whither were the historical novelists to turn for theirs? The directive force came from Britain just as it had in the middle of the preceding century at a similar period of hesitancy in the development of French fiction. The brilliant success of Scott produced an immediate and decisive effect on the French novel. Beginning with *Guy Mannering* in 1816, the Waverley novels were translated into French as they appeared. In 1820, Pichot, who introduced Byron to Frenchmen, collaborated with Defauconpret and Artaud in a translation of Scott's novels which was terminated in 1832. They were so much in demand that a sixty-volume octavo edition was issued between 1822 and 1829, and other translations continued to appear throughout the whole nineteenth century. No other English writer has ever enjoyed such a vogue in France.

Scott's novels with their vivid picturesque detail and romantic adventures were joyously received not only by the Romantics but also by the traditionalists. It is easy to understand why. Scott prided himself on the accuracy of his documentation, and, as is shown in his *apologia*, he regarded this aspect of the historical novel very seriously. It was for him primarily an exact reconstruction of the *mœurs* of the past. This positive and pseudo-didactic trend of his art it was which made such a strong appeal to the French Classics. For the Romantics, however, what mattered was that there was ample food for the imagination in the pageantry of the scenes and in the bravura of the adventures described by the great Scotsman. Here indeed was a cadre apparently elastic enough to embrace the whole range of humanity. Here, seemingly, the fancy could rove at its sweet will unhampered by rules of any sort. So indeed it appeared to these enthusiastic devotees, but was it really so?

In the 1822 crop of historical novels there was one, the *Héritière de Birague*, by a young man flaunting the somewhat pretentious *nom de plume* of Horace de Saint-Aubin. His real name was Honoré de Balzac. The *Héritière* passed, amongst a crowd of similar productions, as unnoticed as it deserved to be. In this novel we have the Balzac of the early imitative period with little, even in the descriptive passages, to suggest his later genius. The picture of manners of the period, which is that of Richelieu, is poorly executed and betrays unfamiliarity with the material at the author's disposal. The characters of the comte de Morvan and his wife Mathilde are obviously suggested, as is the theme, by *Macbeth*. The mysterious cloaked stranger who materialises at the stroke of midnight and who, as later transpires, is the imperfectly murdered father of the count, is painfully reminiscent of the melodrama of Pixérécourt and the terror novels of Maturin. Indeed the only human and probable figure is that of the hard-drinking swashbuckler, Captain de Chanclos, and even he is not original, so closely does he recall Pigault-Lebrun's Baron de Felsheim. Balzac is clearly ill at ease in the milieu he has chosen; yet in the character of the villain, the cold, ruthless, intriguing Italian, the marquis de Villani, there is the promise of better things. As we shall see, Balzac quickly realised that his knowledge of the past was as yet too imperfect to afford scope to his talent for characterisation and description of a creative sort; so, abandoning this type of novel, he turned his attention to the manners of a more recent period.

In 1826, says the *New Monthly Magazine*, English novels were very popular in Parisian society. "Independently of the Galignani reprints, not only the Scotch novels, but every work of fiction which has the slightest success in England is immediately translated into French." The knowledge and appreciation of English literature had indeed enormously advanced since 1822, when the public hissed the English actors under the vague impression that Shakespeare was Wellington's aide-de-camp! Now Cooke drew great crowds to the Théâtre de la Porte Saint-Martin, whilst to round off the *entente cordiale* the French comic actor Potier played before George IV. in London. *The Times* and *Morning Chronicle* were widely read in Paris, and young Frenchmen instead of going to Switzerland made pilgrimages to Scotland. Byron's *Don Juan*, of which a prose translation had just come out, and Scott's latest novel were the fashionable topics of conversation in Parisian *salons*. The great Sir Walter himself crossed the channel in 1826 and was presented to Charles X. It was during this stay that he received a visit from one of his most successful imitators, the poet-novelist Alfred de Vigny, who brought with him a dedication copy of his historical romance *Cinq-Mars*. What Scott had done so splendidly for the period of Louis XI. in *Quentin Durward* De Vigny did, but not splendidly, for the reign of Louis XIII.

Cinq-Mars is one of those exasperating novels which just misses the mark; why, it is difficult to say. The central character, Richelieu, is powerfully conceived and dominates the scene. De Vigny in one of his letters confesses that when he wrote *Cinq-Mars* Richelieu was his *ennemi intime*, and he is indeed a striking and sinister figure. He is more than a man: he is the symbol of ambition, the destructive force which, in De Vigny's eyes, sapped the foundations of monarchy. For that the Royalist author could not forgive him, and De Vigny's political and aristocratic bias darkens the whole novel. This subjective strain it is which differentiates him so sharply from the cool and objective Scotsman, and the Richelieu who emerges at the last page is improbably villainous just as Cinq-Mars is improbably sentimental.

De Vigny's style is dramatic, and certain episodes, for example the trial of Urbain Grandier, are alive with movement. But the plot lacks dramatic interest because the author chose his theme badly. The outstanding events in the life of the hero are of course well known to the reader before he opens the book. De Vigny tried unsuccessfully to reinforce the political intrigue by a love story, but unfortunately the heroine, Mlle de Gonzague, is anæmic and passive. The poet of *Eloa* and *Moïse* possessed a mind of philosophic cast. Observation, the first requisite in a novelist, is not his strongest point. Temperamentally, too, he was ill-equipped for the task of the historical novelist which is to evoke the bustle, colour and passions of the crowd. De Vigny has a poetic sympathy for the common people, but he cannot, like Sir Walter, reproduce their language or enter into their thought. And, though he was himself a soldier—perhaps because he was—he cannot, like Charles Reade for instance, stage a siege so that the reader has the enjoyable illusion of fighting side by side with a Denys. In a word, *Cinq-Mars* lacks local colour, which is a nice way of saying that it is an historical novel without a soul. Local colour cannot be added as an afterthought like a sort of seasoning to the repast, and this is precisely the impression one obtains from *Cinq-Mars*. To take an example, John Milton reads his *Paradise Lost* in Marion Delorme's *salon* to an audience which includes Molière, Corneille, Descartes, and sundry other equally illustrious men! De Vigny's description of this scene, like Milton's reading, is lamentably uninteresting. How could it not be? How could any novelist make Milton and Molière talk, not as they probably did talk, but as the reader expects them to? Here we have the essential defect of the whole novel. It is too historical. There are too many great and well-known characters and consequently very little room is left for the *romanesque* or purely fictional element that gives life and suspense to novels of this type.

Cinq-Mars reflects De Vigny's passion for the nobility, but it would be hard to find in *La Chronique de Charles IX.* any echo of the intimate opinions of its author, Prosper Mérimée. Writing of this work in the London *Athenæum* of 1837, Jules Janin the critic complains:

> It is the fault of this writer that, cold at all times, and ever self-possessed, he narrates all these dangers and terrors without any appearance of being moved by them himself. He seems as if he were an entire stranger to the book which he is writing, so little care does he take to arrange his plot, to dispose his incidents—so completely does he leave to themselves and to fortune those happy fictions which he is unskilled to turn to their full account.

Yet it is because of this "self-possession" or objectivism that Mérimée has given us one of the few French historial novels which we can still read with pleasure. *La Chronique de Charles IX.* has not the philosophic depth of *Cinq-Mars*, nor the impassioned movement of Hugo's *Notre Dame*, but it admirably reflects the tension of the political atmosphere on the eve of the massacre of Saint Bartholomew's Day. Mérimée deliberately limits his field of vision to the court and factious nobility of the two parties, Huguenot and Catholic. The reward is a series of very clear-cut portraits and a love intrigue round which crystallise incidents and characters. Very unobtrusively, too, the cool and indifferent attitude of the author produces a feeling of revulsion against religious fanaticism, an impression which is fortified as the characters develop. Bernard Mergy, the young and ardent Protestant, loses his religious fervour in the arms of his passionate mistress, the Countess de Turgis, who in turn finds that love is greater than proselytising zeal. Bernard's brother Georges, who is an atheist, goes over to the Catholic side because of an insult at the hands of Condé, but throws down his sword rather than take part in the massacre of Saint Bartholomew. Mérimée's most trenchant comment on the whole sorry business is the tragic death of Georges Mergy, who falls into an ambush prepared by his own brother and in his last moments is tormented by a priest and a Calvinist minister who squabble over his deathbed.

Mérimée knows his period, and his interpretation of the events leading to the massacre is the result of a careful study of contemporary memoirs. He has a horror of dogmatism and realises that his business as an historical novelist is not to express historical verdicts, but to sketch a probable picture of past manners and events. "I only say, suppose this supposition," he quotes from Byron, and most of his readers will find his suppositions plausible and very interesting. He has avoided, too, the common error of thrusting the big historical characters into the foreground, and his Coligny and Charles IX. are delineated with a fine sense of perspective. As a novelist Mérimée can give lessons in technique to any of his contemporaries, but his creative powers are limited. This he knew well, for his artistic instinct is keen and *Charles IX.* is his one long novel. He immediately abandoned this fictional form for the *nouvelle* or short story in which, as every schoolboy knows, he is an artist. *Mateo Falcone* and the *Vase étrusque* are masterpieces of their kind, models of psychological skill and classic restraint, for Mérimée is really a traditionalist only superficially touched by Romanticism. He continued the school of Courtilz de Sandras and above all of Hamilton, for in the *Chronique de Charles IX.* we catch an echo of the scepticism and airy persiflage of the age of the late seventeenth-century *libertins.*

At this stage in our narrative writers like Mérimée occur as a timely reminder of the fact that literature and in particular the novel was by no means entirely given over to Romanticism. The old materialistic, positive spirit was still very much alive, and there were many "Classics" or traditionalists of Mérimée's stamp who were, like the Romantics, attracted to the historical form of novel. One may perhaps be excused for harping on this subject, but it is one which needs elucidation since to so many critics an historical novel is another name for a Romantic novel. Surely this is a mistaken view. An historical novel is essentially very *romanesque* because it depicts a type of life and manners remote from the life and manners of our own environment, but it will not be a Romantic novel in the French sense unless it is coloured by the emotional and subjective outlook on life, which we have noted as so characteristic of the Romantic novelist. There were many lesser historical novelists in this period of confusion and flux, and their works reflect the whole spectrum of artistic tints, from the extremely sombre and violent Kératry, with his popular *Dernier des Beaumanoir* (1825), to the objective and analytic Henri de la Touche, whose successful *Fragoletta* (1829) is a cool and realistic picture of Revolutionary manners and intrigue in France and Italy. Generally speaking, in the Romantic historical novels psychology and intrigue are subordinated to local colour and action of the melodramatic sort, whilst in the works of the traditionalists the contrary is the case. In these the interest is not focused on a great canvas displaying a multitude of coloured details, but rather upon the destinies of two or three individuals whose passions furnish the dynamic force which makes the novel throb. Undoubtedly, however, the influence of Scott is everywhere evident in the new care with which historical background is now sketched in, and even when, as in *Fragoletta*, it is merely suggested, it is suggested with a fidelity and with an instinct for essential values almost totally absent in the late seventeenth-century historical novels of the school of Mme de Lafayette.

In the first-rate novel perfect harmony and balance is maintained between milieu, character and action, and defective art in historical novels is usually the result of too much rather than of too little attention to the creation of milieu. Most of Scott's French imitators, as we have seen, handled their local colour clumsily, looking upon it as an ornamental adjunct merely and not as an essential and inseparable part of the novel. The *Mercure au XIXe Siècle* for 1829 noted this abuse of local colour. "I confess," said its critic, "that my gratitude towards all our young Walter Scotts would be most fervent if I were quite certain that they knew their history . . . but I have learned to my great disenchantment, alas! that the taste of the century being for things which are as far removed as possible from our actual usages, writers manufacture the extraordinary with the intention of passing it off as the result of long bibliographical researches. Some are honest, but often they transport into the fifteenth century what belongs to the ninth or tenth; they take a few characteristics from all the centuries of the French monarchy and out of all this they make a harlequin's coat which they clap on to their hero." D'Arlincourt's *Ipsiboë*, a wretched imitation of *Ivanhoe*, is a typical instance of this false conception of what constitutes local colour. Almost every page swarms with archaisms grubbed up in medieval books and the text is invaded by an array of footnotes which would excite the envy of a Ph. D. candidate. Local colour, points out the *Mercure*, became a fetish with the Romantics, "a sort of Balkan peninsula placed between the partisans of Romanticism and the fortified citadels of the Classics."

Balzac, as has been noted, felt unequal to the heavy labour of documentation involved in the task of reconstructing the *mœurs* of the seventeenth century, and the local colour of the *Héritière de Birague* is lamentable. But he made very honourable amends in *Les Chouans* (1829) which deals with the Royalist insurrections of Brittany in 1799. Here was material so recent as to be almost immediately accessible to the observation, for there were many still living who had played a part in the events so dramatically resuscitated in *Les Chouans*. Off dashed Balzac to Fougères, where, aided by his father's old friend, General de Pommereuil, he ransacked the countryside for human documents and returned to Paris, his mind saturated with facts and impressions. Three months later appeared *Les Chouans* under the title of *Le Dernier Chouan*. It was rather coolly received by the critics, though the *Mercure au XIXe Siècle* praised it with the reserve that it was too "prolix."

Posterity has been more just and discerns in this work the deep thrumming note which opens that magnificent symphony, *La Comédie Humaine*. In this novel Balzac for the first time is really himself. He has passed beyond the stage of conscious imitation to listen only to the inner voice of his genius. Doubtless the success of Scott and De Vigny inspired him to use the form of the historical novel, but I can detect no significant echo of either in *Les Chouans*. With consummate art he spins his web of motives, passions, plot and counter-plot, darting backwards and forwards like a giant spider from Paris to Brittany, from Brittany to London, embracing all Europe almost in the toils of his imaginings, yet never for a moment allowing the interest to wander from its focal point. With that marvellous dual gift of analysis and synthesis he grasps his subject in all its aspects, local and universal. Seized with material which was passing from actuality into history he fuses it in the furnace of his imagination, hammering it on the anvil of genius into a brutal and convincing image of universal truth. That is his great secret: the power of rendering the improbable not only probable but natural. Marche-à-Terre, presented by any other novelist, would be a monstrosity as incredible as Han d'Islande or as ludicrous as the Solitaire. In *Les Chouans* he appears as the natural product of an atmosphere in which everything is extraordinary but perfectly credible. The same is true of the action which centres round the love of Le Gars, the Royalist leader, for Marie Verneuil, the ex-actress and emissary of Fouché. Where an inferior novelist would have made the mistake of concealing Marie Verneuil's mission till the dénouement, Balzac begins by making us a present of all the facts. Moreover, all the other characters know them too, and soon very cunningly the author by his ingenuous frankness makes it seem the most natural thing in the world that the Government should subsidise an inflammable courtesan and send her invested with plenary powers into one of the most critical zones of operations. It is only the big artists like Balzac who can do these things with impunity.

He avoids also the temptation of "romancing" the Chouan rising which he views as brigandage masquerading as a war. Whilst he fully appreciates the other motives that actuated the rebels, their religious fanaticism, their lust for revenge, their loyalty to the monarchy, the dominant passion in his eyes is the desire for loot. But in creating his central figures, Le Gars and Marie Verneuil, he has realised too that no insurrection is complete without its Romantics who seek in the dangers of troublous times an escape from the world of drab commonplace. Balzac saw in the Brittany of 1799 an admirably probable setting for the type of love that appealed to his imagination: elemental passion veering in a moment from loathing to adoration, the tigerish love that can only thrive where the ten commandments are temporarily in abeyance and where there are no social obstacles to its free expansion. There is a strong dash of Romanticism in *Les Chouans*, as indeed there is in all Balzac's early work, which like a seismometer faithfully registers the disturbances that convulsed intellectual France from 1830 to 1840.

Hugo's *Notre Dame de Paris* (1831) possesses the very qualities absent in *Cinq-Mars*—an exciting plot, stirring pictures of crowds in action and a wealth of fascinating details which vividly illustrate the manners and customs of fifteenth-century France. Hugo is a master of broad and telling effects, and *Notre Dame* has almost the stature of an epic. This illusion—for it is one—is produced by his original idea of imparting a life and soul to the great cathedral, which assumes the rôle of a character, the dominating character of the book. Notre-Dame is the rock round which the waves of the action surge and beat and eddy, and not for a second does Hugo allow us to move outside its shadow. Quasimodo, the hunchback, is its familiar genius, for to the author's Romantic mind the squat, misshapen body and inarticulate soul of the bell-ringer personify the cathedral. Quasimodo and Notre Dame are inseparable, and when he leaves it to seek out Esmeralda's body it is to die. Frollo, the priest, who is obsessed by his mad lust for the gipsy dancing-girl, also possesses symbolic meaning. He is the servant of Notre Dame, his true mistress. When he betrays her to adore another she ruthlessly punishes him. And at the close of the novel, when the great tumult of the mob has died away, when Quasimodo, Frollo and Esmeralda are dead, the cathedral looks down impassively on the corpses of the *truands* who measured their puny strength against hers—impassive, inexorable, like Destiny carved in stone.

It is rare to find a novel which, like *Notre Dame*, appeals to readers of every intellectual category. It has all the defects of popular fiction. The psychology of the characters is crudely sketchy; their actions are not always clearly motivated, and too great prominence is given to melodramatic or purely physical incident. That is why *Notre Dame* is such a remarkable success as a film, for it is ideally suited to the art of the cinema. On the other hand few historical novels offer such a splendid illusion of the period which they attempt to portray. No one, not even Scott, has so well reproduced the local colour, the costumes, manners, architecture, indeed the very spirit of an epoch, as Hugo has done in this novel. Certain scenes, the performance of the mystery-play, the *Cour des Miracles*, Quasimodo on the pillory, the attack on Notre Dame, hum with vitality, radiate colour. And if the characters lack the fine shades which we get, for example, in a Stendhal, the whole conception is so grandiose that Hugo's deficiencies as a psychologist almost pass unnoticed. Somehow, too, one feels that a minute analysis of human motives and conduct would here strike a dissonant note out of tune with an age the key-note of which is action and not introspection. Did Hugo unconsciously realise this when he painted his Louis XI. in primary colours, presenting only the bold dominant traits—avarice, cruelty, superstition, treachery and patriotism? This, I fancy, was accidental, and because Hugo's vision of life was a synthetic one; Balzac, the greater genius, combined the synthetic and analytic. This is, however, true only of their characterisation, since in the realm of the picturesque Hugo is a painstaking artist and a remarkably well-informed one. His costumes and interiors are executed with the meticulous fidelity of a Flemish painter.

As to his limitations as a psychologist, we have a good example in Frollo, who is of the stuff that Balzac loved to handle, a priest tortured by the demon of the flesh, an assassin and a dabbler in the occult. One has only to imagine what the creator of Troubert and Vautrin would have done with this material to realise the shortcomings of Hugo's Frollo. Where is the germination of passion, the gradual corrosion of the spirit as evinced in a steady remorseless march to climax and dénouement? The psychological life of Frollo is scarcely revealed at all. His obsession for Esmeralda is such that at first he nurtures a sadic desire to see her burned as a sorceress. His jealousy for her lover, Phœbus, drives him to attempt murder. At this stage surely a trifle like rescuing her from prison should not deter him, but instead he passively lets her go to her execution, from which she is saved by Quasimodo. When she is in sanctuary he tries to violate her; then, in order to rescue her, concocts an elaborate scheme whereby his own brother, aided by the poet Gringoire, excites the underworld of Paris to storm Notre Dame. Only when the riot is at its height does Frollo think of smuggling Esmeralda out at a side door to a boat waiting at the wharf. He then makes love to her in his peculiar way, which is to offer her the choice between yielding to him or being handed over to the hangman. Frollo's conduct is in fact a mass of improbabilities from the moment when disguised as a monk he asks Phœbus to let him spy on the latter's love-making with the gipsy to the final scene in the tower of Notre Dame when he gloats with satanic glee over the corpse of Esmeralda dangling on the Place de la Grève. In fact the Frollo of the beginning is exactly the Frollo of the closing pages: he is, psychologically speaking, static. In creating him it seems clear that Hugo was influenced by recollections of Goethe's Faust, but Frollo, far from presenting the spectacle of a man whose soul is the battle-ground of virtue and vice, of religious and profane love, leaves the final impression of an unpleasantly erotic archdeacon in a state of constant terror lest his doings should come to the official notice of the authorities.

Stendhal, in a letter to an English friend (24 December, 1824), comments as follows on the prevailing mania for historical novels: "All the writers who aspire to celebrity in France are hastening to publish their imitation of Scott. M. de Salvandy has given us his *Alonzo*; M. Félix Bodin, his *Le Père et la Fille*; M. Trognon his *Childebert III.*; M. Kératry, his *Le Dernier des Beaumanoir.* All these works have been vigorously *puffed* by the authors themselves in the journals which they edit." Eight years later he estimated the number of Scott's French imitators at two hundred, and he was not exaggerating, for in the period from 1820 to 1840 it was rare to find a novelist who did not try his hand at this species of fiction. Inevitably, too, the historical novel attracted a large number of writers who strictly speaking were not novelists at all, but chroniclers like the celebrated "Bibliophile Jacob" (Paul Lacroix) who patiently explored the annals of France for interesting facts and details which they clumsily threw into novel form. It is in such productions that one sees the great harm which this mania for historical fiction was doing to the novel in general by atrophying the creative powers of the novelist. As the *Revue française* of 1829 pointed out, the exaggerated cult for reality in historical fiction tended to paralyse the imagination. Writers no longer dared to create, but were content to follow the line of least resistance, resuscitating the manners of the past, but making no advance in the exploration of the soul. The only hope for the French novel lay, as the *Revue française* correctly surmised, in a departure from this sheep-like imitation of Scott into that virgin field, the history of contemporary manners. As it happened, it was in this direction that original novelists like Stendhal, Sand and Balzac were already moving.

The *Flâneur* for 1836 gives a recipe for concocting historical novels which aptly describes the formula adopted by Scott's imitators. "To make an historical novel, you rummage in the archives of some town; you unearth the usages and customs of that town, the names of the *échevins*, the prerogatives of the corporations, the scandalous chronicles of the time; add to this a hopeless love, four or five orgies, duels, a seduction, two adulteries and a more or less threadbare dénouement and you have an historico-dramatic or quasi-historico-dramatic novel. The essence of the novel will always be the same; it will consist of a requited or unrequited passion, murders, adulteries, marriages . . ." Such novels, says the *Flâneur*, differ only in local colour the recipe for which is as follows: "*France Under Charles VI.*: A scene with Maillotins; description of a Court of Love; a cartel; squires and ladies; a good dagger. *Louis XI.*: A jest of Olivier le Daim's; a smutty adventure of the Cardinal de la Balue's; a student's riot. *Louis XV.*: Half a dozen orgies; as many duels; three pannier dresses; . . . three *lettres de cachet*; two seductions, etc."

Henri Beyle, or, as he is better known, Stendhal, disapproved strongly of this Romantic abuse of local colour. Indeed, he disapproved of everything connected with the Restoration. As a lieutenant of dragoons, and later as an army auditor, Stendhal roamed all over Europe in the wake of Napoleon, a cool and sardonic observer of epic events. His war experience, naturally enough, accentuated his cosmopolitan outlook on humanity and made him acutely suspicious of sentimental manifestations of any sort. He acquired, therefore, a distaste amounting almost to a loathing of the emotional Romantic idiom, or as he termed it, "la phrase à la Chateaubriand." Although one of the first to interpret the beauties of Shakespearian drama to his countrymen, he disassociated himself peremptorily from the melodramatic and Hugoesque extravagances of the Romantic coterie of 1830. Indeed his interest in contemporary French literature was slight, and he wrote to Balzac in 1840 that apart from a few novels by Sand and some short stories by Frédéric Soulié he had read nothing in French since 1810. Taken literally, this is of course an exaggeration. Essentially, it is true, for Stendhal's great passion was Italian literature and art, which he knew from first-hand observation. With English literature he was also well acquainted, and as a young man conceived a great admiration for Byron, whom he met in Italy in 1816, and classed along with Napoleon and the sculptor Canova as one of the three greatest men he had ever encountered. Yet what attracted him to Byron was not so much the latter's poetic talent as his *byronisme*: his aristocratic disdain of public opinion, his revolt against the cant of contemporary society and above all his sublime egotism, which struck an answering chord in the heart of Stendhal, who was himself an intense individualist.

This individualism of his, however, is not the individualism of Romantics like Rousseau or Chateaubriand. It finds its outlet, not in lyricism or in melancholy and tragic introspection, but rather in a cold restrained irony which colours his whole attitude towards life. Stendhal's individualism finds its most natural expression in a species of intellectual iconoclasm which inspired in him an instinctive distrust of accepted ideas on life and art. Like Descartes whom he admired, he discovered that three-fourths of the so-called "truths" which the ordinary man adopts without examination are inaccuracies, consecrated by tradition and intellectual sloth. This is why he approved of the restless probing analytic method of Marivaux. "If you prepare yourself by reading every morning twenty pages of Marivaux's *Marianne*," he wrote to Mme Gaultier in 1834, "you will understand the advantage of accurately describing the movements of the human heart." For him as for Marivaux, amour-propre is the motive force of all human conduct, and in his analytic study, *De L'Amour*—which is, style apart, pure Marivaux—as in his three great novels, *Armance* (1826), *Le Rouge et le Noir* (1830) and the *Chartreuse de Parme* (1838), all the variants of amour-propre—egotism, vanity, pride, etc.—play a decisive role in the comedy of human life.

The fundamental weakness of man, as Stendhal sees him, is lack of intellectual sincerity. Most of our unhappiness could be avoided, he thinks, if we practised what he calls *beylisme*, which is essentially anti-Romanticism. It is the knack of seeing ourselves in our proper perspective in relation to the rest of humanity, stripped of the illusions conjured up by our imagination. Julien Sorel, in *Le Rouge et le Noir*, sees himself as a second Napoleon, but since, under the Restoration, a military career holds out no prospects of power or glory to this ambitious and monstrous egotist, he enters the Church. The son of a carpenter—there is deliberate malice in the mental contrast suggested by the phrase—Sorel seduces the wife of the man whose children he tutors, and by dint of patience and dæmonic energy becomes private secretary to a great nobleman, M. de La Mole, whose patrician daughter he finally brings to heel after a long and intricate campaign of duplicity and self-discipline. Yet in the end he dies on the scaffold for having in an outburst of ferocity attempted to murder his first mistress. The whole elaborately constructed edifice of lies and hypocrisy which compose his existence collapses then, because for one fatal moment he was his true self, the vindictive and envious peasant lad whose imagination was corrupted by the *Mémoires de Sainte-Hélène*. Imagination blinded him to the reality of life, to the fact that under a regime like the Restoration, governed by aristocrats and Jesuits, not even the ambition and the will-power of a Julien Sorel can make a Napoleon of a plebeian. This complex character, who offers more than one affinity with Stendhal himself, is the victim of the very passion which carries him from his father's sawmill to the Faubourg Saint-Germain, for it is his rage at an insult to his amour-propre that prompts him to shoot Mme de Rênal, who exposed his secret ambition to M. de La Mole. Yet before setting out to kill her he hands back Mme de Rénal's letter to his second mistress, Mathilde de La Mole, with these words: "I cannot blame Monsieur de La Mole; he is just and prudent. What father would wish to give his dear daughter to such a man?" Thus at the very moment when his vindictiveness is being translated into action it is not his passion but his habit of hypocrisy which finds utterance in speech. And so inveterate is this habit that even in the condemned cell, twenty-four hours before his death, he cannot be sincere with himself. Like Harpagon, who caught himself robbing Harpagon, Julien Sorel in his last moments is as hypocritical as if someone were present to listen to his words.

Stendhal detested hypocrisy and stupidity with equal ferocity. *Le Rouge et le Noir* is a bitter attack on Jesuitism, which to him was the incarnation of hypocrisy, and in *La Chartreuse de Parme* he exposes the incredible pettiness, vanity and intrigue that underlie the pomp and circumstance of court life. But his true originality reveals itself in his conception of love and in particular in the opposition of love and self-esteem. His novels are indeed the practical application of the theories which are so meticulously exposed in the treatise, *L'Amour*. Each of his women represents a different aspect of love. Mme de Rénal becomes an adulteress because of too much sensibility and pity. Her anxiety about Julien's shirts is her first step to destruction. Mlle de La Mole, the *femme forte*, falls because of her Romantic imagination, in which she dramatises herself till she has the illusion of being like one of her noble ancestresses, a *grande amoureuse*. Armance is attracted to Octave by a curious blend of emotions. Having just acquired several millions he is the "catch of the season," and Armance, who is poor and acutely sensitive, openly shows her contempt, thus creating in Octave a passionate desire to gain her esteem. It is the realisation of her injustice which by a counter-swing arouses her love for Octave. When she is convinced that his moodiness and misanthropy are not the insolent *ennui* of the spoiled bachelor, but the reflection of a hidden tragic sorrow, Armance's love becomes passion, a passion all the more violent because it has encountered the resistance of her amour-propre. In the *Chartreuse de Parme* Stendhal has attempted, in the portrait of Gina Sanseverina, a daring and original psychological study. Gina is, like most of the characters in the novel, completely amoral. She might have said, as did Octave in *Armance*: "I have no *conscience*. I find no trace in me of what you call a *sens intime*, no *instinctive* repugnance for crime. When I abhor vice it is quite simply as the result of a rational process, and because I find it harmful." Gina is in love with her nephew, Fabrice, but as she never examines her feelings she is never conscious of the significance of her love, and if she were it is extremely doubtful if she would experience any remorse. All her education has been intellectual and positive, not moral and spiritual. Living in the present, her whole existence is devoted to the protection and advancement of Fabrice, who good-naturedly leaves his future in her hands. So when Gina suggests that he prepare himself for an archbishopric Fabrice dutifully carries out the elaborate programme arranged by his inventive aunt and her lover, the prime minister Count Mosca. Clélia Conti, with whom Fabrice actually falls in love, is a rational young woman with a high sense of her moral duties as laid down by her confessor. To save Fabrice she becomes an accomplice to the drugging of her father, the governor of the jail where Fabrice is imprisoned, and in a fit of remorse makes a vow to the Virgin that she will never see her lover again. With typical irony, however, Stendhal makes her salve her conscience by receiving Fabrice at night so that literally she does not see him. Superstitious to the end, she regards the death of their love-child as divine punishment for her having broken her vow by allowing Fabrice to share her vigil at the child's bedside by candlelight.

Stendhal presents life as a bewildering spectacle of disorder, a human comedy in which none of the actors remember their cues or speak their lines as we should expect them to. This is because the majority of human beings act not from logic or reason but from passion. Logically Fabrice should be pining his heart out in his lofty prison on the Farnese rock, but by one of Stendhal's impish contrasts, whilst his aunt and her friends are moving heaven and earth to gain contact with him, Fabrice's one fear is lest Clélia will fail to come that morning at a quarter to twelve to feed her birds in the aviary beneath his window. When Fabrice kills the strolling actor Giletti, his first words are a request for a mirror to see if his face has been damaged by the hilt of Giletti's dagger. The description of Waterloo is a classic example of Stendhalesque irony. At the crucial moment when the emperor rides past, Fabrice, who has drunk too much brandy, cannot see Napoleon because of that accursed extra glass! In all Stendhal's novels this contrast between imagination and reality occurs, a sardonic leitmotiv in the symphony of existence. The universe is a badly synchronised mechanism. The people who ought to love each other love someone else, a futile and lavish waste of energy and passion. We prepare for catastrophes which never happen or happen in unexpected ways.

To-day, of course, this attitude of mind, which in Stendhal was natural and sincere, has been perverted into a technical formula by every novelist who has not the wit or patience to observe life for himself. As a result we get—what we never find in Stendhal—improbable situations and conduct artificially dragged in with no regard for psychological probability, in order to stage a paradoxical contrast. This is not only bad art, but unprofitable art, since the reader gets to know the technique as well as the author, anticipates all the moves and speeches and ceases to be astonished. Even a Chesterton will soon fail to interest us when we learn like him the trick of looking at life standing on our heads or how to run through the alphabet of logic backwards. An ironical incident depicted by Stendhal, however, stands the test of meditation. Indeed, once the reader has recovered from his preliminary shock of surprise he realises that, given the psychology of the characters involved and their particular situation, Stendhal's version of what happened is the only one consistent with probability. The great and sincere artist feels such things instinctively. In this connection Stendhal's letter to Balzac on the genesis of the *Chartreuse de Parme* is illuminating. After the amusing *boutade* that he read two pages daily of the *Code civil* in order to preserve the naturalness and clarity of his style, he adds: "I take a character well known to me. I leave him the habits which he has acquired in the art of setting out in his daily pursuit of happiness, then I give him more *esprit.*" The final phrase is interesting because it is an unconscious reflection of Diderot's famous remark on the difference between artistic truth and the truth of life. Our realistic novelists, when they fail, do so because they neglect this essential artistic truth. A novel, like a play, is not a transcript but a synopsis, a condensation of experience, an interpretation of life; and the novelist, like the playwright, must retouch and exaggerate the realities which he has observed, because the novel, like the play, has its "optics." Only the great artists achieve to perfection this difficult business of transferring reality from its great and natural cadre to the miniature, artificial cadre of the work of fiction. The temptation to use all the material is too great, and the average novelist has not as a rule the self-discipline to discard the irrelevant though interesting matter and to retain only the significant and vital traits which produce the illusion of complete life. In the case of the *Chartreuse* Stendhal accentuated the natural psychological features of his characters by lending them *esprit*—the only form of "make-up" which would not clash with their peculiar individuality. Realising his limitations, he was careful not to spoil the bold relief of the finished work by the addition of descriptive details of costume or milieu. In the same letter to Balzac he wrote: "For a year I have been told that I must sometimes distract the reader with descriptions of costume or scenery. . . . These things bore me so in others. . . . I should exaggerate!" He was quite right. Black and white, not colour, was his artistic medium. Balzac, working on a greater scale, nearly always succeeded in preserving the proper proportion both in characterisation and in reproduction of milieu. That is why he is *hors concours* and also possibly why he has not so many imitators as Stendhal, whose influence on the French novel since the eighteen-sixties has been very great, though in his lifetime he was appreciated only by Balzac and Mérimée. It is said that he was fond of describing himself as "un observateur du cœur humain." This is exactly what he was. With him the novel of psychological analysis acquired new vitality, and tragic passion, as distinct from lyrical and pathetic sensibility, re-entered fiction for the first time since *Manon Lescaut.* Once again we encounter men and women who feel profoundly enough to do instead of talking about doing—amoral egotists, but intensely alive and elemental.

CHAPTER V

CHANGING VALUES

SAINTE-BEUVE, like Jules Janin, and for that matter like all the critics of the Restoration, exaggerated the influence of the *coup d'état* of 1830. According to him, the Revolution of July "demobilised" the forces of Romanticism, a judgment which a century of perspective has shown to be fallacious, for the change of dynasty in no way altered the trend of Restoration literature. On the contrary, it hastened if anything the full flowering of Romanticism by creating an atmosphere favourable to the development not only of a Romantic literature and art which were already well advanced, but also of a Romantic philosophy, sociology, and religion. Nowhere perhaps is this general fermentation in French thought so luminously revealed as in the astonishing luxuriance of the French novel during the reign of Louis-Philippe.

By 1830 the Romantic type was already adumbrated, though no great novelist had arisen to exploit its psychological possibilities and thus to carry on the work so ably begun by Chateaubriand, Constant and Nodier. Naturally enough, the progress thus far achieved by the Romantic novel was primarily extrinsic, not intrinsic. Drunk with colour and sensation, the *Jeune-France* writers found a facile medium of expression in picturesque description and melodramatic invention, whilst in the atmosphere of bygone days they sought an illusory escape from the unsatisfactory world of actuality. In their pursuit of sensation they drifted farther and farther from normality, eagerly sacrificing psychological truth to obtain astonishing and dazzling effects. The strange supernatural tales of the German Hoffmann, first made known to the French by the translations of Loève-Weimar in 1829, enjoyed for some years a vogue which almost rivalled that of the Waverley novels. Soon dozens of *contes fantastiques* testified to the popularity of this new species of fiction, so ill-adapted, nevertheless, to the peculiar genius of the French. The *Edinburgh Review* for 1833 makes the following appropriate comment on these Hoffmann imitations:

> The authors take care indeed to have their punchbowls surrounded in the most approved style with a plentiful supply of blue flames through which imps and *homunculi* flutter in profusion, serpents twine along the smoke up to the ceiling, faces grin upon the reader from the knocker of a door, lidless eyes glare upon them from bodiless heads; the hazy confounding effect in short of the *Fantasiestücke* and the *Golden Pot* is imitated with an elaborate *niaiserie*; but, alas! the true elixir which Hoffmann possesses, be it from the devil's cellar or not, is still to Messieurs Janin, Balzac, Charles Rabou and their brethren as a vessel sealed with Solomon's seal.

Of Janin's and Balzac's share in this agreeable madness we shall presently speak, but in the meantime let us turn to another vogue, also of foreign origin. In 1827 Fenimore Cooper during a sojourn in Paris received a flattering letter from Eugène Sue with a dedicatory copy of his novel *Plick et Plock*. So far as I know, the disgruntled American never acknowledged the gift nor made the slightest attempt to make the acquaintance of his French rival, of whom he ignores the existence in his correspondence. None the less Sue contrived to survive the slight and became the Cooper of France. With his *Atargull* (1831), *La Salamandre* (1832), *La Vigie de Koalven* (1833), to mention but three titles from his stupendous repertory, he founded what was called *le roman maritime*. As in all his works—who has not heard of the *Mystères de Paris* (1842) and *Le Juif errant* (1844)?—Sue built up a European reputation and a nabob's fortune by catering to the popular lust for melodramatic adventure. His sea stories are a hotch-potch of blood-curdling incidents and extravagant descriptions of foreign lands which he had, for the most part, never seen. In his novels planters, pirates, ferocious tars, *grands seigneurs*, easy midshipmen and easier ladies love and fight and murder each other. The secret of his success is that of Dumas the elder and I suppose of every popular novelist—movement. His plots are improbable and incoherent, his characters absurd, but Sue's admirers cared not a fig for that so long as he treated them to a continuous cinematograph display of murder, rape, robbery with and without violence, arson and treason, enlivened from time to time by his peculiar flashes of savage humour. Yet despite all his defects he was the first nineteenth-century French novelist to inspire his readers with a love of the open-air novel of adventure. Fashionable people like the critics of *La Mode* might wrinkle their noses and sniff at this *littérature saumonée*, jeering at his "drawing-room sailors, his boudoir *matelots* and his corsairs perfumed with tar and rose-water." Sue smiled and pocketed the cash. There is indeed a Gilbertian flavour to his pirates, but unlike the late Lord Goschen he did have some "notion of the motion of the ocean," having served as an apprentice to a ship's doctor on the Mediterranean. Corbière, the author of the *Pilotes de l'Iroise* (1832) and another Cooper adept, was not so successful. Like Sue he used the *roman maritime* as a vehicle for exciting strong emotions, but with him the picture of nautical manners disappears completely beneath a lava of horrors.

These imitations of Hoffmann and of Fenimore Cooper, like the early work of Hugo, reflect in varying degrees the Romantic craving for the unusual and sensational. In the novels of Jules Janin the same tendency is visible, but with this author it assumes the form of a perverted realism. Janin, a really notable critic, lacks the novelist's power of seizing and developing the essential traits in a character or situation. A fervent admirer of Diderot, for whose *Neveu de Rameau* he wrote a sequel called *La Fin du Monde*, his principal novels, the *Âne mort ou la Femme guillotinée* (1829) and *La Confession* (1830), are strongly reminiscent of Diderot's pungent wit, incoherent, vivid imagination and his critical, paradoxical view of life. The *Âne mort* was written, Janin tells us, to show how terror can be inspired without resorting to the supernatural. It is difficult to find the Ariadne's thread in this labyrinth of horrors, which symbolises Janin's revolt against the pleasant Theocritean conception of life as reflected in the amiable French pastoral novels of the seventeenth century. Humanity, for Janin, is morally and physically disgusting, so to illustrate this thesis he makes his heroine a strumpet and his hero the public hangman, Charlot, as he is affectionately called by his intimates. The novel opens with a picture of the abattoir at Charenton, the famous *barrière de combat* where elderly horses are mauled to death by dogs to the exquisite delight of the populace. With obvious relish Janin proceeds to describe the morgue, the operating-theatre at Salpetrière, and the execution of Henriette the prostitute, who is seduced by her jailer. Her last thoughts are not for her child but for her pet donkey, so wickedly torn to death by the savage curs of Charenton. The *Confession* is more coherent though its psychology is equally fantastic. Anatole, the hero, is intended, says Janin, to represent "the moral *gêne* of a man who feels the need for a belief and can no longer find this belief in the sanctuary because it is nowhere." That is the theory. In point of fact Anatole is a sombre imbecile who strangles his wife on his wedding night because (1) he cannot remember her first name, (2) she will grow old and ugly and (3) or else will deceive him. Having performed this husbandly office he is seized with remorse, and the remainder of the novel deals with his long and at first unsuccessful search for a priest worthy to hear his confession. At last he finds his man, a proscribed Jesuit priest. However, by this time Anatole has fallen in love and no longer wants to confess, but the priest, who by a strange coincidence knows of the crime, drags confession from him.

Anatole loses his reason for a time, but recovers and enters the priesthood, living happily ever after, save when occasionally to his unspeakable remorse he misses a vigil. Janin is not a good novelist, but his work is interesting to the student of the novel because it reveals very clearly the origin of the nineteenth-century realistic novel which was soon to supersede the subjective productions of the Romantic school. And more important still, it shows that close affinity between Realism and Romanticism already so noticeable in novels like Hugo's *Dernier Jour d'un Condamné* and which will be even more obvious in the work of Balzac. Carlyle used to refer to Romantic literature as "the literature of despair," and indeed it may be regarded as a despairing effort to escape from the drabness of reality into a world of the ideal. But as we have pointed out, there were many, and Janin is one of them, who could not shake off the chain riveting them to the world of actuality, writers devoid of that gorgeous power of self-hallucination which afforded to so many a way of escape from present reality into the dream country of the distant past or a visionary future. Janin was one of those frustrated Romantics. He too had the vision of an ideal beauty, but it was obscured by the ever-present consciousness of a reality that he could not forget, and as a result, he shut his eyes to the beauty which does exist in humanity until the ugliness of life filled his field of vision, assuming forms as fantastic as were ever dreamed of by a drunken Hoffmann. Long before Zola, De Maupassant and our modern supernaturalists, he nursed the illusion that a novelist can interpret the truth of life by steadfastly suppressing his imagination and deliberately starving his æsthetic sense. Hating actuality as much as the Romantics, he jibed at their foolish attempts to take refuge in the colour and romance of the Middle Ages, their novels of "ghouls, gnomes and salamanders" the "solitary trances of the heroes of the psychological novel who live like René outside all society." The curse of Romantic literature, it seemed to Janin, was too much imagination. "In regard to novels," he wrote in his preface to *La Confession*, "and the same is true of all the arts of imagination and of thought, to imagine nothing is the only resource left to us." In theory then he was a reactionary, but only in theory, for the *Âne mort* and the *Confession* present a world peopled with beings as unreal, as hideous as those strange creatures conceived by the brain of Hoffmann or the etcher Gustave Doré, but which with a slight adjustment of the focus might readily pass muster as the creations of a Zola.

A flock of minor novelists, following the lead of Janin and of Hugo, turned their attention to the life of the lower classes in search of new sensations and incidentally broke new ground in the field of the novel. Thus Signol in his *Lingère* (1830) offers some admirable pictures of Jewish manners and a series of excellent impressions of Parisian Bohemia almost equal to anything done by Henri Mürger, who later annexed this province in his *Vie de Bohème* (1851). Masson and Brücker in their *Contes de l'Atelier* (1829) and in *Le Maçon* (1834) wrote with great realism of the domestic life of the working classes. *Le Maçon*, though of course a fourth-rate novel, already announces the school of Zola. In certain scenes, for instance when he pictures the Place de la Grève at dawn or reports the conversation of the mob at an execution, Brücker reveals himself as a precocious naturalist. The short story called *La Mère* in the *Contes de l'Atelier* displays real artistic power. It is an unforgettable and ironic account of the keeper of a bawdy-house who manages to bury her past; becomes a respectable *mère de famille*, marries her illegitimate daughter to a genteel young bourgeois and finally dies mourned by her grateful family, who erect to her memory a tombstone with the inscription, "Ici repose une bonne mère."

The Romantics were all more or less victims of the Rousseauistic fallacy of the natural goodness of the *peuple*, and it was largely thanks to this illusion that the French novel became for the first time democratic. The works of Brücker and Masson, which are not particularly tinged with this prejudice, are therefore exceptional, since most of the novels of popular manners written in the thirties are strongly subjective and philanthropic, contrasting as a rule the primitive virtue of the people with the refined viciousness of the aristocracy. Closely associated of course with this attitude is the cult of the criminal, which explains the popularity of such foreign works as Zschokke's *Le Galérien*, the metaphysical and virtuous German convict who elicited from the sardonic critic of the *Universel* the appropriate and eloquent comment, *Que diable faisait-il dans cette galère?* It is interesting to note how the subjective element, the thesis, in such novels operates to the detriment of art. Touchard Lafosse's *Homme du Peuple* (1829), for instance, which he calls a *roman de mœurs*, is not a novel of manners at all, but a Romantic plea for the rights of the lower classes, containing occasional arresting descriptions of humble life, but ruined by the author's demagogic garrulousness. "The novel is a tribunal," said the *Revue de Paris* in 1832. "To-day the novelist believes himself to be a statesman like the journalist and politician." This critic probably had in mind inferior novelists like D'Arlincourt, Rey-Dusseuil and Pigault-Lebrun, who were now using the historical novel form for Legitimist propaganda, thereby illustrating the truth of Stendhal's favourite dictum that politics in a novel is like a pistol shot in the middle of a symphony concert. Yet outside the domain of party politics there was scarcely a novelist of the Louis-Philippe period who did not at some time use fiction as a channel for disseminating his pet theories on religion and social reform. The social novel, which is the nineteenth-century counterpart of the eighteenth-century *roman philosophique*, was indeed founded by the Romantics, and whilst one or two writers of the calibre of Balzac and Sand succeeded in producing artistic masterpieces in this difficult genre, the great majority gave birth to abortions which were neither good novels nor good treatises. This is no condemnation of the social novel *per se*, because a great novel like a great play is all the greater if it is suffused by the glow of generous hatred of a social evil. It is great, however, not because of its choice of a social theme, but because of its artistic treatment of that theme. The temptation here is to arrange life to suit the exigencies of the thesis, a fundamental error which not even the artistic skill of a Bourget can redeem; for nothing is more calculated to chill the reader's sympathy and forfeit his interest than the spectacle of a group of characters carefully selected to illustrate various aspects of a social problem. A novel composed in this manner becomes a clever exercise in dialectic, the outcome of which is obvious from the beginning. Moreover, as the novel progresses its mathematical structure becomes painfully evident, and the flesh and blood characters shrivel before our eyes into the semblance of robots obediently talking and acting at the dictates of a thesis. Life as seen through the medium of such a novel becomes improbably free from complexity, and its men and women seem unreal because their conduct is governed by intellect and not by passion. Again, and perhaps this is the greatest defect of all, the novelist is too apt to attribute to his characters a force of insight which they could not naturally possess, making them, for instance, see the relationship of their own particular situation to the vast social problem which he is discussing. Yet in real life how very few of us are capable of such a form of synthetic thinking! It is this error in psychology which vitiates many of the novels of that gifted artist George Sand, the first great representative of the social novel in French, who in this capacity exercised such a profound influence on Dostoïeffsky and Tolstoi.

The twentieth century claims to have evolved a completely objective type of literary criticism, the critic having now acquired, it would seem, the scientist's gift of impersonal and impassive observation. Yet when we examine any particular application of this scientific method, the fallacy of any such objective system of critical approach to literature becomes immediately evident. It is peculiarly so in regard to the work of George Sand because everything she wrote is the idealised reflection of her spiritual and moral aspirations and perplexities. And since most of her novels are a condemnation of the social order, the scientific critic, to fulfil his rôle, must begin by severing the fibres that unite him to that social order. In a word, he must divest himself of the mass of traditions, prejudices and ideals composing his individuality, a feat of imagination which may indeed be possible, but which in the case of George Sand has nevertheless not yet been achieved if we may judge from the contradictory impressions produced upon our minds by the many and varied critical studies and articles on this novelist.

Her contemporaries, who possessed only one critical standard, the moral one, had a very simple task. I quote the following appreciation of her work from the *Quarterly Review* as a fair specimen of orthodox opinion in 1836.

> We have had, and we still have, some conscientious doubts whether we should mention this author at all, but we have been determined to do so by having found *his* works in our London circulating libraries. Whether we shall have sufficient influence to put them into the *Index Expurgatorius* we know not; but at least we may be

permitted to mention in *Albemarle Street* what is sold and circulated in *Piccadilly* and *Bond Street.*

Madame du Devant—for, although we decline taking severer measures, we must at least condemn her, as the Parliament of Paris did the Chevalier d'Éon, to wear her petticoats—Madame du Devant, we say, is a closer follower of Rousseau than any of the writers we have been mentioning. *They* have adopted the principles of the *school—she* mimics the very gait and manners of the *master.* The majority of her novels are founded on a single plot—the plot of the *Héloïse—an ill-assorted marriage and an adulterous amour*; and the very unequal conflict between duty and passion is conducted in a *burning* style, both of sentiment and language, obviously kindled at the guilty flame of *Julie* and *St. Preux.* But she has in some respects gone far beyond her model. Rousseau never ventures to exhibit the actual scene of guilt, however vividly he paints its preliminaries and consequences. Madame du Devant has no such scruples. Rousseau, moreover, in the note which he adds to the conclusion of the *Héloïse*, adduces, as a kind of palliation to the immorality of his story, that at least it is not aggravated by the addition of "*noirceurs*," "*crimes*," "*horreurs*"; and he expresses a contemptuous pity for both the heads and hearts of the authors who deal in such deplorable dramas. But Madame du Devant has not only repeated the main incident of the *Héloïse* in several different novels, but finding, we suppose, that frequent repetition deprives even adultery of its zest, she thinks it necessary to stimulate the palling appetite of her readers with "*noirceurs*," "*crimes*," *et* "*horreurs*" beyond what even the corrupt head or corrupt heart of Rousseau could have imagined.

It is a remarkable testimonial to the originality and precocity of George Sand that she continues to arouse in critics of the school of M. Seillière sentiments of equally violent hostility. Her bold and subversive theories, fearlessly—or, as her detractors would say, cynically—expressed in all her novels of the combative or anti-social phase, produce a sense of irritation which has led many to depreciate the artistic value of these works. Yet in *Indiana* (1832), in *Valentine* (1832) and in *Jacques* (1834), to select at random three of the best-known early novels, she imported qualities that revitalised fiction—enthusiasm, sincerity, lyricism, and above all a new interpretation of love, which this arch-Romantic conceives as a religion, indeed, the only religion, transcending all social or moral laws. She is, as the *Quarterly* notes, a lineal descendant of Rousseau, but he, it will be remembered, tried to compromise between the claims of passion and those of that social institution called marriage, in his *Nouvelle Héloïse*. Moreover, Jean-Jacques with all his fine pretence of egalitarianism was at heart an early Victorian in his attitude towards woman, for whom that great feminist, George Sand, demands absolute liberty in her emotional life. She is the first novelist to grapple with the problem of unhappy marriage, and this of course she was admirably qualified to do because of her own unfortunate marital experience. *Indiana* and *Valentine* discuss the question from the point of view of the woman; *Jacques* from that of the man. In *Indiana* the solution is, bluntly, free love, though with the death of the brutal husband, Colonel Delmare, every obstacle to a legal union had disappeared. In *Valentine* both the hero and heroine die, victims of society, but in *Jacques* the husband commits suicide rather than stand in the way of Fernande's union with Octave. Summarised in this way the dénouements of *Indiana* and *Jacques* appear of course unconvincing and maybe preposterous. Yet, if we follow the character development step by step there is nothing in the final decision arrived at by these two which is at all factitious or unexpected. Indiana and Jacques are Romantics and therefore exceptional beings. Their attitude towards society is one of revolt because in society they see merely an annoying barrier erected between them and an ideal. Indiana, whom the author presents as the prototype of "woman suppressed by the laws," is an impulsive, passionate creature who in her ignorance of the world expects to find ideal happiness in marriage. She finds it neither with her husband, the apoplectic ex-cavalry officer, nor, for that matter, with her lover Raymond, the man of the world, but with her cousin Ralph, who is like herself a misunderstood Romantic. Jacques, on the other hand, enters marriage prepared for the worst, convinced as he is that he is predestined to unhappiness in this as in every other social relationship. "I have lived in vain," he tells us; "I have never found any harmony or similarity between me and anything that exists. Is it my fault or that of others? Am I dried up and devoid of sensibility? Am I incapable of loving? Have I too much pride? It seems to me that no one loves with more devotion and passion; it seems to me that my pride yields to everything and that my affection resists the most terrible tests." His attitude towards marriage is one of complete disillusionment, and he tells Fernande before the ceremony that the marriage vows are an empty farce. "You are going to swear to be faithful and to obey me; that is to say, never to love anyone but me and to obey me in everything. One of these vows is absurd; the other is infamous. You cannot answer for your heart even if I were the greatest, the most perfect of men." The only really binding vow, he avers, is the one not demanded by the law;

that the husband should respect his wife's individuality. Such are his principles, and at least he follows them with courage and consistency. Yet, sincere as is his love for Fernande, his marriage is an egoistic experiment, since he has nothing to lose and everything to gain should it prove successful. His sense of justice, which like all his other sentiments is exalted, tells him that his own life is not too high a price to pay for failure. It is easy to dismiss Jacques as a madman and to pooh-pooh his suicide as incredible. But he is not mad: he is simply the product of an epoch, a victim of the Romantic malady, and as such accurately and logically conceived. He is the *homme fatal* destined to unhappiness and doomed to blight the peace of mind of all who come within the aura of his spiritual influence.

Jacques is generally supposed to be George Sand's reply to the criticism that she was prejudiced against men, a criticism to which her amorous life was the most suitable retort. Her opinion of her own sex as expressed in *Indiana* is by no means flattering. "Woman is an imbecile by nature. It seems that to counterbalance the eminent superiority which her delicate perceptions give her over us, Heaven has purposely placed in her heart a blind vanity, an idiotic credulity." It is this vanity, this "idiotic credulity," which is the secret of woman's unhappiness as it was of George Sand's. That is why in her novels one is so constantly shocked at the intellectual disparity between her fictitious men, of whom so many are nincompoops, and her women. To quote again from *Indiana*: "Sometimes the men who are most incapable of any ascendancy whatever over other men, exercise a boundless influence on the minds of women." These words aptly describe Sand's own experience, her relations with the demagogue Michel de Bourges, with the stupid Italian doctor, Pagelli, the spineless Sandeau and the fretful lily-like Chopin. In every case she was betrayed by her "idiotic credulity" against the promptings of a fine intelligence. And in all her love adventures she found the man lacking in sincerity or in moral courage, and this impression colours all her male creations of the second plane, but not her heroes, who are endowed with precisely those qualities in which she had found her lovers so sadly deficient. It is a pity that in effecting the transposition from reality to the ideal she always pitched her key too high.

The secondary male characters, however, are admirably executed. It would be hard to find, for instance, a more finished portrait of the *homme sensuel moyen* than the Raymond of *Indiana*, an excellent study of a difficult type analysed with much understanding. "Raymond," says M. Doumic in his life of George Sand, "is a frightful little cad who starts as lover to Indiana's maid, continues by making love to the mistress of poor Noun and ends by leaving the former to make a rich marriage." Now that is exactly the opinion expressed by the average decent man when his attention is drawn to the conduct of the Raymonds of real life. But surely the novelist worth his salt can do better than that; and in this case George Sand is decidedly worth her salt, for she unfolds another and much more complex

Raymond than the one who is revealed to the casual passer-by and to M. Doumic. Raymond, carried away by his senses, does seduce Noun, but he does not realise the significance of his action till he receives a badly spelt letter from the *femme de chambre*. Then only does he feel the sting of remorse and shame. Yet it is not the content of the letter, but the ill-formed handwriting and childish orthography which effect the moral change in him. Is not this true and well-observed, this conception of what constitutes the reality of life? Is it not almost always seeming trifles which make our conscience vibrate and not the resonant pompous principles like Honour, Duty, which are mere empty abstractions till they are illuminated and interpreted by the so-called little happenings? Raymond is Sand's conception of a very ordinary man, torn between a false conception of honour and an ideal smouldering beneath a rubbish-heap of social prejudices. With great dramatic power she arranges a situation admirably contrived to throw Raymond's moral conflict into stark relief. Noun, who is *enceinte*, asks him to come to Lagny, the country-house of Indiana, who with the rest of the family is in Paris. In Indiana's room, Noun, arrayed in her mistress's finery, makes a desperate bid to regain Raymond's love by an appeal to his senses. He betrays his ideal love after long resistance, not because he is dominated by lust, but simply because he has not the moral courage to be brutally frank. His education has been entirely social, not moral, and in this crisis habit is stronger than instinct. Instinct warns him not to yield, but the habit of what he would call decency prevents him from humiliating Noun by telling her the truth.

Nevertheless, it is by her leading characters that we must finally appraise George Sand's creative ability. Her own theory of character portrayal was to seize upon a sentiment, in her case almost always love, which she idealised and invested with all the strength to which she herself secretly aspired and all the tragedy she had ever experienced. The type, the fictitious man or woman incarnating this sentiment, was then deliberately exaggerated to the limits of probability and sometimes beyond. According to her theory there must never be any compromise, no pandering to chance. Her hero "must either die or triumph. One must never be afraid of allotting him exceptional importance in life, strength above the ordinary, charms or sufferings far exceeding the common run of human things and even to some extent beyond the probability admitted by the average intelligence." This ideal type she next tried to place in a cadre of reality vivid enough to throw it into relief, but it nearly always happened that, in her Romantic novels at least, the chief characters, which she over-idealised, dwarf and obscure their cadre of reality. So in *Lélia* (1833) there is no reality whatever, scarcely even the reality of an intrigue to link together the symbolic figures which pour forth their torrents of lyrical invective against man and social institutions. *Lélia* is not a novel but a rhapsody, a Romantic *feu de joie*. It is the incoherent expression of George Sand's Romantic despair, an apocalyptic vision born of her burning day-dreams. Of dream-stuff, too, the characters, moving in an unreal world where there is no time and no space. Lélia is not a woman but the spirit of Illusion, a sexless Lilith who may not be measured by human standards because she is above good and evil. Two men, the Poet Sténio and the Priest Magnus, are the victims of Lélia's strange and astringent sweetness. Sténio in despair turns to Lélia's sister, the prostitute Pulchérie, falls then under the corrupt charm of Don Juan and finally commits suicide. Magnus under the influence of his obsession becomes insane, strangles Lélia with his rosary and disappears. Only one character remains to mourn the death of Lélia and Sténio. This is Trenmor, the ex-convict, who leaves their tombs to go in search of Magnus, to comfort and if possible cure him, for Trenmor, the former criminal, symbolises Pity in this queer fantasy. *Lélia* is an enigma to the critics, as it was probably to the author herself, if we may judge from the *Lettres d'un Voyageur*, in which she explains her book very obscurely as "a frightful crocodile very well dissected, a bleeding heart laid bare, an object of horror and pity." Doumic calls it her *coup de folie romantique*, adding that it is "in some sense the sum of the themes which were then current in the personal novel and in lyric poetry," a remark which whilst no doubt true applies equally to almost all Sand's early novels. May we add one more stone to the cairn of conjecture? Is not Lélia simply George Sand's Romantic vision of herself divested of that "idiotic credulity" of which she speaks so bitterly in *Indiana*? Lélia has passed through the credulous phase with its inevitable sufferings. She has conquered the devil of the flesh and now the rôles are reversed, for it is Man in the figures of the Poet and Priest who grovels at her feet. But having lost the power to love in the grosser, physical sense she finds herself spiritually isolated, for not even the Poet and Priest can rise above the sexual conception of love. In turn she seeks in Art, in Nature and in Religion an anodyne, but in vain, till Magnus with his rosary opens the gates of her prison. *Lélia* is not the first essay at a Symbolist novel in French, for it is an interesting reversion to type, a throw-back to the poetic and allegorical fictions of the Middle Ages, those tales of passion and death in which Woman and love are fraught with a rare and mystic beauty. There is the echo of such a spirit in George Sand's conception of Lélia and of her courtesan sister Pulchérie, "vierge dans un corps prostitué à toutes les débauches."

Maxime du Camp, in his curious *Souvenirs littéraires*, describes the fluttering of excitement which George Sand's early novels aroused in the dovecots of the Saint-Simonians, the most fascinating perhaps of the many nineteenth-century sects which undertook the regeneration of social France. In the religion of the Saint-Simonians there was not only a God the Father but a God the Mother, and, on the death of Saint-Simon, Enfantin, an employee of the P.-L.-M. railway company, assumed the title of *Dieu le Père*. All efforts to find a spouse, however, had been unavailing. The candidate had indeed to possess rather special qualifications. One of the conditions of appointment was, for instance, that she be prepared to reveal all the feminine mysteries so far hidden from man, in order to furnish the elements indispensable to the formulation of a declaration of the rights and duties of woman. The Saint-Simonians were convinced that the complete happiness of humanity is impossible without absolute equality of the sexes. In his lifetime Saint-Simon had written to Mme de Staël asking her to aid him in giving mankind a new Messiah. She smiled, says Du Camp, but did not reply. Under the godship of Enfantin a similar invitation was extended to George Sand, but curiously enough she did not accept, despite the flattering rôle attributed to woman in the Saint-Simonian formula: "Man remembers the past; Woman foresees the future; The Couple sees the present."

However, it would have been impossible for George Sand, with her credulous and impetuous nature, her generous sympathy, to have stayed long aloof from the great humanitarian movement whose ideals were reflected in the activities of Fourier, Proudhon, Leroux and Lamennais. Writing of George Sand in the *Revue des deux Mondes* in 1857, Mazade said: "Her political and philosophic inspirations at a certain moment are solely the reflection of her friendship and her entourage. They are ideas which she received the day before—ideas which she embraced successively or simultaneously and reproduced with the docility of an *enfant terrible*. . . . This is the explanation in her novels of the growing invasion of a quite factitious element, of the social and revolutionary spirit, that is to say, the substitution of a systematically false ideal for the direct and accurate observation of human life and sentiments." It is this factitious element which permeated all her works from 1839 till 1847. Detached from the contemplation of her own spiritual sufferings, she now directed the forces of a powerful imagination towards the construction of a dream society which was to be reared on an unshakable foundation of universal brotherhood and love. Under the influence of the mystic socialism of Lamennais and, particularly, of Pierre Leroux she unpent a flood of writings in which, under the guise of fiction, we find the reflection of all the Utopian theories dear to the Romantic humanitarians of her time: metempsychosis, spiritualism, satanism, freemasonry, communism, seasoned with fantastic adventures reminiscent of the old *romans noirs* and relieved by occasional pages of great descriptive beauty. Such are *Spiridion* (1839), *Consuelo* (1842) and the *Comtesse de Rudolstadt* (1843), regular *romans-feuilletons* in the manner of Sue and Dumas and Soulié, save that where these authors melodramatised the world which exists Sand melodramatised one which existed only in her own overheated imagination and in that of her dangerous, crack-brained gentlemen friends. A passionate disciple of Jean-Jacques, she sucked up avidly the socialistic doctrines of Lamennais and the communistic ideas of her idol, Leroux. Her prejudice in favour of the lower classes, already obvious in *Valentine*, was by 1840 crystallised into a definite thesis, which she exposed in *Le Compagnon du Tour de France*, and the same motif with lessening emphasis can be heard in *Le Meunier d'Angibault* (1845), in *Le Péché de Mon-*

sieur Antoine (1847) and, *diminuendo*, in the idyllic and lovely stories of rustic life of which *La Mare au Diable* (1846) and *François le Champi* (1846) are perhaps the most notable examples. This thesis is the Romantic doctrine fathered by Jean-Jacques that the *peuple* is the sole legatee of that primitive virtue, that *bonté naturelle* which existed before civilisation brought evil to mankind. The voice of the people is the voice of God and, since the proletariat enjoys the special confidence of the Deity, the State must listen to its commands and govern according to its divinely inspired wishes. Thus we have in a nutshell, stripped of several thousand superfluous words, the gospel of Pierre Huguenin, the carpenter-hero of *Le Compagnon du Tour de France*, whom the author naïvely compares to Christ, though Pierre is if anything a shade more perfect than Jesus. Huguenin envisages a future where there will be no class distinctions, but gives us no very clear idea how this millennium is to be attained. As a preliminary step, however, the aristocracy as represented by Yseult de Villepreux humbly beseeches the favour of being admitted to the ranks of the People. Yseult, in declaring her love for Huguenin, compares herself to those neophytes of old, who prayed to be baptised as a first step towards becoming Christians. The people is not only the repository of virtue but of art. Amaury, the "Corinthian," as he is known to his lodge brothers, is a "natural" artist, for according to the Romantics art, like virtue, is a sort of grace which arrives from heaven *tout fait*. But alas! Amaury falls a victim to the wiles of Josephine, a sensual little bourgeoise who has married into the nobility. When their amour is discovered, Josephine, oddly blind to the moral advantage of marriage with a joiner, gives up Amaury, whose silence is purchased by a travelling scholarship to Italy. Ironically enough Josephine is the only person in the book who finally emerges with any shred of character—in the artistic, not in the moral sense. The others are garrulous marionettes, except perhaps La Savinienne, who in a fumbling way represents the stoical and inarticulate woman of the people. As one peruses novel after novel of George Sand's Hyde Park period one marvels at the "idiotic credulity" of a sincere and great artist who prostituted her talents as a novelist and imperilled her style in a domain which belongs not to art but to politics. In her case Stendhal's "pistol-shot" simile is quite inadequate. Her symphony is drowned in the roar of an artillery barrage.

In the early novels of George Sand the shrill and aggressive cry of revolt against society is tempered by a softer note when she gives expression to that passionate love of nature which wove itself into the tissue of her childhood's reveries. Submerged for a while beneath the passionate illusions of an ideal love and an ideal society, her sweet memories of Nohant survived the flood and, when the murky waters receded, bloomed again with almost spring-like freshness. Almost, but not altogether; for even in those much-praised rustic novels we too often surprise the accents of that old Hyde Park voice, jangling so strangely in the soft and simple speech of her Berrichon peasants. Her admirers, and many, too, who have no sympathy with her Romantic philosophy, vouch for the accuracy of her pictures of peasant life. Most, however, will agree that in *La Petite Fadette* (1840), *Jeanne* (1844), *La Mare au Diable* and in *François le Champi* the characterisation is vitiated by a Romantic tendency to over-idealise reality. Fadette, Landry, Germain, Marie and François le Champi use the vernacular to express ideas and sentiments which are not theirs but George Sand's, and, pathetic as they are in their sweet resignation, they would be much more pathetic and infinitely more natural if the author had remembered that in reality what strikes the intelligent observer as truly pitiful in the life of the humble peasant is his complete unconsciousness of the harshness of his destiny. He himself is incapable of that intellectual process which consists in relating his particular situation to an abstract idea like Justice or Humanity. When as the result of education he bridges the gap he is apt to forfeit our sympathy. But when, as in George Sand's novels, the humble peasant is represented as discovering the language of the social philosopher, presumably by a species of divine or Romantic inspiration, he not only forfeits our sympathy but shocks our sense of probability. Artistic beauty is sacrificed to a thesis.

This defect is redeemed to a great extent by the art with which she portrays the natural beauty and the quaint old-world customs of the Berrichon region. Here George Sand reveals herself unmistakably as the first great French nature novelist and the first, too, of that school of *régionalistes* who since her day have translated the spirit of provincial France into fiction. And it is when she forgets her humanitarian propaganda to describe, as in *La Mare au Diable*, a village wedding in Le Berry, that her peasants are most sympathetic and most natural. So it is in all her rustic novels. Landry in *La Petite Fadette* is most convincing in realistic scenes like the wooing of Catherine or when dancing *bourrées* with Fadette after vespers. François le Champi is an authentic peasant in the outwitting of the village bad woman, but he is not so probable in the idealised rôle of lover to his adoptive mother Madeleine. What is truly admirable in these novels is the unobtrusive manner in which the beauty of nature gradually emerges, for there are practically no long descriptive passages. A word here, a phrase of apparently no significance, a pool with water-lilies, a farm fringed by walnut-trees, a freshet with a boy's toy watermill, sodden, mist-wrapped woods—little by little the atmosphere of the country envelops the novel, permeating the interstices between the characters, filtering into their language and their gestures until the reader has the illusion not merely of seeing Le Berry but of having been born and bred a Berrichon.

Though George Sand will continue to be read only, I fear, as the novelist of Le Berry, this fact should not blind us to her real significance in relation to the development of the novel as a whole. "Art," she once wrote, "is not a study of positive reality; it is a search for ideal truth." In her case this search carried her into an ideal world whither to follow her one must possess the magic carpet of her imagination. Yet sometimes she remained close enough to "positive reality" to reveal to a future generation the promise of a type of novel in which the ideal and the real may be presented in a state of fusion, as that wonderful complex organism in fact which is life itself, where ugliness and beauty, good and evil, truth and falsehood swim in a rhythmic, coloured flux. Her error as a novelist, the error of all the Romantics, was in the assumption that a passion, to be great and intense and therefore worthy of the artist's consideration, must be freed of all the ties which lash it to society. With this Romantic conception of love, then, she often created unreal men and women, unreal because life offers no such simplification of its problems. On the contrary, what interests us is not the passionate hero and heroine who live in a social vacuum, but the spectacle of the passionate hero and heroine in their struggle to strike a compromise between their passion and their real situation, their social ties. As a result of this initial artistic error George Sand minimised the importance of these social bonds. That is why Jacques, for instance, or, to take a more flagrant example, Lélia, captivate us only up to a certain point. Once the particular articles of their Romantic creed have been enumerated they cease to interest us as real human beings. What Flaubert called "the umbilical cord" is severed. The essence of the Romantic nature of course is its individualism, its horror of social laws, but unless the author can place it in an environment which will throw into dramatic relief the conflict between that nature and life he has failed as a novelist.

In *Indiana*, in *Valentine*, in *André* and in other novels George Sand showed that she could achieve this polarisation of character which is produced by the action of social institutions, particularly the institution of marriage. By her new conception of the rôle of woman in society she opened a new vein of profit to the novelists who came after her, a vein which they have not been slow to exploit. Had she continued as she began, she would have been a genius like Balzac or Stendhal, for the greatness of a novelist lies not in finding simple explanations of the problems of existence but on the contrary in interpreting the infinite variety and complexity of life. The poet can lead us into a land of the imagination, where for a time the tired spirit has a respite from the feverish reality of every day, but, alas! we cannot breathe long in that ethereal atmosphere. Soon or late we must return to earth. The novelist fulfils a similar function it is true, but his realm is closer to the reality of our daily life, and perhaps his art is thus more difficult, for we ask him to show us the ideal that lies glowing beneath the dross of drab reality. George Sand too often showed us an ideal which by no effort of the imagination can we associate with humanity as we see it.

CHAPTER VI

BALZAC

At thirty Balzac had already attained a degree of maturity rare in a man of his age. Thirteen years of failure loomed behind him as he wrote in his little room in the quiet rue de Cassini, but his gaze was fixed on the golden mists of the future and on the glory which he knew was his, for if ever a man had implicit confidence in his own greatness it was Honoré de Balzac. Yet what was there in his record to justify this conviction? For three years he had studied law with no success, at last persuading his irritated parents to grant him two years in which to become a great writer. Fifteen months' labour in a garret in Paris produced the still-born tragedy *Cromwell*. It was so bad that even the author realised that play-making was not his forte. However, rather than go back to law, he toiled as a hack journalist and wrote "pot-boilers" for five years. It was now that he fell in love with Mme de Berny, a married woman over twenty years his senior, who surrendered to his passionate love-making. Her influence on Balzac is best expressed in the novelist's own words, written after her death: "She was to me more than a mother, more than a friend, more than any human creature can be to another; her influence can only be expressed by the word *divine*. She sustained me through storms of trouble by word and deed and entire devotedness. She inspired me: she was my spiritual star."

It was she who lent him forty-five thousand francs to finance a business venture which, like others of a similar sort, was a complete failure. Indeed, when Balzac sat at his desk in the rue de Cassini he owed a hundred thousand francs, but what were a hundred thousand francs to a man whose imagination conceived in millions? There are men who appear to require the shock of a catastrophe to liberate their great creative powers, men whose minds make no response to the ordinary stimuli afforded by a humdrum existence. Such a man was Balzac. The steady flow of novels, short stories and articles brought him fame and money, but never enough. Just as his fortune was always insufficient to cover his lavish expenditure, so, too, the praise which men accorded to his greatness always just failed to satisfy his inordinate appetite for glory. Life was always littler than his vision of it.

Lionised in the Paris clubs and *salons*, Balzac was fêted by women like Sophie Gay, Mme Récamier and the duchesse d'Abrantès. The Faubourg Saint-Germain opened its doors to him, and he realised the dream of his life by becoming the lover of an authentic duchess, Mme de Castries, a brief and passionate affair which was painful to the man but precious for the novelist. About this time (1832) Balzac's curiosity and vanity were aroused by certain letters which began to arrive from a foreign admirer, who revealed herself in due course as the Polish Countess Hanska. These letters were obviously written by a woman of exceptional intelligence, for they expressed a belief in Balzac's genius comparable only to the faith that Balzac had in himself, though at this time he was passing through a critical phase. Mme de Berny was no longer a stimulus to his creative powers. His experience at the hands of Mme de Castries was a sore blow to his amour-propre, whilst other affairs with society women left him wearied and dissatisfied. His financial situation, too, was more than usually acute. The love and admiration of Mme Hanska gave him new life. Until his death in 1850 this dynamic woman by her jealousy, her passion and her valuable intellectual collaboration dominated and directed the existence of the novelist, whose naïve and monstrous ambition was gratified by this liaison with beauty, rank, wealth, and Slavonic capriciousness. Mme Hanska's husband died in 1841, but it was not till 1850, shortly before Balzac's death, that he persuaded her to marry him. For seventeen years he loved her, and in loving her he lived the greatest of his novels—the one he never wrote.

From one point of view, the work of Balzac represents the culmination of a psychological change which ever since the close of the seventeenth century had become increasingly reflected in French literature. This movement may be described in its most general terms as the supersession of Cartesianism by the new experimental philosophy which derived from the influence of Locke and Newton. One great idea put forward by experimentalists like Diderot and

Condillac was that there is an intimate relationship between our physical and moral lives and that frequently our physical life explains and directs our moral existence. Foreshadowed already in Montesquieu's famous "theory of climates," this doctrine fertilised the literature of the whole eighteenth and early nineteenth centuries. The philosopher, the dramatist, the historian, the politician, viewed humanity from a new angle. The proper study of mankind was no longer man in general but individual men. It was gradually realised that such factors as social milieu, race, climate, historical moment, might have a profound influence in determining character. The great writers of the seventeenth century, Corneille, Racine and Molière, had interested themselves in the traits common to men of every race and time, paying scant attention to the reproduction of environment, to what we call setting, atmosphere and local colour. They wrote not for their contemporaries but for posterity, and projected their great creations against a background of eternity. The eighteenth-century writer approached the riddle of life from another direction, working back to the universal through the observation of those particular facts of existence which came within the range of his immediate experience. Diderot, in the theatre, led this movement towards reality by advocating the creation of a new type of play which was to emphasise not character but milieu, and in which, he said, the playwright would study, "instead of the eternal passions, which are of all time and of all countries, the problems which confront a man because he belongs to a particular profession or social condition." In other forms of literature the same preoccupation was evident, but in the novel the tendency to depict characters in their relation to their environment was temporarily arrested if not nullified by the vogue for sensibility which in Rousseau's successful *Nouvelle Héloïse* prepared the way not for an objective and realistic type of fiction but for the subjective, idealistic works of the Romantic school. Still, as we have seen, the positive doctrines of the eighteenth-century intellectuals were not forgotten, and the conception of man as a product of his social environment, evolving as it were new moral organs to suit the needs of his milieu, existed side by side with the Romantic vision of a moral and intellectual élite consisting of supermen imposing their individuality upon society and preserving their ego by refusing to adapt themselves to common social requirements. Balzac ranged himself not with the Romantics but with their opponents, the intellectual descendants of Diderot and Condillac. For, though he disagreed absolutely with these men on religion, like them he conceived man as a social animal for whom life meant a constant struggle to gratify his private passions and interests whilst respecting those of his fellow-men.

The Balzac of the Restoration, though he dabbled in Romanticism, never seriously adopted the Romantic attitude towards life. There exists, however, a curious book, written by his friend Jules Sandeau, and printed in 1836 as a preface to the collection of Balzac's early and now forgotten novels. It is called *La Vie et les Malheurs d'Horace de Saint-Aubin*, for

Saint-Aubin, it will be recollected, was one of the *noms de plume* behind which the future author of the *Comédie Humaine* hid his identity in the eighteen-twenties. Sandeau offers the picture of a most Romantic, most exalted young provincial who is infatuated with the poetry of Lord Byron, that "chalice" from which he greedily absorbs great draughts of "love and knowledge, those two poisons of life." Horace spends his nights devouring romances, for he is obsessed by the ambition to become a great novelist. Scott's *Bride of Lammermoor* falls into his hands and the revolution is complete. The stage-coach whirls him off to Paris, where he meets the famous Balzac to whom he shows his maiden effort, a novel called *L'Excommunié*. Balzac, in return, reads him a few of his *Scènes de la Vie privée*, and poor Horace in despair resolves to write no more. This little parable symbolises rather neatly the transition from Balzac, the author of the melodramatic *Vicaire des Ardennes* (1822), *Argow le Pirate* (1824) and other *romans noirs*, to the Balzac of the *Comédie Humaine*, the germ of which lies hidden in those crude and juvenile productions. The *Vicaire des Ardennes*, which was suppressed by the censorship, is a recast of *Paul et Virginie* with an incest theme obviously suggested by *René*. *Argow le Pirate* is a brigand tale much in the manner of Ducray-Duminil's *Victor*, though immensely superior in technique. It is usual to dismiss *Jane la Pâle* (1825) along with these other early novels as the regrettable and somewhat inexplicable indiscretion of a young genius who has not yet found himself. Yet, in spite of its glaring crudities, *Jane la Pâle* is well worth reading as a precocious example of the Balzacian conception of passion. Briefly, it is a study of the tenacity and the ineffable unselfishness of love in the hearts of two romantic women. Jane, the daughter of an old artist, is separated from her fiancé by the perfidy of the latter's best friend. The fiancé, a young nobleman, marries another woman who is madly in love with him, but tells her of his former passion and supposed betrayal. Later, on learning of his friend's treachery he returns to Jane, whom he discovers living in Tours, and on the eve of his wife's confinement contracts a bigamous marriage. His legal wife obtains a post as companion to Jane, in whose house she instals herself with her child. An extraordinary situation now arises, for Jane soon learns that her maid is in love with her husband. When she discovers the identity of the former she is seized with a mortal illness, and the novel ends with a scene in which the two women, forgetful of their strange relationship, attempt to console the remorseful hero. What is really remarkable is that Balzac almost succeeds in convincing the reader of the probability of these dramatic events: they appear as the logical result of a dynamic passion fastening like a Fury upon a human life, twisting it into the queerest shapes. To Balzac, as to the abbé Prévost, the passion of love is a thunderbolt that can in a moment destroy the carefully erected edifice of principles and experiences which we call a good education.

That sensitiveness to actuality which is the secret of Balzac's power as a novelist of manners explains the readiness of his response to the numerous vogues current in the fiction of the Restoration. This sensitiveness to intellectual environment accounts for the imitation of the melodramatic novelists already alluded to, and, if due reserves are made for Balzac's originality, it explains also the *Chouans*. Nor did he escape the influence of the Hoffmann cult, since *La Peau de Chagrin* (1831) is based on a fantastic and supernatural hypothesis, the magical property of a wild ass's skin which grants the owner's every wish, subject, however, to the fatal stipulation that the fulfilment of every desire shall shorten his life by a certain span. Still, whilst paying lip-service to the craze for the *genre fantastique*, Balzac wove over the flimsy network of fancy a splendid tissue of solid reality, a gorgeous tapestry of Parisian manners at the close of the Restoration. This is a work of Rembrandtesque and violent contrasts, wealth clashing with poverty, vice with purity, ideal love with cold sensuality.

The universal, insatiable curiosity of Balzac tempted him away sometimes from the contemplation of the real into a world of chimeras. Thus, in *Le Lys dans la Vallée* we discover a Balzac infatuated with the cobwebbed mysticism of Saint-Martin. In *Séraphine*, that abortive fruit of untold labours, he appears as an adept of Swedenborgianism—"my true religion," as he told Mme Hanska in 1837. *Ursule Mirouet* is saturated with spiritualism, or *magnétisme* as it was then called, most unfortunately too, since the whole action of the novel is made to hinge on a supernatural theme. For all this, to see in Balzac one of the hierophants of Romanticism is to misunderstand him utterly, for no one possibly has reacted with greater vigour against the individualistic and anti-social influence of the Romantic school. It is also possible, however, to dart to the opposite extreme and, like M. Doumic, to represent Balzac as the protagonist of objectivism in art. In his excellent study of George Sand M. Doumic says of Balzac:

> Here is the novelist of the objective school who comes outside himself and ceases to be himself in order to become someone else. Instead of that external world to which Balzac adapts himself Aurore [i.e. George Sand] tells us of an inner world, the emanation of her fancy, the reflection of her imagination, the echo of her heart and which is still herself. Such is precisely the difference between the impersonal novel which will be that of Balzac and of the personal novel which will be that of George Sand, the difference between the realistic art which submits itself to the object and the idealistic art which transforms it as it chooses.

Now, however true this may be of Balzac's treatment of man's material environment and of the purely physical aspects of his men and women, we have only to regard any of his great types, his Goriot, his Vautrin, his Esther Gobseck, for instance, to realise the limitations, and indeed the inaccuracy, of M. Doumic's generalisation. In creating these types Balzac did not "submit himself to the object." On the contrary, far from remaining impersonal, he was every whit as subjective as George Sand. Esther is an idealised courtesan, Vautrin an ideal individualist, and the same magnificent exaggeration is visible in the monstrous avarice of Grandet and in the maniacal paternal love of Goriot. Balzac, just like Sand, for this was her formula also, takes a sentiment or a passion and abandons it to the fertilising heat of his imagination, so that it finally emerges as a something almost superhuman but still obviously human and probable. It is this alchemy which transmutes Vautrin into a monster criminal and Grandet into a Goliath of avarice, but it is precisely the same process which makes Jacques a model of abnegation and Indiana the type of Romantic martyr to the passion of love. In the case of both Balzac and Sand it is the transfusion of the author's personality which lends colour and vitality to these creations. Both were themselves passionate and imaginative to an intense degree. Both believed implicitly in the potent force of passion, and it is this conviction communicated to their creations which explains their inimitable energy. But whilst to the Romantic Sand passion was a unique, a tremendous and mysterious force far removed above all considerations of petty social morality, to Balzac, the Classic, passion was a dangerous thing productive of incalculable harm to society. It is this fundamental attitude of his mind which reveals what he meant when he wrote to George Sand: "You seek man as he ought to be; I take him as he is. We are both right. These two roads lead to the same goal. I too love exceptional beings. I am one. I need some, besides, to throw my common beings into relief and I never sacrifice them unnecessarily. But these common beings interest me more than they do you. I exaggerate them. I idealise them *inversely* in their ugliness or their stupidity. I lend to their deformities frightful or grotesque proportions." Yet Balzac did not merely magnify the passions of his characters; he revealed as no other novelist has ever done the surprising extent of the social zone which can be devastated by the influence of an unbridled passion.

Balzac viewed passion, then, essentially as an anti-social force, and here lies precisely one of his claims to originality as a novelist. Others, like Prévost in his *Manon Lescaut* and Rousseau in his *Nouvelle Héloïse*, had portrayed the classic conflict between passion and reason, but the tragic consequences affected only one or two individuals. Balzac, on the other hand, with his greater vision, reveals the repercussions of a passion the gratification of which produces unhappiness in the most unexpected quarters. His work acquires thereby an almost cosmic significance. It is doubly tragic, since it frequently reveals not only the terrible punishment that overtakes the guilty man, a punishment out of all proportion to his fault, but also the suffering which overtakes innocent people who are associated with him by economic or other ties. *La Cousine Bette* is an admirable instance of the working-out of this Balzacian conception of tragedy. The baron Hulot is an elderly man of fine intellect and generous instincts. His family has a magnificent reputation for probity, and he holds a high office in the State. But his ruling passion is women, and to support his mistresses he dissipates the family fortune, squandering his daughter's dowry and his wife's inheritance to satisfy the rapacity of the evil Mme Marneffe. He sacrifices his dignity as a Councillor of State to obtain advancement for the husband of his mistress, who subjects him to blackmail. Finally, his credit exhausted, he sends his brother-in-law, Fischer, to Africa in charge of a criminal enterprise the object of which is to speculate in Army supplies. The affair comes to light and Fischer commits suicide. The dishonour kills baron Hulot's own brother. His wife, a saintly and beautiful character whose only fault is that she loves her husband too well, commits the magnificent sin of offering herself to the infamous Crevel, a financier who has sworn to avenge himself on Hulot by seducing the baroness. At seventy, Hulot, whose passion has now become a mania, is surprised by his wife in a sordid amour with a Breton cook, a bovine creature whom he marries on the death of the baroness, which occurs shortly after this shameful incident. In *Cousine Bette* we see passion destroy the family, which Balzac regards as the social unit. "The family," he says, "will always be the basis of societies. In losing the solidarity of the family society has lost that fundamental force which Montesquieu discovered and called honour." To Balzac the most evil result of the Revolution was the appearance of a new society composed, not as hitherto of families whose joint interests were identical with that of the state, but of mutually suspicious individuals whose ambitions were fundamentally anti-social and egotistic. He saw in the passing of parental authority and religious discipline the removal of two great sources of national unity and order, and all his big novels picture the disastrous consequences of these social changes. Passion, individualism, egotism destroy the family and in so doing undermine the social fabric. That is the moral of *Eugénie Grandet*, of *La Cousine Bette*, of *La Recherche de l'Absolu*, of *La Muse du Département* and of *Père Goriot.*

Before Balzac, the French novelist had practically confined his attention to one passion, love, and thereby he gave a false interpretation of life. Balzac, whilst appreciating the great part played by love in human existence, reduced it to its proper proportions and threw light on other motives of conduct. The dreadful avarice of a Grandet; the foolish social ambition of César Birotteau; the blind inferiority complex of Cousine Bette; the inordinate paternal love of Goriot; the perverted family instinct of De la Baudraye; the Mephistophelian love of evil for the sake of evil incarnated in Vautrin; the intellectual passion of a Claës in his mad search for the Absolute; the romantic cravings of a Louise de Chaulieu; the sinister and obscure vindictiveness of an abbé Troubert: these themes indicate to a slight extent the gulf which separates Balzac from his predecessors, and enable us to measure in some degree the fertility of his creative genius. It is obvious to the most perfunctory student of the French novel that Balzac profited greatly from the failures of the craftsmen who went before him. M. Lebreton, in an authoritative work, has traced the influence on Balzac of Scott and the so-called "terrifying" school of novelists headed by Ann Radcliffe. It is certain too, I feel, that an examination of the lesser novels of the eighteenth century, in particular those of Restif de la Bretonne and of the marquis de Sade, will reveal further sources of inspiration, since Balzac, profound student of life at first hand, was also an omnivorous and retentive reader. No one, I think, is a better example of the truth of the old adage that practice makes perfection. "Constant work," said Balzac, "is the law of art as it is of life: for art is idealised creation." The proofs of his books are illuminating in this respect. They went back to the printer's so covered with erasures, emendations and new matter as to be almost illegible. His productive power was enormous. *César Birotteau* was finished in a fortnight. Sometimes he wrote six novels in a year, one of which at least was usually a masterpiece. We must recollect, too, that he revised some of his books fifteen times. Naturally his work bears traces of over-production. As in Shakespeare, there are passages where clearly the pen ran on whilst the imagination stood still. Sometimes, having begun a novel, he resumed it years later, giving it a denouement which has no logical connection with his original hypothesis; as in *Une double Famille*, which is a masterpiece of inconsequence, since the heroine, originally an adoring and faithful mistress, is for no reason at all transformed into a cynical trull. Little flaws like these are often to be met with in Balzac: the marvel is that they are not more numerous or more serious. In every great edifice you will find some stone scored with hasty chisel-marks.

Much has been written about Balzac's realism: his novels, it is said, reflect real life. But if one means by this that Balzac is content to transcribe into novelist's language the multitude of human emotions, actions and physical facts that make up Life the definition is sadly inadequate. The author himself insisted on this point in his introduction to the *Comédie Humaine*. "By drawing up the inventory of the vices and the virtues, by collecting the principal facts concerning the passions, by selecting the chief events in society, by composing types, by uniting the traits of several homogeneous characters, perhaps," he said, "I might succeed in writing the history, neglected by so many historians, namely the history of morals and manners. But," he went on, "it is not enough to describe. The novelist must find the reasons of these social consequences, he must surprise the hidden meaning in the immense assemblage of figures, of passions and events. After having sought, I do not say found, the reason, the social motive force, must one not meditate on the natural principles and observe in what respect societies depart from or approach the eternal rule — Truth and Beauty." For Balzac this social force, this dynamic source of all human activity, is passion. "Passion," he said, "is all humanity. Without it religion, history, the novel, art would be useless." So all his novels, besides being faithful reflections of some aspect of social life, are also illustrations of the workings of a passion. Balzac does more than reflect life: he interprets it, and this is surely the highest function of the novelist. *Les Paysans* shows admirably the cumulative and resistless force of a combination of petty passions which in the course of time break down and destroy a social system that has behind it all the authority of law and government. The rich landowner, Montcornet, is eventually forced to sell his estate and to leave the district after a stubborn but hopeless battle against that terrible coalition of childish spites, little jealousies, repressed class hatreds, land greed, vindictiveness and the passive resistance to discipline which composed the peasant mentality of post-Revolutionary France. Here indeed we have Balzac the realist tearing aside the veil with which Romantics like George Sand had obscured the true character of the French peasant. He saw in the peasant the nearest approach to primitivism to be found in our highly developed civilisation. In him he saw thrown into high relief those depraved tendencies which to him are essentially human and which, unless repressed by some strong moral authority like religion or education, will inevitably lead to chaos. That is why he constantly preached the need for restoring Catholicism, and it is here of course that he breaks with the eighteenth century and joins hands with the great religious teachers of the seventeenth century, Bossuet and Pascal. Yet even here, in a subject that lay very close to his heart, he was too great an artist to be a fanatic. If in *Ursule Mirouet* he portrays in the abbé Chaperon the saintly, charitable and human priest whose example welds together the dissentient elements in a community, his Fontanon of *Une double Famille* is a narrow bigot who by his interference in the domestic affairs of the Granville family sets husband against wife and dissolves a household. Side by side with the simple and guileless abbé Birotteau of the *Curé de Tours* we have Troubert, in whom the priestly attributes of silence, secrecy and humility conceal a gangrenous mass of ambition and of vindictiveness with a genius for intrigue which an Alexander VI. might have envied.

There is in many of Balzac's characters a tigerish cruelty like Troubert's, a thoroughness in their destructive methods which makes them, like Troubert, dissatisfied until they have completely annihilated their enemies. For to Balzac, passion is an incurable thing, implacable as the Fate of the Ancients. If you examine the structure of his great characters you will observe they change for evil, rarely for good. The truly passionate characters seldom indulge in death-bed repentances, and this is well observed. The baron Hulot and Cousin Bette carry their vices to the grave. Grandet expires dreadfully, clutching at the glittering crucifix held out by the priest; Goriot's last words, "O mes anges," reveal the sublime persistence of the great folly of his life; Claës in the *Recherche de l'Absolu* is killed by a newspaper report that the Absolute has been discovered. Gobseck dies in a house full of rotting provisions which he kept rather than sell at too small a profit. The cynical Bridau of the *Rabouilleuse* is hacked to pieces by Arabs, deserted by his soldiers who have suffered under his inhumanity. Vautrin is an exception, for on the death of his protégé, Lucien de Rubempré, he renounces his feud against society and becomes an element of order and repression, an ending which appears at first sight banal and improbable. In reality this dénouement is the only one consistent with probability. Vautrin's original obsession was to avenge himself on society, and the young poet Lucien was the instrument which he fashioned for this purpose. But Lucien became his creation, the living expression of all that Vautrin dreamed he would be and never was—his "visible soul." As he saw the young poet develop, Vautrin's idea of vengeance gradually yielded to a greater passion, the passion of the artist for his masterpiece, nay, even more gigantic than this, for was he not moulding a human destiny? Lucien is imprisoned and, in despair, commits suicide. Vautrin, like Macbeth when his magical defences collapse, realises for the first time that there are limitations even to his dæmonic genius for corruption. He is too old to begin again, and, moreover, he has glimpsed behind the organisation called society an inscrutable directive force compared to which his own efforts seem futile and puny. There are two courses open, resignation or suicide, and he chooses the former. Vautrin had set himself up as a god and he committed the supreme blasphemy of attempting to enslave the will of a fellow-man. The destruction of his creation, Lucien, by a greater power is a magnificent example of poetic justice.

Balzac is the first great French writer to break away from the aristocratic attitude towards society so typical of the *ancien régime*. He is also the first to emphasise the economic interdependence of the various classes, and to throw into light the tremendous part played by money in human existence. The eighteenth-century novelist preserved a gentlemanly and hypocritical reticence in regard to lucre, though it is true that *roturiers* like the abbé Prévost had the poor taste to draw attention to the financial embarrassment of their heroes. But, in general, the tradition was that so stoutly maintained by our fashionable English novelists. Heroes were able to devote their entire time to amorous intrigue unimportuned by creditors or bailiffs' men. Debts were divided into two categories, debts of honour, i.e. card debts which were paid, and *dettes de justice*, or debts to tradesmen which were not. The usurer was regarded as an amusing bugbear, the financier as a figure of fun. Towards the end of the century, however, we notice in the works of writers like Restif de la Bretonne, the existence of classes to whom life was hardly so amusing—artisans, farmers and peasants, hitherto ignored by authors save for satirical purposes. Yet, on the whole, the literature of the eighteenth century, despite its social pre-occupations, pictured the manners and morals of only a small section of the nation. Balzac began to write in an age when all the old social values had been reversed by the Revolution and by the Napoleonic regime. Never had France witnessed such kaleidoscopic changes, such a re-shuffling of titles, classes and fortunes as during the upheaval of 1789 and the advent of Louis-Philippe in 1830. Here was ample raw material indeed for a novelist of manners, but material so tremendous in quantity, so bewildering in diversity as to strike dismay into any but a Balzac, who alone possessed the type of intellect capable of mastering it, a mind in which the analytic and synthetic faculties were balanced to a nice degree and splendidly reinforced by a peerless imagination. In this new society, as Balzac saw it, the dominating passion was the lust for money, whether as an end in itself or as a means to the gratification of other passions. The power of money obsessed him to an extraordinary degree, and this attitude of mind was fortified by his personal experience of law and debt. It has often been said that if you take away the money interest from Balzac's great novels you deprive them of their chief appeal, but this hypothesis implies that the money interest in these works is a background or setting, something which silhouettes the action or the characters, whereas in reality money is part of the tissue of the novels and, as in life itself, is inextricably bound up with human existence. Less able men have written novels about a disputed inheritance, a bankruptcy or a struggle on the stock market, but their works seem lifeless, the characters and situations artificial, compared to Balzac's. They lack the social significance, the breathless suspense, the intensity and the illusion of reality of which the great Frenchman possesses the secret. The theme of *César Birotteau* is very simple. A perfume manufacturer is led by social ambition into speculation. His solicitors abscond and he ends in the bankruptcy court. The shock changes his whole character, and slowly and by a fine effort of will he sets out to build up his shattered fortune and to recover his commercial honour. Handled by Balzac the story of this rehabilitation assumes almost epic proportions. Open this book and you step into the Paris of 1820, the Paris of commerce, of political intrigue, of financial and legal chicanery, the Paris of tortuous, mean streets, of dim and dusty back shops, where usury, crime and squalor rub shoulders with industry and honest trading, where life seems to move with accelerated tempo and where the smallest action, the most trivial word, unchain consequences of terrible import. The ordinary ethical standards have no meaning in this society, which is not a society but an assemblage of opportunists unrestrained by any moral code, ignorant of any law save that of experience which has taught them that to yield to an impulse of generosity or mercy may result in social annihilation. Birotteau discovers that his bookkeeper, Du Tillet, has embezzled three thousand francs, but he himself replaces the money, pretending to have made a mistake in checking his balance sheet. This generous act converts the envious and ambitious Du Tillet into an implacable enemy whose hatred pursues Birotteau throughout his whole career. The inference which Balzac would have us draw is that if an individual infringes a social law, however estimable be his motive, the consequences may be disastrous. Birotteau, the idealist, compounded a felony and reaped not gratitude but hatred. "A pessimistic attitude towards life"—such is our first impression, but on second thoughts we see that it is Balzac the realist who is right. Du Tillet abused his master's confidence: his theft was premeditated and carefully executed. His actions sprang from fundamental viciousness, not from boyish folly. It is therefore illogical and quixotic to expect in a nature like this the stirrings of gratitude and repentance.

In *Eugénie Grandet* the question of money seems to overshadow the novel as the figure of the miser overshadows Saumur, like some great tree which makes a desert of its environment. But interwoven with the story of Grandet's monstrous avarice is the lyric poem of his daughter's love for her cousin Charles. But for the miser's character this would be the banal story of a pure love unrequited, the sad but common tale of a desertion. As it is, Eugénie's love blossoms in an atmosphere charged with the indescribable oppression and sordidness of greed, a flower of rare beauty and perfume in this swamp of moral corruption. The real drama lies not in the sinister picture of Grandet's financial activities, not in the slow cancerous spread of his avarice as it permeates the social organism, but in the clash of two characters, in the sudden volcanic outburst of resistance in the daughter, a resistance inspired by love and reinforced by that tenacity of will which she has inherited from her father. The miser surprises her holding a richly ornamented casket entrusted to her by her lover. Mechanically he begins to prise off the gold from the glittering trinket, but recoils before Eugénie, who, seizing a knife, exclaims: "If your knife touches a single particle of that gold I will kill myself with this!" In the duel between avarice and love, love wins. The dénouement contains the tragedy, which is that the object on whom this great love is lavished is pitifully unworthy. And so Eugénie, after soaring for a brief and glorious moment into the empyrean, flutters broken-winged back to the drab reality of Saumur.

No two critics have ever agreed on the question of Balzac's ability to depict feminine characters, yet all assume that the answer to this question is of momentous importance to his reputation as a novelist.

Are we not here confronted with a fallacy that has its roots in French tradition? In the seventeenth and eighteenth centuries the French novel was largely exploited by woman for the glorification of woman, and this was natural enough in a society where woman played a predominant rôle. From the *Astrée* to the *Nouvelle Héloïse* the novelist is exclusively preoccupied with the analysis of feminine sentiments and emotions, listening with the strained attention of the specialist to record the slightest murmur of the female heart. But in Balzac's day woman no longer exercised the glorious supremacy which she had enjoyed under the old regime, and public opinion relegated her to a useful but unspectacular position in the state. Napoleon's attitude towards woman was quite Victorian. He liked to see her as the potential mother of future citizens rather than as a delightful but disturbing emotional factor in the community. This, generally speaking, was also Balzac's attitude, and when we reflect upon the essentially social character of his outlook on humanity, we must not expect to find in his work that minute analysis of the feminine heart so typical of a Marivaux, a Rousseau or a Proust. This does not mean that Balzac is incapable of tracing the great psychological changes that love can produce in the female mind. Did he not discover the woman of thirty? But it is notable that his genius fails him when he ventures into the penumbra of contradictory desires and suppressed emotions which announce the dawn of love in a virginal heart. In reality, the young girl is accorded a relatively minor part in the vast *Comédie*

Humaine. Eugénie Grandet, often regarded as his finest study of a *jeune fille*, presents peculiar traits. A girl in point of years and in ignorance of love, she has at twenty-three the serenity and the determination of a much older woman. She is a striking example of the effect that an abnormal milieu may exercise upon individuality; and if you regard the characters of Eugénie, her mother and of the servant Nanon, you will detect in all three a similarity, a lack of personality, an almost animal docility and stoicism which comes from their exposure to the pervasive influence of Grandet's avarice. Where Balzac redeems himself here is by his genius in portraying the liberation of Eugénie's individuality by her love for her cousin. Yet her love, or rather her passion, is abnormal, as indeed it was bound to be in one repressed as she has been. In its origins it is almost wholly sensual, for she is first attracted to Charles, not by affinities of sentiment or intellect, but by his purely physical attributes, by his exoticism when he ruffles his gorgeous Parisian plumage in the sad purlieus of Saumur. This scented exquisite appears to her, to quote Balzac, "like a creature descended from some seraphic region." He arouses in Eugénie emotions delicate but voluptuous. From that moment she is his devoted slave, lavishing upon him a love that has in it all the fierce protectiveness of unconscious maternity. Her passion for Charles is the primitive passion of a strong-willed ingenuous woman for a weak and selfish man.

Balzac has of course often depicted the conventional type like Césarine Birotteau who plays the colourless rôle of the adored only child and obedient fiancée, but he is only really inspired when he portrays young girls who are the victims of some abnormal vice or passion, as, for instance, his Rosalie de Watteville in *Albert Savarus*. The psychology of the average intelligent *jeune fille* did not really attract him. Rosalie de Watteville falls madly in love with Albert Savarus, a Byronic and sombre young lawyer, who swoops down upon the provincial town of Besançon wrapped in a mantle of mystery. Having discovered, by intercepting his letters, that his destiny is bound up with that of an Italian princess married to an elderly husband, Rosalie plots to detach him from his noblewoman. Failing to capture him by her own charms, she forges a letter purporting to come from the princess and giving Albert his dismissal. The latter, broken-hearted, retires to a Carthusian monastery, and the princess, believing herself deserted, marries again on her husband's death. Rosalie is disfigured by an accident and devotes her life to charity. Thus baldly outlined, the story sounds not only improbable, but mildly absurd. Yet, passed through the crucible of genius, it emerges almost purified of its intrinsic flaws. Rosalie is of course a monster, but a fascinating monster, and Balzac makes her credible by showing her as the product of an unusual milieu and as an example of atavism. She has been brought up in complete ignorance of life by a stern mother, whilst from a rascally grand-uncle she has inherited an iron will and a romantic audacity. Outwardly calm and serious, a model of filial obedience, she is in reality a pent-up volcano of ambitions, and her subsequent conduct is the outcome of her upbringing at the hands of this suspicious and devout mother, who is not, however, too devout to be secretly jealous of her own daughter's youth and beauty. Again and again Balzac insists on the problem which confronts all parents in their relations to their daughters during those critical years when a carelessly dropped phrase, an unconsidered act, may change a girl's whole future. In none of his novels has he shown such complete understanding of this question as in *Modeste Mignon*, which was certainly inspired by Mme Hanska, if not actually partly composed by her. Modeste, the daughter of wealthy parents, was engaged to be married until a financial crash put an end to the engagement. Her father went abroad to seek another fortune, leaving her in the jealous care of a faithful secretary and his wife, for Modeste's mother is blind. There is a reason for this unusual supervision, since Modeste's sister, Bettina, had been seduced and betrayed. From Bettina, Modeste had acquired an insatiable curiosity regarding the mysterious passion of love, a curiosity which she tried to satisfy by devouring the works of Goethe, Byron, Schiller and Rousseau. Finding in her domestic circle no one in whom she can confide, and knowing that she is an object of constant supervision, she goes to literature for the sympathy which she cannot find in reality. Soon her life becomes entirely a life of the imagination, and she visualises herself as the heroine of some great love drama, now a brilliant courtesan, now a famous actress, or again a heartless coquette driving her adorers to despair.

This phase passes into one of religious mysticism in which she devoutly believes that if she faithfully carries out the duties prescribed by the Church, God will send her a man of genius, a Byron or a Schiller, for a husband. By chance one day she sees in a window a lithograph of Canalis, her favourite poet, with whom she engages in a clandestine correspondence. Modeste is one of Balzac's most wonderful feminine creations, because whilst she is obviously drawn to illustrate the evils of Romanticism, her personality stands out boldly from the background of provincial society which the author has as always sketched in with a wealth of detail. She is the most convincing of Balzac's *jeunes filles*, and nowhere else has he shown so vividly the pathetic reluctance with which youth abandons its romantic dreams as in the contrast between Modeste's exalted adoration of genius and the sordid, shoddy reality of Canalis's egotism. "If I had a daughter who threatened to become a Mme de Staël," says one of the characters in this novel, "I would wish her dead at fifteen." The phrase expresses Balzac's detestation of Romanticism, which he regarded as the most corrupt element in the society of his day. In the thirties of the last century Romanticism was a social problem, though, as we know now, its importance in literature was happily out of all proportion to its place in life. There was, however, much talk of women "completing their lives," or as we should now say, "expressing themselves." This was the era of "misunderstood women" looking for the *homme fatal*, the predestined twin-soul, for since Rousseau it had been the habit to disguise eroticism in Platonic and mystic terms. In the *Mémoires de deux jeunes filles mariées* we have in the proud and passionate Louise de Chaulieu the ultra-romantic girl of 1823, who falls wildly in love with her tutor Henarez, a noble Spaniard of Moorish descent, "her African lion" with the smouldering eyes, who passes his nights perched on the garden wall gazing at the windows of his beloved's room. It is significant that Balzac selected a foreigner as his hero, a foreigner in his readers' eyes being presumably *capable de tout.* In marriage these two maintain an impossible note of exaltation, and the wretched Henarez is dragged half over Europe in the vain attempt to find in nature a setting worthy to harmonise with his wife's romantic temperament. Finally, worn out by Louise's jealousy and by the incessant drain upon his emotions, Henarez dies. After a brief period of self-recrimination his widow remarries. This time it is with an artist, Gaston, whose debts she pays and for whom she builds a beautiful country-house near Paris, a house which is really a cage, for Louise is determined that no one shall intrude on their happiness. There is to be no more travelling: Gaston is younger than she. But one day he escapes to Paris, really to help an impoverished sister-in-law, but his wife, after spying on him, is convinced that he has a mistress. In a passion of jealousy she gives herself tuberculosis; this is done, explains Balzac, by getting into a state of perspiration and afterwards standing in a pond. Too late, of course, she discovers her mistake, but dies certain that she will be able to resume her idyll with both husbands in Paradise, which, like all

Romantics, she regards as a place of assignation. I have analysed this, one of Balzac's worst novels, to show how inane a great writer can become when he hangs a novel on a thesis. The whole story is designed to illustrate the Balzacian doctrine that in marriage a woman must sacrifice her will and subordinate her individuality to her husband's. Both Louise's husbands were like herself, Romantics, so that in Balzac's language there was no mixing of the species. The law she infringes is that which governs the relationship between the individual and society at large.

There is a static quality in the character of a good woman that has proved a stumbling-block to many a novelist, for whilst it is comparatively easy to portray immoral women, the good ones are apt to degenerate into angels. However, in the *Lys dans la Vallée*, Balzac has achieved the impossible, and his heroine, the virtuous Mme de Mortsauf, is human and thoroughly interesting. In creating this admirable character the novelist had before him the image of Mme de Berny, whom he idealised. Mme de Mortsauf is a saintly woman who by her purity converts the ardent Félix de Vandenesse into a Platonic, though passionate admirer. Henry James, whose pronouncements on Balzac are always dogmatic and frequently inaccurate, dismisses Mme de Mortsauf as "an attorney in petticoats" and "a kind of fantastic monster," thereby betraying a complete inability to understand the moral beauty of Balzac's conception. Mme de Mortsauf is married to an elderly neurotic, incapable of administering his affairs, but who has to be constantly humoured into thinking that all his wife's suggestions are his own. Saddled with this maniac and with two sickly children, this admirable woman shoulders the responsibility of managing the affairs of the household and of the estate whilst her life is further complicated by the temptation to yield to the passionate advances of Vandenesse, the only person who knows what a hell her life is. This temptation she resists. What apparently annoys Mr. Henry James is that a woman should be able to do a man's work and remain perfectly feminine. By the way, the same eminent Victorian, criticising another of Balzac's good women, the Baroness Hulot in *Cousine Bette*, makes the fantastic statement that: "Mme Hulot is a saint who offers herself to a man she loathes in order to procure money for her daughter's marriage portion." This misrepresentation of the facts amounts to a confession that Henry James had not read the novel very carefully, for the true situation as presented by Balzac is that Mme Hulot offers herself to Crevel in order to get the money to save her brother's life and her husband's honour, motives much more powerful and convincing than that alleged by Henry James.

Bad women are numerous in the *Comédie Humaine*, more numerous, think some, than they are in real life. It is true that they create the illusion of dominating Balzac's novels, pushing their way to the front of the stage, but is not this the very impression which they give in life itself? Novelists would starve but for this fact. Balzac thoroughly enjoyed describing wicked women; it was one of the ways in which religion affected him. But there was another reason —his unfortunate experience with Mme de Castries; and it was to restore his amour-propre that he created the duchesse de Langeais, who appears in three of his novels. Like Mme de Castries, she is the type of *allumeuse*, the cold, insolently beautiful woman who deliberately arouses in men desires which she has no intention of satisfying, extracting infinite amusement from their rage and discomfiture. Montriveau, one of her dupes, is within an ace of branding her with the cross which then decorated the shoulders of convicts. He spares her, however, and she falls hopelessly in love with him. That is what Balzac would have liked to happen to Mme de Castries! There are echoes too, of Mme de Castries in the plebeian Flore of *La Rabouilleuse*, whose moral and physical ascendancy over the pitiful Rouget is one of the most revolting though most human situations ever described. Flore is a duchesse de Langeais of the people, and in transposing this character from the highest to the lowest social plane Balzac achieved an artistic *tour de force*, throwing into crude relief the cold malevolence which is the essential trait of such natures. To Balzac women like these were infinitely more evil than the professionally immoral woman who is gently treated in the *Comédie Humaine*. The courtesan Esther in *Splendeurs et Misères* is romantically rehabilitated by her disinterested love for Lucien; but as a rule Balzac's courtesans are, like Florine and Josépha, good-natured and extravagant trollops who make no pretence of loving their protectors. Their honesty redeems them in the eyes of the novelist, for whom the real social pest is the middle-class married woman of the Mme Marneffe type who exploits her respectable status, using it as an added lure to squeeze the last sou from her infatuated dupes. Mme Marneffe is the feminine counterpart of the usurer, though instead of money she hires out her physical charms. Apart from that, her methods are the same, and in employing them she displays the same inhuman cruelty, the dreadful mercilessness which remind one irresistibly of the boa-constrictor.

The greatness of Balzac lies in this. By an extraordinary feat possible only to a genius, he was able to adapt the artistic procedure of the great dramatists to the purposes of the novel. Whilst retaining the minute descriptive method of the novelist who, unlike the playwright, is practically unhampered by considerations of space and time in his character construction, he succeeded in imparting to his creations the stature, the universality and the intensity which one had hitherto associated with a Shakespeare, a Corneille or a Molière. No novelist, French or English, prior to Balzac, achieved this. Gil Blas, Tom Jones, Des Grieux are not to be compared with the great Balzacian types like Goriot, Vautrin or Grandet. And the reason for this relative and very honourable inferiority is that they are too human. This is no paradox. Of course, Balzac excels as a novelist of manners: as a painter of the manifold and seething human activities composing social life he has few rivals. But his great figures are superhuman. No one in real life was ever a miser on the plane of a Grandet. Nor was there in real life a man so possessed by the mania of paternal love as a Goriot, or a criminal of the immensity of a Vautrin. If we would find parallels we must go to great drama, where Harpagon, Lear and Mephistopheles present the superhuman qualities reproduced by the great Frenchman. Balzac benefits by that state of mind peculiar to those witnessing great drama. For the moment, petty and local considerations of probability, drawn from our limited experience of life, are swept aside as we behold the actions of a being who is just human enough to appeal to our understanding and sufficiently superhuman to captivate our imagination. Reason assures us that no such being exists, but imagination persuades us that he might; and, after all, the immediate appeal of art in fiction as in drama is not to the reason but to the emotions. The rational verdict comes as an afterthought, but then the effect desired by the artist has already been attained.

CHAPTER VII

THE DECAY OF IDEALISM

For Balzac, as for all great novelists, art was a long and tireless effort to strike a just compromise between an ideal and a reality. Life presents itself to us simultaneously in two ways: as directly observed experience and as remembered experience, which is not at all identical with the other but infinitely richer and subtler. For the experience which we evoke from the past is a vastly more complex thing than when it first moved into the zone of our observation. During that sojourn in the mysterious caverns of the memory it has undergone a certain change. The imagination, moving like a busy shuttle backwards and forwards across the warp of actual fact, has woven a pattern. So warp and weft, ideal and real are inextricably blended into that close-knit, many-coloured fabric which we call life. Now, the business of the novelist is to interpret life in all its complexity, to create, as it were, a miniature pattern that shall give his reader the illusion that he is witnessing the grandiose and mysterious process by which life itself is evolved from the loom of time. The art of the great novelist, therefore, must always be a compromise since, however strenuously he tries, in M. Doumic's phrase, "to submit himself to the object," his interpretation of life must always be coloured by the reflection of that inner vision which results from the action of the imagination upon remembered experience.

Bad art in the novel invariably arises from a deliberate and a misguided attempt to offer a simple interpretation of life, and this the novelist achieves by isolating and analysing one of life's elements according to a preconceived system. Such was essentially the procedure of the Romantic, as it was later of the self-styled Realist, who was a frustrated Romantic. To both of these, existence was a disillusionment, a sordid affair completely different from their ideal conception of it. Both systematically denigrated society, but not in the same way, for whilst the Romantic steadfastly turned his gaze away from the reality of life towards a dream world peopled by supermen created in his own image, the Realist, whose impotent imagination afforded him no such escape, derived a peculiar consolation from the contemplation of what is ugly, gross or vulgar in humanity. By wilfully ignoring the beautiful and spiritual elements in human nature he attained a sense of superiority which, added to his false conception of life, links him with the Romantic. Both, in fact, lack that spirit of compromise, that sanity of outlook so typical of the great humanists. Romanticism and Realism are thus equally remote from the real and the ideal: they lie therefore outside the domain of great art in the novel, which is bounded on either side by these two vital sources of inspiration.

At its birth Romanticism contained within it the germ of its own destruction; and, as we have seen in the case of so many novels, the exaggeration and distortion of truth was liable to assume at one moment the form of brutal realism and, at the next, to find expression in mystic and beautiful idealism. This duality which is inherent in Romanticism was peculiarly evident in "frenetic" novels like *Bug Jargal*, and even more so in the imitations of Scott's historical novels. Again, the Romantic fallacy of the divinity of the people produced not only the idealised and absurd picture of the lower classes presented by George Sand, but also the gross and brutal etchings of the dregs of humanity that we find in the works of Masson, Brücker and Signol. The Romantic craving for the sensational and the exceptional, coupled with a malicious and cynical desire to shock the stolid bourgeois, was responsible for the ghastly realism of Janin and of his disciple Arnaud Frémy, who in his *Deux Anges* (1833) attains the nadir of horror. In common with other journals, *La Mode* in 1833 protested against the "sensations de cours d'assise et d'échafaud" which formed the chief attraction of such novels. The *Quarterly Review*, with characteristic and touching solicitude for the moral welfare of the French, launched in 1836 a formidable attack in which its critic produced statistics to prove the connection between the increase of murder, rape and suicide in France and the ultra-realistic character of that nation's fiction. In approaching, then, the question of the rise of Realism and Naturalism in the French novel of the second half of the century one must constantly bear in mind this dual nature of Romanticism. For when we think of Romanticism we unconsciously associate it with that lyrical and idealised attitude towards life and morality which was but one of its aspects, and we are prone to forget its other positive element that found an outlet for the hatred of actuality—in what has been christened Realism, an attitude towards humanity often just as remote from truth as the most etherealised idealism. Balzac by his genius produced some order where there had been chaos. Like the wizard of a fairy-tale he hacked a way through the swamps and luxuriant undergrowth of the Romantic forest and with a touch of his magic wand liberated truth and beauty from the enchanted and fantastic shapes to which they had been long condemned, restoring them finally to their natural semblance. But this Herculean labour took many years to realise, and those of his contemporaries who sensed Balzac's greatness failed to grasp the secret of his originality. And, when they tried to follow his example, they imitated and exaggerated not the essence of the master's work but those mannerisms which he himself had inherited from his predecessors. Was not this very natural? The centripetal force of genius is rarely exercised upon its own generation, and there is little evidence that in Balzac's productive lifetime, which covered the whole reign of Louis-Philippe, his example did much to consolidate the increasingly disparate tendencies then active in the novel. Nowhere can these tendencies be better discerned than in the trend of popular fiction during this period. The rise of industrialism, which began at the Revolution of 1830, besides providing new and rich material for the student of contemporary manners, was responsible for the apotheosis of the Press, now about to exercise a great influence on the novel. Tempted by the liberal remuneration offered by the new cheap dailies, novelists like Dumas, Soulié and Sue prostituted what talents they possessed in the service of *Le Siècle*, *Le Constitutionnel*, *Les Débats* and *La Presse*, which catered to the taste of the masses by publishing serial novels called *romans-feuilletons*. Another circumstance accelerated the spread of the newspaper serial. The French publishing houses could not compete against the piratical methods of their Belgian colleagues, who flooded France with cheap reprints of the latest novels. Charpentier and others lowered their prices, but by that time the newspaper serial was firmly established in the popular favour, so that the publishing houses were forced to reprint old novels and to refuse new ones.

The three novelists I have mentioned, the kings of the *roman-feuilleton*, enjoyed an immense vogue which in the case of Dumas still has repercussions. *Monte-Cristo* and *Les Trois Mousquetaires* seem to possess a perennial charm for the very young and the very old, but who now reads Soulié's *Mémoires du Diable* (1840)? Yet in his day Soulié was adored by thousands and rated far above Balzac or Sand. Eugène Sue's *Mathilde* (1841) is now unknown, though most of us have heard our grandfathers wax enthusiastic over *Les Mystères de Paris* (1842–3) and *Le Juif errant* (1844–5), classified in their day as masterpieces. Certain common traits distinguish all these writers—a baneful fecundity, a certain verve and facility of expression, a complete ignorance of psychology and a gift for inventing the most incredible adventures. They picture life as a continuous melodrama. Their heroes are all supermen like Dumas's Dantès or Rodolphe of the *Mystères de Paris*: social rebels who are a law unto themselves and employ their unlimited wealth and power to punish enemies and rescue friends. As a sample of the various Romantic tendencies struggling for mastery in the novel during the forties, Sue's *Mystères de Paris* is extremely interesting. Like Sand, Sue took himself very seriously as a social reformer and, says a contemporary critic, Lemayrac, he used to display with pride letters from workmen who attributed to him an evangelical mission resembling that of Jesus Christ. What endeared Sue to the lower classes was his familiarity with their language, habits and prejudices. With cynical gusto he exaggerated and travestied life, wallowing complacently in the trough of low realism, presenting a monotonous procession of fantastic monsters each incarnating some form of monstrous vice. When, on the other hand, he tried to portray the beauty that exists even in the slums of humanity, his Romantic imagination, careering to the opposite extreme, invested his characters with a crude and false sentimentality. His Fleur de Marie, the prostitute who has retained the delicacy and fragrance of her natural virtue in the sink of her foul environment, is a typical instance of Sue's Romantic manner. One can observe in the works of such popular authors the persistence of that anticlericalism which was the chief source of inspiration of the eighteenth-century propaganda novel. Soulié, Sue, and, to a lesser degree, Dumas made great capital out of the unpopularity of the Church. In the *Juif errant*, in particular, Sue abandoned himself to a systematic and violent campaign against the Jesuits, whose sinister influence is represented as the chief obstacle to the establishment of the Utopia promised by socialists like Fourier, the head of the Phalansterians, or Cabet, the author of the *Voyage en Icarie* (1840). Valueless as literature, Sue's vast *romans-feuilletons* are precious historical documents, since they reflect and magnify the characteristics of the Romantic novel of the forties, that is to say at the period of its dissolution. What emerges clearly from all his work is the subjective character of Romantic realism, which has its origin in that detestation of the actual state of society and that Utopian dream of perfection which lie at the roots of the *mal romantique*.

When the old seventeenth-century *romans comiques* described the manners of the lower classes, their realism was always objective and satirical. The Romantics, initiating what Hugo called *la littérature démocratique*, now employed realism as a weapon of criticism and propaganda. A critic, writing in *La France littéraire* in 1838, notes that the Romantics of 1830 mistook the state of society then for its normal state and, impressed by the general condition of despair, "created for themselves ideas on life and on its purpose which presented some semblance of truth in that they were based on facts whose immediate influence was undeniable but which became mere hypotheses whenever one tried to draw from them conclusions as to the future and the moral existence of humanity. Having no fixed convictions, they made a god of the vice whose effects they saw everywhere. *They unleashed Caliban.*"

With the notable exception of Balzac, whose influence was as yet slight, and of Stendhal, who remained unappreciated until the sixties, the French novelists of the Louis-Philippe period behaved like an army of stragglers seeking a rallying point. In the general disorder they veered erratically from the most fantastic realism to an equally fantastic idealism, following now one false leader, now another, but ignorant of the fact that a Napoleon was in their midst. In this strange confusion originality was apt to receive scant recognition, whilst mediocrity was often acclaimed as genius. Only thus can one explain the deference paid even by critics to Alphonse Karr's *Sous les Tilleuls* (1832) and the relatively lukewarm reception accorded to Sainte-Beuve's *Volupté*. Karr, who grandfather was Bavarian, tried to graft Germanic Romanticism to the French novel and produced a weird hybrid. There are echoes in *Sous les Tilleuls* of a Wertherish pantheism, but the rustic nature of Karr's novel is rather that of the gentlemen who design stage scenery for the first acts of German student operettas—the quaint little cottage with the green shutters, smothered in roses, clematis and hollyhocks. In the background is Göttingen University, and Stephen, the *schwärmerisch* hero, is a sort of *privat-dozent* who, having obtained the post with apparently no qualifications, is working hard to build up a home for little Magdeleine, the daughter of a doddering old fellow whose mania is botanical philology. The old man is not, however, so completely *gaga* as to allow his daughter to marry Stephen. Magdeleine, led away by her wealthy cousin Suzanne, marries a rich man, and inane comedy is suddenly converted into melodrama, for Stephen seduces Magdeleine and slays her husband in a wood. The novel closes with a picture of the hero, turned resurrectionist, exhuming Magdeleine's corpse to imprint a last impassioned kiss on her decomposed features. This, I presume, is what in a modern Russian novel would be called "stark realism" or "athletic art." Perhaps the most distressing feature of Karr's novel is the attempt to acclimatise the whimsical digressive manner of Sterne and Hoffmann. His *humoristisch* or *ulkig* efforts should be a solemn warning to any other Latin misguided enough to try to interpret the mystery of Germanic facetiousness.

Sainte-Beuve's *Volupté* (1834) is of different metal. Here poet and critic fuse in the novelist, but *Volupté* lacks the dynamic force that comes from a nice balance of physical and psychological action. Like Marivaux and Stendhal, Sainte-Beuve has a genius for psychological analysis, but whilst in *Marianne* and in *La Chartreuse de Parme* this analysis is applied to a number of characters surprised in the manifold activities of daily life, with Sainte-Beuve it is static and subjective. After Senancour he dissects, with painful fidelity to reality, a state of soul: Amaury, the hero, is a victim of Obermann's malady. He too is a hyper-sensitive and a classic example of what the French call *veulerie*, since all his anguish springs from his Romantic lack of energy, from that impotence which makes it impossible for him to realise his gorgeous dream of beauty and of glory. The real theme of the novel indeed is the moral and spiritual disintegration that springs from *veulerie*. Amaury is in love with Mme de Couaën, a chaste and beautiful woman whose husband is obsessed by a futile yet devouring hatred of Napoleon. De Couaën is a dreamer and a fatalist. He is conscious of the power of individual energy, but he has not the courage to traverse "that vague, nebulous, inextricable region" which lies between fatality and individual effort. So his life drifts past in a purposeless suppressed hatred interrupted by one half-hearted attempt at action, a conspiracy that is discovered and for which he is imprisoned.

Long before Proust—for there is much of the *Recherche du Temps perdu* already in *Volupté*—Sainte-Beuve unravelled with Proustian delicacy the shimmering tangle of the adolescent lover's perceptions, desires and sentiments. There are passages in *Volupté* which Proust might have signed, so closely does he resemble Sainte-Beuve in the *timbre* and in the cumulative structure of certain phrases, as also in the interpretation of the hidden realities underlying conscious experience. Did Proust or Sainte-Beuve, for example, write these lines?—

Je ne voulais, mon ami, que vous raconter ma jeunesse dans ses crises principales et ses résultats, d'une manière profitable à la vôtre, et voilà que, dès les premiers pas, je me laisse rentraîner à l'enchantement volage des souvenirs. Ils sommeillaient, on les croyait disparus; mais, au moindre mouvement qu'on fait dans ces recoins de soi-même, au moindre rayon qu'on y dirige, c'est comme une poussière d'innombrables atomes qui s'élève et redemande à briller. Dans toute âme qui de bonne heure a vécu, le passé a déposé ses débris en sépultures successives que le gazon de la surface peut faire oublier; mais, dès qu'on se replonge en son cœur et qu'on en scrute les âges, on est effrayé de ce qu'il contient et de ce qu'il conserve: il y a en nous des mondes!

Again, Proust and Sainte-Beuve envisage love in the same way. For both, the woman is merely the tangible and material symbol of an ideal, unattainable beauty. "Idol and symbol"—it is Sainte-Beuve who writes—"revelation and snare, such has been the dual aspect of human beauty since Eve. Just as within us there are love and the senses, so there exist outside of us two sorts of beauty to correspond to these. The true beauty, more or less complete, more or less complex, is often difficult to perceive in its purity; it is not till later that it appears to us just as the true love within us is slow to emerge." All the tragedy of adolescence, for Sainte-Beuve, lies in the eagerness which leads youth to confuse the symbol and the true spiritual beauty of which it is the reflection. Lost in the contemplation of the lamp under the alabaster, to borrow the author's image, youth lingers too long over the contours. Amaury passes beyond the stage where ideal love and sensuality are fused into that mystic suspense which only the greatest poets can interpret because it is a fleeting echo of the infinite. This is the great crisis in our lives, "this supreme call of the infinite within us, the dolorous protest, in human form, of our immortal instincts and our power to love." For a Romantic like Amaury the crisis can have only one ending, since creative activity, the refuge of the ordinary man, is beyond his strength. Gradually, then, he allows his senses to disintegrate his soul. With clinical thoroughness Sainte-Beuve traces step by step the spiritual *débâcle* of Amaury. Mme de Couaën is in Paris waiting for her husband's release, and Amaury's life is spent partly in the stews of the capital, partly in a quiet house in the rue des Feuillantines where Mme de Couaën lives with her friend, the former Mother Superior, Mme de Fursy. This is but one phase in an *Éducation sentimentale* that ends with Amaury's reception into the Church. And by a strange but very natural combination of circumstances it is to Mme de Couaën that the young priest administers his first extreme unction. How noble and yet how convincing is Sainte-Beuve's account of these last hours! How alien, on the other hand, to the realism of Flaubert in the treatment of a similar theme! Yet each in his way interprets the essential truth of life.

Volupté is a confession, but it is the confession of a repentant Romantic, since Amaury is the Sainte-Beuve not of 1838 but of that earlier period when he dallied with the Saint-Simonists and sat at the feet of Lamennais, that spiritual doctor to a generation of exalted souls. The novel faithfully follows the curve of the great critic's flight from the Wertherism of *Joseph Delorme* back to the sensuous and pagan Christianity of Amaury's last phase.

Alfred de Musset's *Confession d'un Enfant du Siècle* (1836) is a page torn from the passionate life of the poet who loved George Sand. Rousseau, who was a natural liar, used to boast that he had unnecessarily vilified himself in his *Confessions.* This De Musset might have said with truth concerning his novel, for the chivalrous portrait of Brigitte Pierson is a lover's illusion, less like the real George Sand than the picture drawn by that lady of herself in *Elle et Lui.* De Musset's prose-lyric keeps the promise of its title and holds for our generation an interest far transcending that presented by the story of his love affair with Sand. It is in fact a first-rate manual of Romantic psychology, which is analysed with a pitiful and wellnigh intolerable solicitude for truth. The litany is already familiar, yet one point emphasised by De Musset concerns our immediate discussion. Commenting on the disenchantment, the *désespérance*, of the Romantics he speaks of the two attitudes towards life arising from this common state of soul. Some sought an escape in *rêves maladifs*, others in a species of hectic epicureanism. For the latter, life was a brilliant pageant of beautiful courtesans and Lucullan feasts, a cynical and soulless mummery designed to cheat the *ennui* of existence. But there were others, like De Musset's hero, Octave, who passed from one camp to the other, finding happiness in neither. Haunted by a dream of ideal beauty, corrupted by *dandyisme*, they lost the power to love, and like Octave, when love came to them in its most perfect earthly form they prostituted and destroyed it. For Octave is the type of *homme fatal*, as Brigitte is the incarnation of feminine resignation. In the *Enfant du Siècle* the dénouement is the inevitable one. The lovers part, each cherishing a memory, but hopeless as to the future, for in reality there is no dénouement to the Romantic tragedy save death.

Only a few old-fashioned people are familiar nowadays with the novels of Théophile Gautier. Mr. Aldous Huxley, I should imagine, is one of them, for certain passages of his *Antic Hay* and *Point Counter Point* recall the æsthetic and passionless eroticism of *Mademoiselle de Maupin*, though, to be sure, the *dandyisme* of Mr. Huxley, expressed as it is in the biological idiom of our twentieth-century decadents, lacks the jewelled splendour of Théophile Gautier, who was an artist and only an artist. The worship of purely external, sensuous beauty, of form as distinct from spirit, finds perhaps its supreme utterance in Gautier, crystallising finally in the doctrine of *art for art's sake* which, assimilated by Flaubert, emerged eventually as the so-called objective or "scientific" realism of the Naturalists. Yet in the great days of 1830 it was "Théo," arrayed in gorgeous raiment, who led the frenzied mob that bellowed and gesticulated at the battle of *Hernani*. It was he, too, who at a given moment found Hugo's Romanticism too conservative, and was ready to dethrone the master in favour of Petrus Borel, the *lycanthrope*. But this fever abated and Gautier scoffed at what he termed "ces doléances sur les âmes dépareillées, la perte des illusions, les mélancolies du cœur et autres platitudes prétentieuses qui, reproduites à satiété, énervent et amollissent la jeunesse d'aujourd'hui." Yet he was always a

Romantic by his gorgeous vision of life. Beauty was his idol. He adored form, colour, harmony and perfume with Oriental passion. The spiritual troubles of his generation exasperated him beyond measure, because they clouded the luminous transparence of his ideal image of material loveliness. So it has become a commonplace to speak of Gautier's insensibility, despite these words, to be found in the diary of his intimate friend Ducamp:

> In spite of his exceptional strength and the magnitude of his desires Gautier was a dreamer strayed into the midst of a restless, implacable civilisation which rushed past him and over him and trod him under foot while he, unconscious of the fact, made no complaint. . . . Where would have been the use? No one would have heeded him. "Poor Théo!" he sometimes exclaimed, and we, his friends, knew what depths of unspoken suffering were compressed into that cry.

Little or nothing of this, however, was allowed to stray into his work, though beneath the violence of the preface to *Mademoiselle de Maupin* one can detect the angry frustration of the Romantic whose wings were too feeble to lift him into the ethereal regions. Like Flaubert, he made a virtue of necessity, priding himself on his objectivity, although, as is the case with Flaubert, a Romantic disgust for actuality pervades all his writings. *Mademoiselle de Maupin* (1835) is a brilliant example of decadence. It represents the climax of that erotic and cynical tendency which the *romanciers corrupteurs* of the eighteenth century borrowed from the *Arabian Nights* and invested with the persiflage of their generation. Only, in Gautier eroticism is caparisoned in all the splendour of Romantic prose, and if it is possible to speak of lyricism in regard to purely material beauty *Mademoiselle de Maupin* is a lyric in prose. The only work in English that can give one an idea of the flavour of Gautier's style is Wilde's *Picture of Dorian Gray*. Of human interest, however, there is none in Gautier's novel. It is impossible to pay serious attention to the erethrism of the nymphomaniac Rosette or to the fantastic and dubious travesty of *As You Like It* which is the theme of the second part of this dishevelled production. *Fortunio* (1838), which has more consistence, is an excellent specimen of Romantic *dandyisme*—well defined by the *Revue française* for 1838 as "a systematic and sovereign contempt for ordinary ideas, sentiments, habits and conventions — a profound disgust for the narrow boundaries of real life." *Dandyisme* is actually an offshoot of Byronism, but without Byronic passion. Fortunio and the brilliant courtesan, Musidora, are absolutely soulless. They are figments of an artist's imagination, beautiful and meaningless as the creations of Beardsley or Dulac. Only a Romantic could have conjured up the splendid and exotic visions that crowd the pages of this bewildering book, a veritable orgy of Sardanapalus transported to the Paris of Louis-Philippe.

Possibly no French novelist has ever squandered so much artistic treasure so lavishly in an ungrateful cause, for it must be confessed that not even Gautier's stylistic wizardry can disguise the limitations of the theme. The artistic possibilities of eating, drinking and sexual intercourse are soon exhausted, and in Fortunio there is naught else to hold the interest.

Those who are curious to follow the evolution of *dandyisme* should read Baudelaire's *La Fanfarlo* (1847), which like *Mademoiselle de Maupin* is a satire on Romantic sensibility. The hero, Samuel Cramer, "one of the last Romantics possessed by France," presents a further stage in the progress of Gautier's picturesque sensuality. "Though Samuel had a depraved imagination," writes Baudelaire, "and perhaps even because of that, love was for him less a matter of the senses than of the reason. It was above all the admiration and the appetite for beauty. He considered reproduction as a vice of love, pregnancy as a spiderish disease. Somewhere he has said: 'The angels are hermaphrodites and sterile.' He loved the human body as material harmony, as a piece of beautiful architecture plus movement. And this absolute materialism was not far removed from the purest idealism." The *dandyisme* of Baudelaire is the scientific notation of material beauty.

Thanks to a useful perspective of nearly a century we can see what was hidden to the French novelists of the eighteen-forties. A new type of fiction was rapidly disengaging itself from a swarm of conflicting tendencies. It is clear now that to define Realism as a "reaction" against Romanticism is to be guilty of a species of *simplisme*: it would be equally naïve to describe illness as a reaction against health or unhappiness as a reaction against happiness. Various elements, we have observed, entered into the composition of the Romantic novel. As we approach 1850, the novel of subjective and spiritual trend gives way to the growing popularity of the objective and material novel. Gautier, unconsciously carrying out the ideas of Janin, advocates complete objectivism. Yet the Romantic dream of ideal beauty will not be denied, a circumstance that explains the unreality of Gautier's picture of material life. But in contrast to this æsthetic materialism we have the Romantic Utopians, Sue and Soulié, whose subjectivism leads them to dwell chiefly on the sordid aspects of human nature. Soon we shall witness in the works of Flaubert the sublimation and fusion of these two Romantic and false conceptions of reality. Meanwhile, after 1850, the influence of Balzac begins to make itself felt, and the so-called Realists, ignoring the spiritual and lyrical beauties of the *Comédie Humaine*, reserve all their admiration for its excellent reproductions of middle and lower class life. Their descendants, even more obsessed by the desire to systematise art, evolve their curious doctrine—a blend of objective materialism minus its æsthetic elements, and of misanthropy or frustrated Utopianism.

However, even before the death of Balzac other influences favoured the development of Realism. Industrialism, revolutionised by the exploitation of steam-power, had emphasised the now overwhelming importance of the working-classes and of the small tradesman. The works of Balzac reveal the new powers enjoyed by the moneyed bourgeoisie as a result of the growth of banking and stock-broking. Journalism, inextricably bound up with political finance, catered to the positive and materialistic aspirations of these classes, and to a large extent commercialised fiction.

Everything indicated the spread of a new attitude towards life, an attitude of veneration for that kind of energy which produces immediate and concrete results as distinct from the energy which dissipates itself in futile introspection or mystic reverie. René was supplanted by Joseph Prudhomme. Yet this spirit had many critics. If the more exalted of the original Romantics had regarded themselves as the Messiahs of a new religion, as divinely inspired poet-prophets, there were also materialistic Romantics like Gautier who considered themselves, too, as *âmes d'élite*. Gautier and Flaubert, those high priests of the cult of *l'art pour l'art*, expressed their contempt of the bourgeois, the *épicier*, in fiery language. They placed the artist on a pedestal from which he surveyed the rest of humanity with lofty and Romantic disdain. Naturally, this conception of the Artist as a superman, set aside from the herd by virtue of his unique gifts, was reflected in fiction, just as was that other Romantic illusion of a naturally virtuous and divinely inspired plebs. Signol, in his *Lingère* (1830), had already interspersed his studies of popular manners with sketches of Bohemian life. Signol deserves to be better known than he is, if only as the faithful historian of that motley society which in 1827 frequented *Vauxhall*, *Le Jardin Turc*, the *Théâtre des Funambules* and the *Bal de Sceaux*. His students are at least real, and his grisettes, unlike those of De Musset and Mürger, speak the language of their milieu. The ideal grisette immortalised in De Musset's *Mimi Pinson* does not exist in the *Lingère* any more than she did in the Paris of Louis-Philippe.

It was Henri Mürger, that specialist in Latin Quarter manners, who first invented the fiction of the Bohemian grisette, the Manon Lescaut of the nineteenth-century novel. The type still persists in literature exactly as originally portrayed by Mürger in his *Vie de Bohème* (1851), and by a curious decantation from fiction to real life Mimi and Musette have their imitators amongst the prostitutes of the students' cafés to-day, since it is good business to pander to the literary ideals of those new-fledged *bacheliers* who still model themselves on Mürger's Rodolphe and Marcel. In fairness to Mürger, however, he had no illusions about the *Vie de Bohème*. Marcel, after some years of it, falls back with a thud on hard reality. "As far as I am concerned," he confesses, "I 've had enough. Poetry does not exist solely in the disorder of existence, in improvised happiness, in amours as brief as a candle, in more or less eccentric rebellions against those prejudices which will be the eternal sovereigns of the world. It is not enough to wear a summer overcoat in December in order to have talent; you can be a true poet or artist and still keep your feet warm and have three meals a day." So Mimi's fascinating consumptive cough and camellia complexion land her in the amphitheatre of the Hôpital de la Charité, and Schaunard, Rodolphe, and Marcel become solid and respectable ratepayers, a banal if not very realistic dénouement, since by all the laws of probability they should have gone to keep Mimi company in the hospital. Mürger, for all his anti-bourgeois violence, is a thorough bourgeois at heart. The real theme of the *Vie de Bohème* is not love but money, but where Balzac juggled with millions Mürger fiddles with sous. Perhaps no one has ever treated with more loving detail the great art of *carottage*, no one save Dickens, whose Alfred Jingle remains of course the classic type of *carotteur*. Mürger's great attraction is not his sentimentality but his humour: his chief defect is lack of proportion. Really he belongs to the school of comic caricaturists whence issued Sorel, Furetière and Lesage. His tendency to exaggerate, whilst it produces some unforgettable characters like Schaunard and the Bohemian bourgeois, Barbemuche, is responsible for the false sentiment of his grisettes, Francine and Mimi. Mariette, in his *Le Pays Latin*, is much more convincing because Mürger in creating her reveals the evolution of the grisette from the simple peasant girl to the suspicious and shrewish product of Latin Quarter sophistication. Mariette is indeed a direct contrast to De Musset's poetic Mimi, the dainty, tender-hearted Mimi, who pawns her one dress to buy food for a sick friend, and dies unknown in her attic with her pot of mignonette and her goldfinch.

The contempt for the bourgeoisie was shared by many novelists who had nothing else in common. Henri Monnier, who in 1830 created his Joseph Prudhomme, furnished an immortal type to be recognised again and again under various forms in the facetious literature of Louis-Philippe's reign. Monnier was not so much a novelist as a caricaturist whose drawings and descriptive sketches created a vogue in the anti-bourgeois faction. Mürger and Champfleury owed a great deal to his *Scènes populaires*, as did

Léon Gozlan, the author of *Aristide Froissart* (1843), that successful and jovial satire on bourgeois ideals. But Gozlan, "the lesser Balzac," as he was called, much to his annoyance, was not originally an anti-bourgeois. On the contrary, his *Notaire de Chantilly* (1836) was intended as the first of a series of novels designed to reveal the sacerdotal character of the various bourgeois professions. Thus the notary of Chantilly, Maurice, enjoys the esteem formerly accorded to the priest, and his office is described as a sort of lay confessional. Gozlan's picture of provincial manners has the ring of Balzacian authenticity. But the vivid meridional imagination which sent young Gozlan cruising to Africa in search of romance soon breaks through the narrative of sober fact, and a quite gratuitous Legitimist conspiracy distracts attention from his account of the notary's financial and domestic complications. Gozlan was really himself in tales like the *Histoire de Cent Trente Femmes*, a brutal, red-blooded story of a mutiny aboard a convict ship, and really a classic of its kind. He leaves Sue far behind in the art of graphic description. His ruffians are hairy and genuine ruffians. Do they not at one moment threaten to eat the purser? Sue never rose to these heights.

Gozlan was a great admirer of Balzac, and his *Balzac en Pantoufles* is one of the earliest biographies of the author of the *Comédie Humaine*. Impossible to conceive a bigger contrast to the erratic and paradoxical Gozlan than De Bernard, another of Balzac's intimates. Charles de Bernard made his name with *Gerfaut* (1838), still much in demand in

French circulating libraries. Maybe Balzac did his friend a grave disservice by telling him that he had *la tête épique*, for De Bernard's talent lay in those witty and caustic observations on bourgeois life which lend distinction to *Les Ailes d'Icare* (1840), that excellent and ironic account of the sentimental adventures of a provincial in the Paris of the Palais Royal and the political salons of the Chaussée d'Antin. One wonders to what extent Flaubert was inspired by this work when he wrote his *Éducation sentimentale*. There is a very strong family resemblance between Mme Piard and Mme Dambreuse. Deslandes and Frédéric Moreau are half-brothers, whilst Mme de Marnancourt and Rozanette have many traits in common. But De Bernard's Voltairian spirit of raillery prevents him from exploiting his characters to the full. Like Lesage, he sacrifices psychology to situation, for he has all the comic dramatist's love for *coups de théâtre* and effective "curtains." Nevertheless, *Les Ailes d'Icare* betrays a flair for reality which segregates De Bernard absolutely from the Romantic idealists, Utopians and bogus Realists of his age. With Mérimée he continues the school of the eighteenth-century *conteurs* by his talent for critical and detached observation of human foibles and passions.

Gerfaut is not so good. Here there is a sense of strain, for the theme is too powerful for the author. Bergenheim is a typical feudal survival; unimaginative, slow to suspect duplicity but terrible in anger. His wife Clémence is a product of the Faubourg Saint-Germain, a *romanesque*, but not, like Mme

Bovary, a sex-ridden Romantic. One feels indeed that her love for the fashionable poet Gerfaut arises mostly from boredom, from school-girl hero-worship and to some extent also from a fundamental incompatibility of temperament which alienates her from Bergenheim. De Bernard's ironic manner strikes a jarring note in a tragic narrative of this sort, and he lacks the Balzacian quality of patient analysis which might have transformed the portrait of Bergenheim into a fascinating study of jealousy. As it is, the dénouement—the killing of Bergenheim at the boar-hunt and the suicide of the heroine—produces an impression of melodrama simply because of bad preparation. In short, the whole novel lacks proportion. However, the clash between the two types of civilisation, the feudalism of Bergenheim and the nineteenth-century sophistication of Clémence and Gerfaut, is admirably interpreted, as also is the comic contrast between the Bohemianism of the artist, Marillac, and the naïve cunning of the Lorraine peasantry. De Bernard was a Stendhalian who, in following Balzac as he did in *Gerfaut*, worked against the grain of his talent.

Gozlan, in one of his paradoxes, advances the theory that life is completely undramatic. Exciting events abound in life, but never can one sense beneath them any underlying dramatic unity, for, says Gozlan, men never really provoke critical happenings. Bridges fall, but never as in the story-books when they are being crossed by the villain or the adulteress. "Cæsar was killed coming out of the Senate, but because the conspirators were waiting for him. There is no drama here, merely a brutal event. Had Cæsar killed the conspirators the contrary would have been the case. There would have been surprise, morality, drama." Gozlan belonged to the Flaubertian school for whom "la vie est bête." De Bernard on the contrary was of the school of novelists for whom life is essentially dramatic. Seen through such a temperament as his, existence resolves itself into an exciting combination of incidents naturally grouping themselves into cause and effect, moving with a sort of fatality towards a crisis and a dénouement. It is this effort to dramatise or simplify life which detracts from the reality of *Gerfaut*. Balzac, it may be objected, had the same obsession for what reporters call "the hidden drama" in life; but he also possessed the artist's gift for making his dramatic characters probable, and this he managed by projecting them always against a background of lesser creatures whose lives flow past in a stupid and apparently meaningless fashion.

There is nothing like a sound, tangible hatred for keeping a novelist face to face with reality. To hate the whole universe, as did the Romantics, was to lose contact with reality and to drift into speculation and poetic reverie. On the other hand, the detestation of the bourgeoisie provided the new novelists with an excellent incentive to study the manners of a class which, despite Balzac's exploitation, was still in a process of evolution and therefore rich in material. However, to be original in this field, the novelist had first to divest himself of that mania for caricature which was a tradition in all French novels dealing with bourgeois life. The humanitarianism of Sue and other Utopians led them to interpret falsely the life of the lower classes. Was there not an equal danger that the anti-bourgeois spirit would mar the truth of those novels now setting out to depict the manners of the middle classes? To counteract this subjective tendency there was a rising desire to view life from a completely objective and impassive standpoint, and this ideal was expressed in the doctrine of *l'art pour l'art.*

Ever since 1830 the critics had protested loudly against the novelists' growing fondness for descriptions of unidealised "low" life. Their criticism was not confined to French literature. The *Écho de la Littérature* (1842) sharply rebuked Dickens for the excessive realism of his *Old Curiosity Shop* and remarked: "The novel is a mirror, no doubt, but one should take care not to make it reflect too often the mud on the highway." The same journal, commenting in 1843 on the disquieting trend of contemporary fiction, attributed its gross realism to the influence of the *roman-feuilleton.* "The picture of manners, characters and passions is no sooner outlined than it disappears beneath a multiplicity of little details, tiny facts and petty incidents calculated merely to arouse the curiosity. To-day, since, thanks to these sordid speculations, art, having become a trade commodity, is now a mere rule in proportion—to-day, the great canvases, the big historical studies are consigned to oblivion and, as they are quite unsuitable for such settings, are giving way to dirty sketches and ignoble passions whose colours are borrowed from the walls of the bagnio, from the mud of the filthiest streets of the city or from the *vin bleu* of the most disgusting taverns." These sporadic protests swelled into a concerted howl of indignation against realism in art.

Two men, one a novelist, the other a painter, were singled out by the critics as scapegoats. These were Champfleury and Gustave Courbet. It was not till after the Revolution of 1848 that Champfleury acquired the conviction that he was an original novelist and the father of a new artistic doctrine. Previous to that time he had frequented the Bohemian Café de Momus, where he consorted with Mürger, Baudelaire, De Nerval and other bourgeois-eaters. In his early works, *Chien-Caillou* and the *Contes domestiques*, the picture of popular and Bohemian manners is spoiled by a Hoffmannesque obsession for the grotesque. This caricatural tendency, evident in all his work, found an outlet in Champfleury's *Les Excentriques* (1851), a collection of pen-portraits of Parisian oddities too fanciful to be really interesting. Nor was he much closer to reality in the sentimental *Oies de Noël,* though a certain deliberate drabness of style indicates an effort to suppress the old subjective and fantastic manner. In 1848 Champfleury frequented the Café Andler in the rue de Hautefeuille, the headquarters of a socialist club of artists and men of letters governed by Courbet and called *La Réforme*. Courbet was that prize bore, the peasant who is noisily proud of the fact. At the Andler this incredibly vain but original artist domineered over men like Proudhon, the social reformer, André Gill, the "Red" caricaturist, Gustave Planche, the critic to the *Revue des deux Mondes*, Baudelaire, the poet, Corot, the artist, and Champfleury. The latter it was who by his article in the *Pamphlet* first prophesied the success of Courbet, whose *Après Dîner à Ornans* (1849) brought him notoriety. Seated in his shirt-sleeves, between Gargantuan mouthfuls of sausage and tankards of beer, the painter proclaimed his doctrine that the artist must paint only what he can see. "Il faut encanailler l'art" was his favourite phrase, and he expressed a violent loathing for the slightest suggestion of idealism in art. "Angels!" he once bellowed at a timid colleague. "Have you ever seen an angel? How can you paint an angel? What is it like?" Under Proudhon's influence Courbet's doctrine of complete objectivism degenerated into democratic propaganda, and for that reason, in 1865, Champfleury parted company with him.

Champfleury first seriously attempted to put his vague realistic theories into practice in *Les Aventures de Mariette* (1851). In this uninteresting but faithful account of the amours of a hack journalist and a student's trull there is not a trace of Champfleury's old caricatural style and not a gleam of fantasy. It is certainly realistic in that it has all the objectivity and accuracy of a photograph, but it justifies the remark made by the critic of the *Athenæum français*: "L'écueil du réalisme est de copier la vie au lieu d'y prendre les traits caractéristiques." Yet this drab novel was hailed by the Realist, Duranty, in 1859 as "a sort of *Journal de Dangeau* by the precision of its details, a species of

Mémoires de Saint-Simon by the truth of its revelations." The great "truth" revealed by the *Aventures de Mariette* is that in the Latin Quarter there are lying little sluts like Mariette who are prepared to live for a month with any young imbecile willing to offer them board, lodging and an occasional nocturnal frisk in return for the somewhat dangerous pleasure of their company.

Champfleury was quite unfitted by temperament for the rôle of chief to the Realists which was thrust upon him by circumstances. He had, it is true, a gift for the notation of facts and little traits, but like Furetière and Sorel could never resist the desire to caricature what he saw. A collector of tics and manias, he is only natural and sometimes really funny when, as in *Les Souffrances du professeur Delteil*, he frankly plays the buffoon. Nothing Champfleury ever wrote approaches this faithful account of the impish and horrible occupations of the small boys at the Collège de Laon—the rearing of silkworms and other fauna in the class-room, the concoction of strange dishes in one's desk under the master's nose, and the hundred little joys dear to that malodorous brush-haired and lovable little devil, the small boy. But when, as in the *Bourgeois de Molinchart* (1855) or in *Monsieur Bois d'Hyver*, he tries to ape his idol Balzac, Champfleury is painful to read. The latter novel, which is an imitation of *Le Curé de Tours*, is simply bad Balzac with a moral ending; for the author, despite his careful attention to detail, never gets into the skin of his characters. As in the *Bourgeois de Molinchart*, no synthetic picture of provincial life materialises. Eccentrics crowd out the significant characters, and these do not interest us simply because they are anæmic travesties of Balzacian types.

As a theorist, too, Champfleury is disappointing. His treatise, *Le Réalisme*, is an ill-arranged epitome of his scattered writings on the theory of the novel. Champfleury notes in European fiction the growing tendency to sacrifice idealism as seen in writers like Dickens, Thackeray, Charlotte Brontë, Tourguenieff and Gogol, who prefer accurate observation to imagination or invention. Yet, insists Champfleury, observation can never be absolutely objective. The artist's reproduction of reality will always be subjective; an interpretation and never an imitation, for a writer can never escape his *moi*. Indeed, "artistic truth and the truth of nature . . . tend to combat rather than to approach each other." The business of the artist, then, is to interfere with nature as little as possible. Like Diderot in *Ceci n'est pas un Conte*, he should try to lend an artistic form to observed actuality. He has, however, the faculty of choice: his art indeed lies in this power to discern and select what is truly significant in life. "It is not by an exact description of his costume and features that a novel character becomes visible and remains in the reader's memory; it is by the accentuation and the development of his *moral*." Champfleury could not conceive the possibility of a fusion between the *fond*, the essence, and the form of a work of art. This deficiency led him to decry the picturesque descriptive style introduced by the Romantics, to whom he opposes the colourless manner of an obscure seventeenth-century novelist, De Challes, whose *Illustres Françaises* he hailed as the first great realistic novel. Obviously, therefore, he had no sympathy with the *art for art* school which subordinated idea to form. Style, for Champfleury, was simply a "vain ornament," apt too often to compromise the accuracy of the novelist's observation. The modern writer, he thought, must therefore cultivate deliberate simplicity of expression as a step towards impersonal art. After Diderot and Stendhal there was nothing very new in these ideas, and Champfleury's rôle in the evolution of the French novel was much less important than that attributed to him by critics like M. Bouvier, who in his *Bataille réaliste* refers to his work as marking a date in the history of nineteenth-century fiction. His novels, as we have seen, like his theoretical pronouncements, reveal a lack of originality and the absence of any strong directive principle. He preferred to choose his subjects from middle and lower class life, he tells us in *Le Réalisme*, because "logically it was better to depict first of all the lower classes where the sincerity of the sentiments, actions and language is more evident than in high society." Yet in practice he represents a return to the satiric caricatural methods of the seventeenth century. Again, though he advocated impersonality in art he is less dogmatic than Janin, and certainly much less revolutionary than Gautier and Flaubert, who boldly averred that if the author's thought transpired in his work, the book should be thrown into the fire and that the subject indeed was absolutely unimportant compared to form. An indifferent imitator of Diderot, Hoffmann and Balzac, Champfleury was pilloried as a Realist and feebly attempted to live up to a part which he but dimly understood. The truth is that when he published his theories in 1857 neither he nor his critics regarded Realism as anything more than an attempt to democratise the novel, and that was certainly no innovation.

However, Champfleury and his disciple Duranty did much to establish the authority of Balzac, hitherto not sufficiently recognised. Through Balzac they reached back to Diderot, the true founder of the modern novel. For Diderot, by revealing that vital relationship which exists between the individual and his physical and social environment, enlarged the old conception of realism which the seventeenth- and eighteenth-century novelists had regarded almost exclusively from the point of view of psychology. What was the Balzacian novel, indeed, but the exploitation on a grand scale of this fertile idea? Thanks, then, to Diderot, Balzac added another dimension to the French novel, and, by projecting his creations against a background which was not simply moral but material, he invested them with startling reality. But Champfleury and Duranty did not possess that perspective so essential to a complete appreciation of Balzac's genius. As did Molière's immediate successors, they mistook the shadow for the substance. Molière's imitators had failed to see that his character analysis invariably led to action. By a similar error, Champfleury and Duranty attributed Balzac's success to his gift for the accurate description of bourgeois and popular milieux and manners. They did not realise that in the *Comédie Humaine* the notation of physical elements always subserves characterisation and, moreover, that Balzac with his nice sense of values never fails to reflect those intermittent gleams of the ideal which occur in the nethermost strata of humanity. "The Realism of 1856," as Zola observed in *Le Bien Public* (22 April, 1878), "was exclusively bourgeois." Here is the formula of these early Realists as exposed in Duranty's journal, *Le Réalisme*, which he published with the collaboration of Thulié and of Assézat who, by the way, gave us our most complete edition of Diderot's works. "Realism aims at the exact, complete and sincere reproduction of the social milieu, the epoch in which one lives; because such a direction of studies is justified by reason, by the needs of the intelligence and by the public interest, and because it is exempt from falsehood or trickery. . . . This reproduction must therefore be as simple as possible so as to be understood by everybody."

Duranty's novel, *Le Malheur d'Henriette Gérard* (1860), is an eloquent commentary on the limitations of this or any other literary recipe. The theme is a hackneyed one. Henriette is the daughter of a wealthy bourgeois; Émile, her lover, is a poor clerk. The main interest centres in the long and desperate resistance offered by the heroine in a vain effort to break down parental opposition and class prejudice. Émile is a spineless and whining creature who serves no purpose save that which was farthest from Duranty's mind: he completely alienates the reader's sympathy and justifies the attitude of Mme Gérard. Finally Henriette, after a half-hearted attempt to elope—she returns home because her feet get wet—marries the traditional wealthy dotard. On her wedding-day Émile drowns himself—his first useful and original action—and Henriette in an ungovernable rage accuses her husband and her parents of murder.

Duranty's novel is as accurate as a policeman's report of a street accident and is couched in much the same non-committal and uninteresting language. The speech, the mannerisms and the physical traits of the Gérard family are conscientiously reproduced, but with the sole exception of the son, Aristide, who is so stupid as to be almost attractive, the characters are devoid of personality. They swim like amorphous creatures in a glaucous and viscid milieu. To Duranty, who has not the faintest idea of perspective or proportion, one fact has much the same value as another. True to his system, he makes no effort to select from the mass of material at his command the really significant traits. He reproduces but does not interpret life, for, like all mediocre craftsmen, he confuses the truth of nature with artistic truth. In his zeal to "reproduce" the conversation of his boresome people he forgot that his business as a novelist was, not to bore his reader but to give him a life-like impression of bores in action, which is a very different thing. A novel is neither a mirror nor a dictaphone; it is a work of art, and all art implies a synthesis, a condensation of life.

Zola, writing in 1878 in the *Bien Public*, was naïvely astonished at the curt and hostile notice accorded to Flaubert's *Madame Bovary* by Duranty in *Le Réalisme* for 1857. "How is it," he comically protests, "that the Realists of 1856 did not see the decisive argument which Gustave Flaubert provided for their cause?" The answer to this absurd question is that Duranty and his accomplices were incapable, firstly, of recognising the originality of Flaubert's marvellous style, and secondly, of imagining that a realistic novel could possess a style at all. How could these writers, whose doctrine was a confession of their lack of æsthetic sense, understand a man for whom art was a religion? For Flaubert the choice of epithet, the rhythm of a phrase was everything; the subject, a matter of purely secondary interest. A great artist, he said to his friend Ducamp, can paint with equal effect a snail crawling on a cabbage leaf or Apollo gazing at Venus. Flaubert worshipped form. With Buffon he agreed that "the manner in which a truth is announced is more useful to humanity than even the truth itself." Yet with all his contempt for subject-matter as opposed to style, Flaubert's secret predilection was for the great Romantic themes. So the writing of *Salammbô* was a joy, but an illicit and sinful joy, for according to his credo the perfect work of art can only be conceived in labour and travail. "Literally speaking," he confessed in his correspondence, "there are in me two distinct fellows: one who loves *gueulades*, lyricism, great eagle flights, all the sonorities of the phrase and all the peaks of the idea;

another who digs and burrows into the truth as far as he can, who likes to throw into relief the little fact as vividly as the big one, who would like to make you feel *almost materially* the things he reproduces. The latter loves a hearty laugh and revels in the animalities of man."

Flaubert's life was a long battle between his Romantic instincts and his artistic conscience. One can only compare him to a wanton who has voluntarily taken the vow of chastity. Had he been a Chateaubriand he might have compromised between art and Romanticism, but his austere conception of beauty led him to regard subjectivism and true art as incompatible. "Emotion," he told the Goncourts, "is hostile to literary gestation," and in his two greatest novels, *Madame Bovary* (1857) and *L'Éducation sentimentale* (1869), he wrought to attain that complete detachment which he felt was the only way to achieve his ideal—"the eternal fusion of illusion and reality." The composition of *Madame Bovary* was a prolonged gehenna. Again and again in his letters Flaubert expresses the nausea inspired in him by the self-inflicted task of "entering at every moment into skins which are antipathetic to me." Why then did he choose to write about these characters? The truth is that the bourgeois not only revolted but fascinated him. Like every Romantic he was profoundly out of sympathy with his age, which was an age of industrialism, of political intrigue and general Philistinism. Flaubert lacked the humanistic spirit of tolerance; and that very subjectivism which he abhorred betrays itself in the misanthropic tone of *Madame Bovary*. Indeed, it compromises the artistic integrity of the novel. Every character presents some aspect of stupidity or vice. Charles Bovary is a uxorious dupe, Emma a randy *précieuse*. Homais is an ineffable blockhead, the abbé Bournisien a clod-dish and ignorant priest. Léon, the semi-idealist, has no moral courage, whilst Rodolphe is a selfish and cowardly sensualist. Ducamp once spoke of Flaubert's "myopic" manner, and with a good deal of justice. His observation has astounding depth but lacks Balzac's lateral sweep. No one could plumb what he called the *moral density* of a character like Flaubert, and there is not a person in *Madame Bovary* whom the reader can readily forget. Individually, Emma, Charles and Homais are perfect. They are ready to walk out of the novel into the streets of life. One does feel them *almost materially*, to quote Flaubert's phrase. And still there is something wanting in the ensemble: the general picture of provincial life is askew, and this is so because the author allowed his pessimism to blur his vision of humanity. Even if we agree with Flaubert that humanity is composed entirely of fools and scoundrels, it is hard to imagine a village in France with inhabitants so utterly incurious as to the escapades of the doctor's wife. Everything happens too easily. Granting the extraordinary obtuseness of Charles and the astonishing fertility of Emma's inventive powers, why does not Flaubert reckon with that dynamic social force—village scandal? In reality a hundred tongues would have wagged, a hundred village Baziles would have ripped shreds from Emma's reputation and Charles would have been inundated with anonymous letters. But Flaubert, who knew his limitations, preferred to restrict the zone of his observation and action, a species of myopia which is really dangerous because it deprives the novel of that oblique perspective which gives such spaciousness to the *Comédie Humaine*.

The melodramatic ending of *Madame Bovary* is not typical of Flaubert, for whom life was stupid and not at all dramatic. As is well known, however, the plot was borrowed from real life. Indeed, Flaubert told the Goncourts that a few days before his conversation with Ducamp and Bouillet, he had chosen quite a different theme: it was the latter who reminded him of the incident forming the basis of the Bovary intrigue. In the *Éducation sentimentale*, on the other hand, he followed his natural bent, choosing an undramatic form. The public, which insists on a beginning, a middle, and an end in its novels, preferred *Bovary* to the later work chiefly, as Flaubert said disgustedly, because of its *côté vaudeville*.

Were it not presumptuous to criticise Flaubert as a psychologist, one might ask why Mme Bovary commits suicide at all. After her first affair she thought of doing so, and this, after the shattering of her Romantic ideals, was quite probable. She carried to the second amour fewer illusions; desire was still as keen, but it was now more physical and less ideal. The realisation that Léon had grown tired might have filled her with bitterness but not with despair. There remains the money question. Blackmailed by Lheureux, the bailiff in the house and exposure a mere matter of hours, it might be urged that suicide was the only solution. Possibly, in the case of a business man whose professional honour is at stake, this might be true; but Mme Bovary, as Flaubert insists, has no money sense at all, whilst as to exposure, she has too much contempt for her husband to fear his recriminations—if one could imagine the lamb-like Charles daring to indulge in recriminations. No, women like Emma do not commit suicide so long as there is an unattached male left. In reality she would have cajoled the bemused husband and moved to another village. The dénouement is not satisfactory, for it is only at coroners' inquests that temporary insanity is accepted as a motive for *felo de se*; the novelist is required to furnish more satisfactory reasons.

Untrammelled by dramatic considerations, Flaubert is more at his ease in *L'Éducation sentimentale*, and here he attempts the history, not merely of a marriage, but of a social era. This is in the Balzacian tradition, for here is breadth as well as depth of observation. It is, I feel, a more powerful novel than *Madame Bovary*. Flaubert displays a broader sense of human values, and the presence of that admirable creation, Mme Arnoux, lends the work balance which is lacking in *Madame Bovary*. There are, it is true, few poignant incidents, yet could anything be more profoundly tragic than the cumulative impression of so much courage, love, energy, and talent slowly running to seed? Frédéric Moreau, after all his dreams of love and fame, ends as a discontented little bourgeois *rentier*. The ambitious Deslauriers rises for a moment above his class, but sinks back into the poverty and obscurity of a petty clerkship. The Arnoux retire to the country to start a new life and to face the task of paying off their debts. Only Rozanette, the courtesan, and the slimy, prudent Martinon emerge with any show of affluence, and that is the result, not of careful planning, but of pure chance. The appalling thing is that of all these men and women who work and scheme and suffer in the pursuit of happiness not one attains it. For Flaubert, as for Shakespeare, "Life is a tale . . . told by an idiot, signifying nothing." Frédéric and Deslauriers ponder over the problem of their failure. "I had too much logic," says the latter, "and you too much sentiment." And so they drift back to memories of youth. One stands out vividly, a school-boy escapade. Once after much discussion they had plucked up courage to enter a brothel, each bearing an enormous bouquet culled from Mme Moreau's garden. Timid and stammering they presented their flowers to the giggling drabs, then suddenly overcome with remorse and fear, bolted. "That," mused Frédéric, "was the best thing that ever happened to us." "Perhaps you are right," said Deslauriers. Some critics, like Taillandier of the *Revue des deux Mondes* for instance, have severely rebuked Flaubert for the cynicism and bad taste of this ending, which is, on the contrary, an artistic *tour de force*. That last wistful phrase completes the cycle of Frédéric's life. With him we are once more carried back over those sordid futile years to the glorious morning of existence, that perfect season fragrant with illusion, unsmirched by the knowledge of reality. That, we realise with Frédéric, was the happy time. His mistake lay, not in too much logic nor in too much sentiment nor in any reasoned system of living, but in the failure to see that it is as futile to chase happiness as to follow the rainbow's end. For the ideal is always the memory of illusion, always in the past, though by a strange trick of imagination its glowing tints are reflected on the horizon of the future. Like Frédéric and Deslauriers we run breathlessly over the broken ground after our pot of gold until exhausted we stop and, turning round, behold it shining—behind us. To the connoisseur in wines there is one glass which is perfect to degust: the first or the last of the bottle. In Prévost's *Manon Lescaut* it is the first—the marvellous opening in which the author royally makes us a present of the dénouement: in *L'Éducation sentimentale* it is the last, the ending, with that tantalising suggestion of the magnificent novel which he might have written, entitled, perhaps—who knows?—*La Vie en Fleur.*

There is an interesting letter written by Flaubert in 1844 to Louis de Cormenin recording his first impressions of Plutarch's *Life of Heliogabalus*. Enthusiasm rises in a spray of iridescent epithets—"Asiatic," "feverish," "romantic," "frenzied," "delirium by torchlight," all of which admirably characterise his own *Salammbô*. This "purple" novel, as he loved to call it, satisfied Flaubert's Romantic craving for colour and sensation. But what of the other *bonhomme*, the objective Realist? To quiet him, the Flaubert of the *gueulades* and the "eagle wing-beats" subjected himself for years to an enormous, a Benedictine documentation. Read his letter in reply to Sainte-Beuve's criticism of *Salammbô*, an amusing letter spiky with recondite references, which make Sainte-Beuve the savant of Port Royal look like a sheepish and careless undergraduate wilting under the blast of a professor's erudition. According to those competent to judge, like Louis Bertrand, Flaubert has succeeded in recapturing the spirit of Oriental mysticism. To the layman, *Salammbô* will remain a series of gorgeous frescoes, of rutilant and sonorous epithets like Gautier's "golden horsemen galloping over brazen bridges." But the characters, Mathô, Spendius, Salammbô and Hannibal, have not the old Flaubertian individuality and relief. They melt into a background of surging, swaying bodies, black, brown, bronze and white; of flashing battle-axes and droning slings; of faces agonising, exultant or twisted with hate; of massive elephants ploughing like grey battleships through waves of human flesh; of dim temples dedicated to horrid and obscene mysteries. This is a novel in the grand manner, an Oriental *Notre Dame* dominated by a city on a rock, a novel of crowds and not of individuals, a novel to quaff in huge heady draughts, but not to toy with in analytical mood. For all its rational, erudite preparation *Salammbô* is a haschisch nightmare, one of those stupendous orgies by which Flaubert the ascetic, the devotee of Art, was wont to purge himself of his vaporous and primitive repressions. The Goncourts often comment on his morbid infatuation for De Sade, and there is indeed something really sadistic in the gusto with which Flaubert describes the mass butcheries of humans in *Salammbô* and of animals in *Saint Julien l'Hospitalier.*

Were any further argument needed to expose the fallacy of the traditional but false opposition of Romanticism and Realism, it is surely to be found in the work of Flaubert. Here is plainly visible the dual nature of Romanticism. *Salammbô* is an escape from the drabness of the nineteenth century into an ideal and gorgeous world of the imagination. *Bovary* and the *Éducation sentimentale* reflect in their sombre tints the frustrated Romantic who shuts his ears to the insistent clamours of the *moi* in order to grapple with reality. Romanticism is always the expression of an acute consciousness of the disparity between the actual and our ideal of it. In varying degrees of intensity it is always a protest against life and never an acceptance of reality. Molière, Rabelais, Montaigne accept life for what it is and with all its shortcomings. Flaubert never does. On the other hand, he shuns the Utopian visions of the Romantic humanitarians, Hugo, Sand and Sue. Thereby he attains to a more objective and unclouded view of reality, even in his moments of deepest pessimism. This he did, however, by rigid self-discipline, with the strange result that he has been arraigned for insensibility and cynicism. He was not insensible, but he distrusted his own emotionalism lest it prejudice art. Therefore his novels lack that spiritual *élan* which distinguishes the works of Balzac and of Molière. On the other hand this absence of warmth is compensated for by the astonishing penetration of his observation and above all by the perfection of his style, which is an instrument of rare precision.

What is it that lends such vitality to Flaubert's prose? Is it not the discovery that there is no such thing as "still life"? Chateaubriand and Senancour, in objective mood, recorded the sensitive heart-beats of Nature. In the forest scenes of *Atala* there are moments of intense awareness, of purely objective sensibility. But they are of fleeting duration. Inevitably the insatiable *moi* reasserts itself, ever striving to fuse with the object—the eternal Romantic obsession which enslaves Nature and sees Nature as a mere prism reflecting the changing moods and the yearning desires of the human soul, blurring her contours and her colours. Flaubert, in *Madame Bovary* and in the *Éducation sentimentale*, avoided this by steering a middle course between Pantheism and Romanticism, retaining always the detachment of the true artist. In consequence he was able to surprise that secret life of the external world which is revealed only to the patient observer. Balzac, it is true, possessed the power of objective contemplation, and his magnificent descriptions of man's physical environment add immensely to our knowledge of his characters. Still, the physical world for Balzac was always a background or a setting to humanity. For Flaubert it is more: it is another life evolving parallel to human life, a rhythmic and musical accompaniment illustrating the theme of existence. All of us remember—for how can we forget it?—that passage where he describes Charles Bovary's visit to Emma at her father's farm—the dust gently moving across the flagged floor, the embers blued by the sunlight. Or again, the vision of Emma framed in the doorway whilst the water softly drips from the eaves on her iridescent silk parasol. Remember, too, the garden scene where the guilty Mme Bovary, swooning in her lover's arms, is startled by the soft thud of the ripe peaches on the grass.

This is not "nature description." It is vastly more significant, infinitely more subtle. Flaubert possessed to an uncanny degree the sense of that relativity which links us to our physical environment, that intermittent invasion of human consciousness by material elements which have apparently nothing to do with our immediate psychological state, and yet that ever afterwards persist in the memory; nay, without which we should probably never recall the thoughts or actions with which they synchronised. There is nothing symbolic about the dropping water, the dust, the falling of the peaches. They belong simply to that category of things, trivial in themselves, but which like coloured buoys mark the shoals and currents of our emotional life. And, in selecting for his purpose moving things, the swirling dust, the raindrops, the falling fruit, Flaubert emphasises in a subtle and original way the old theme of the transience of human existence and the eternal life and activity of the material world. What fascinated him was the constant intervention of the so-called inanimate objects in human affairs. Nature, static and evocative in Balzac, Flaubert endows with movement. Recollect the opening pages of the *Éducation sentimentale*, depicting that resurrection of the physical world which all of us may witness, like Frédéric, if we take a trip on a river-steamer. The narrative of the hero's spiritual birth evolves to the accompaniment of shifting curtains of poplars. of rising, dipping and gliding hills studded with red-roofed villas and woods racing down to the riverside. It swells into a rhythmic and glorious recitative comparable in beauty to the Proustian miracle of the steeples of Martinville.

CHAPTER VIII

CALIBAN AND ARIEL

In his excellent *Le Naturalisme français*, M. Martino has made a gallant attempt to demonstrate that Realism and Naturalism "designate . . . different artistic doctrines." What he really shows is that the Naturalism of 1880 is the Realism of 1860 masquerading as a science; for in the early years of the Third French Republic the name of Science was one to conjure with. At last, it seemed, the key to the Absolute was within human grasp.

The term *naturalisme* was not a new one, though towards the end of the Second Empire its old meaning of materialism was altered in order to conform to the new scientific spirit. *Naturalisme* was now employed to describe the doctrine of a school of writers who desired to transfer to literature the objective methods of the experimental scientist. One can find it still used in its old sense in the preface to Victor de Laprade's *Idylles héroïques* (1859), when he says that "the excess of Naturalism leads to two errors which seem irreconcilable and which none the less have many points of contact: Realism and a sort of Mysticism." In 1863 Sainte-Beuve gives to the adjective *naturaliste* its new connotation. "The naturalistic philosophers," he writes, "tend to introduce into everything, to proclaim in everything the processes and the results of science." The reader of to-day, untroubled by critical niceties and basing his judgment on general impressions, sees Naturalism as an exaggerated form of Realism, treating with more crudeness of a lower stratum of humanity. And, after all, is his diagnosis not perfectly right?

De Mazade, in the *Revue des deux Mondes* for 1860, defined Realism as the battle-cry "of a whole school of painters and novelists which has adopted Balzac as its god and of which M. de Champfleury, the author of *Les Amis de la Nature*, is one of the prophets." He echoes the general objections hurled at the new doctrine. "It is the substitution of a servile tracing for the free and fertile interpretation of nature. It is the cult of detail instead of a large and superior study of the characteristic phenomena of the moral world. . . . If your work is only an obstinate and minute transcription you will never equal nature. If this material fidelity of imitation is the sole object, the sole merit of the novel, it is merely the old theory of *l'art pour l'art* complicated by a disturbing predilection for all the vulgar spectacles of life." Commenting on the spread of Realism, he adds: "It is [to be found] in the analysis of the passions, in the description of manners, of luxury, of the equivocal elegancies of a certain type of fashionable life, as it is sometimes in the descriptions of a drab bourgeois home or in stories of peasant life." Essentially, then, Realism was not "a different doctrine" from Naturalism. If in practice the Naturalists departed from their theory and concentrated more and more on the observation of low life their profession of faith always was at bottom identical with that of the Realists, namely, the objective examination and the impersonal reproduction of the real. The Realists of the Second Empire were not yet conscious of being "scientific": the Naturalists of the Third Republic were, and this consciousness led them to invent a new jargon to describe their system. This does not alter the fact, however, that their method was fundamentally that of their predecessors. If a homely simile is permissible, the Realists were like the men who thought that oranges are an indispensable article of diet. Someone told the Naturalists about the vitamins and the orange somehow became a globular, dark yellow citrous fruit rich in vitamin C. But it was the same old orange.

This erosion of literature by science had its origins in the great "philosophic" movement of the eighteenth century, which, as M. Daniel Mornet has so clearly proved, was really a struggle between rationalism and empiricism. On the eve of 1789 advanced intellectuals like Diderot, Condillac and Helvétius had renounced Descartes for Bacon. They substituted for the old Cartesian *a priori* system of reasoning a method based on the objective observation of facts—in short, what the nineteenth century called experimental science. That this spirit was never completely submerged by Romanticism can be seen from the works of the Utopian socialists, Saint-Simon, Fourier, Proudhon, who, for all their ideology, yet built upon a solid subsoil of reality. Similarly, as has been mentioned, the Romantic novelists, even in their wildest flights into the realms of a mystic idealism, did not by any means always abdicate the objective sense of reality. This scientific attitude towards life inspired the positivist philosophy of Auguste Comte, whose *Cours de Philosophie positive* (1839–42) exercised a very profound influence on the thought of his time. Early in the century, indeed, the discoveries made by Cuvier and Saint-Hilaire in the domain of the natural sciences were enthusiastically received, in particular by Balzac. Yet until the middle of the Second Empire the gulf separating science from literature was still unspanned. Champfleury's Realism was extremely local and cannot be called scientific, though of course, indirectly, like the positivism of Comte, it had its roots in the sensationalism of the eighteenth century. Towards 1850 a liaison was effected between scientist and man of letters. Sainte-Beuve, whose critical system had been slowly following the curve of the new intellectual movement, openly declared himself for Realism. Taine, in his celebrated essay on Balzac (1858), had already proclaimed his admiration for the new doctrine. In 1864 he created a sensation by an article on Stendhal which was regarded as a veritable manifesto on behalf of Realism. "A novel," he had already declared in 1861, "is simply a collection of experiments." In the introduction to his epoch-making *Histoire de la Littérature anglaise* (1864), Taine, by the enunciation of his famous doctrine of *la race, le milieu et le moment*, virtually claimed for history and literary criticism the authority of an exact science. In the following year he extended the freedom of the new city to the novel. "If the novel tries to show us what we are, criticism tries to show us what we have been. Both now constitute a great investigation into mankind, into all the varieties, all the situations, all the periods where human nature has flourished or degenerated. By their seriousness, their method, their rigorous exactness; by their future and their hopes, both are approaching science." Two works, Darwin's *Origin of Species*, translated in 1862, 1873, and 1876, and above all, Claude Bernard's *Introduction à la Médecine expérimentale* (1860), excited the curiosity of men of letters. In a few years the novel and the stage were transformed into laboratories for the conduct of researches into human nature. Taine's phrase, "Vice and virtue are products like vitriol and sugar," was accepted by Zola as an axiom and eagerly repeated by his admirers. Immature scientific theories and formulæ were avidly snapped up by credulous novelists with that touching faith in the pronouncements of science which is an eternal subject of wonder and embarrassment to the scientist himself. Such was the state of the public mind that if Berthelot had said he could repeat the miracle of Lazarus it is possible that many would have believed him.

As exposed in this brief summary it may appear as if the transition from Realism to Naturalism in the novel was effected, as the war communiqués used to phrase it, "without incident." Such was not the case. It might seem, too—and this is certainly the impression given by writers like M. Martino—as if the French novel from 1860 to 1890 was absolutely dominated by Realism and Naturalism to the exclusion of Romanticism and Idealism. This was also not the case, and M. Martino's assertion that "in reality 1830 put an end to the brief conquests of Romanticism" is not at all borne out by facts, as has indeed been partially shown, I venture to hope, in these pages.

A good deal has been said by various writers about State opposition to Realism. Now, as is well known, the effect of censorship upon literature has always been to facilitate the spread of new ideas. Flaubert was prosecuted for *outrage à la morale publique et religieuse*, and triumphantly acquitted. Immediately, of course, there was an upward leap in the sales of *Madame Bovary*, and the author was acclaimed as the high priest of Realism, an honour which he violently repudiated to the end of his days. Other novelists of the same school were molested at various times during the Second Empire, but the Goncourts exaggerate when they speak of a "white terror." The Realists were looked on with disfavour, and where possible the Government of Napoleon III. tried to limit the sales of their "immoral" works by forbidding the hawking of them. It would be an exaggeration, however, to speak of persecution and an absurdity to suggest that the evolution of the novel was checked by the famous decree of 17 February, 1852. The object of this measure was to censor not literature but political journalism. In nearly all cases where the novelist was prosecuted or harassed it was because he published in a journal hostile to the government. It is indeed questionable whether *Madame Bovary* would have been attacked had it not appeared in the *Revue de Paris*, whose editor, Laurent Pichat, was a political suspect. Nevertheless, if at the same time a blow could be dealt at Realism, then looked upon by the censorship as a vague form of socialism, it was felt by the authorities that no particular harm would be done. Obviously the policy of every government is to pander to the opinion of the majority, and in the sixties that opinion was inimical to Realism.

What was Flaubert's position in regard to the new doctrine? One can well understand his distaste at being associated with the shoddy bourgeois Realism of Champfleury and Duranty. On the other hand, it can be argued that his method was that of the scientist. It was his admiration for the documentary, historical system of the Goncourts, and not only his sympathy for their sense of word values, that drew him into close and cordial relations with these Siamese twins of literature. Flaubert was a regular attendant also at the notorious Magny dinners, the so-called *dîners des athées*, where he met Taine, the Goncourts, Sainte-Beuve, Tourguenieff and Zola. But Flaubert retained his intellectual independence, and as the years recede the originality of his conception of realism becomes more apparent. When, in 1875, he wrote to George Sand: "I execrate what is commonly accepted as Realism although I have been made one of its pontiffs," he was expressing the great artist's instinctive horror for *clichés* and schools. "With regard to my friends," he went on to say, "you add 'my school.' But I am ruining my temperament by trying not to have a school. *A priori*

I reject them all. Those whom I often see and whom you designate are seeking for everything I despise and care only moderately for what torments me. I regard as very secondary the technical detail, local information, in short the historical and exact aspect of things. I am seeking above all beauty, and in that my companions are only moderately interested." The Realism or Naturalism of his contemporaries seemed, then, to Flaubert a very superficial thing. The inner truth and beauty of life, he knew, could not be revealed by any ready-made artistic formula. Nor could he visualise a truth divorced from beauty. Certainly humanity as he saw it was morally and spiritually ugly, but could he not comfort himself by contrasting the spiritual squalor of mankind with the loveliness of man's material environment—a subtle, savage principle of irony which he passed on to his young disciple, Guy de Maupassant?

Romantic Utopians and Romantic Realists—both had an ideal. Hugo and Sand dreamed of a perfect society founded on universal brotherly love. Zola's millennium was to be brought about by experimental science. "We are, in a word," he wrote in 1880, "experimental moralists, showing by experience the way in which passion behaves in a social milieu. The day we possess the mechanism of this passion it can be treated and reduced or at least rendered as inoffensive as possible. Therein lies the practical utility and the high morality of our naturalistic works, which experiment on man, which dismount and reconstruct the human machine piece by piece to make it function under the influence of milieu. In the course of time, when we possess all the laws, the only thing we shall have to do will be to act upon individuals and milieu if we want to arrive at the best social state." The Goncourts' *Journal* reveals what Flaubert thought of Zola's Utopianism. He himself was no such optimist. George Sand once reproached him with the hopelessness of his outlook on life, and he replied: "You are right, absolutely right. But really, now, you do not light up my darkness with metaphysics, either mine or anyone else's. The words, religion or catholicism, on the one hand; progress, fraternity, democracy on the other, do not respond to the spiritual demands of the moment. The new dogma of equality preached by Radicalism is belied experimentally by physiology and history. I cannot see to-day the means of establishing a new principle any more than of respecting the old ones. So I seek but cannot find that idea whence all the rest must depend."

What is the *Éducation sentimentale* if not a faithful picture of the intellectual and social chaos of the France of the Louis-Philippe as Flaubert saw it? And was his vision so very much clouded by his pessimism? In the unfinished *Bouvard et Pécuchet* he satirised with equal cruelty the scientific credulity of the late Empire and early Republic. Was it odd that he should view with sardonic scepticism the application of science to art which paraded so pompously as Naturalism? Flaubert's originality lies in his refusal to sacrifice his artistic ideal. Where his companions rushed to enlist under the banner of Science, Flaubert the artist preferred to keep his intellectual independence. Let Zola, if he cared, serve as laboratory boy to Claude Bernard. Let the Goncourts devil for the scientific historians of social manners. Flaubert had a nobler, a more aristocratic idea of the novelist's function. For him the novel was interpretation and not merely stenography. The novelist, like the scientist, must be impersonal, but art is not the mere reproduction of observed facts: it is the discovery of a form which will express that "fusion of illusion and reality" called life. That was what Flaubert meant by beauty. That was his conception of a realistic novel, and it is one which carries us planes above the Realism or Naturalism of the Goncourts and of Zola, into a region where chronology and systems are of small moment.

There is nothing harder than to know precisely what the term Realism signified to the critic of the early Second Empire. In general, of course, it was applied to any novel offering an unidealised picture of lower or lower middle-class life. Yet in 1858 we find Montégut of the *Revue des deux Mondes* referring to Ernest Feydeau's *Fanny* as the *roman intime de la littérature réaliste*. Another writer, Merlet, coined the phrase "Byronic Realism," a much more satisfactory epithet, for in *Fanny* the major chord is Romantic. Theme, hero, situations are all exceptional, whilst the conclusion too is in the most approved Romantic tradition. Still, Montégut was not entirely wrong. *Fanny* is a *roman intime*, that is to say, a psychological novel of passion in the subjective manner of Constant's *Adolphe*, where, to quote Sainte-Beuve, the author's sentiments "leap straight from the heart to the manuscript." And again there are passages where, in his rendering of material environment, Feydeau is as objective and as painstaking as the Goncourts. Montégut's error is simply that of many modern critics who persist in the implication that Romanticism excludes Realism, whereas in fact there is no earthly reason why a Romantic writer should remain consistently subjective.

Fanny enjoyed a resounding *succès de scandale* owing to the originality of its theme and the startling nature of the crucial scene. The whole interest centres on the strange psychology of the hero, Roger, who is jealous of his mistress's husband. Those who have seen Henri Becque's *La Parisienne* know the rich dramatic possibilities of such a situation, but Feydeau, a diffuse writer and indifferent psychologist, cannot rise to the level of his theme. Roger's character, instead of developing, remains static after the first few pages. We see a Romantic introvert tormented by his insatiable egotism. Until he meets Fanny's husband his amour-propre is satisfied. The imagination of the Romantic is a protective barrier which he erects between his *moi* and reality, so that when Roger thought of the husband it was always with a sort of complacent or triumphant pity. His first visit to Fanny's house brings swift disillusionment: the husband of reality is a young man of great intellectual and physical energy, whose attitude towards his wife is a perfect blend of deference and conjugal solicitude. From that moment Roger's jealousy gives him no rest, and he tortures Fanny with questions as to the most intimate details of her domestic life. That is well observed, because men like Roger are fairly common and jealousy and decency rarely run together. But Feydeau commits two gross psychological errors. The first is the sudden revelation that Fanny's husband is in secret a despot with an ungovernable temper. That is quite probable. What is not probable is that Fanny could have kept that fact from her lover throughout a year's intimacy. Yet during all that time she complacently lends herself to all his caprices and satisfies his ignoble curiosity. Secondly, Fanny is made to acquiesce in Roger's monstrous proposal that she should cease conjugal relations with her husband. Feydeau tries to justify this by explaining that the latter insists on his wife lending her dowry as security in a business speculation. What Feydeau fails to understand is the rôle played by amour-propre in human relationships. Only a violent loathing of her husband could have made it probable that Fanny would so completely betray him, and she is too passive to nourish such a hatred. And even in adulterous women, unless they are fundamentally vicious, and Fanny is not, there is a barrier which not even a lover may cross. It is the amour-propre of a sensitive and intelligent woman. What prevents Feydeau from being a really fine novelist is his radical lack of good taste. Now, bad taste nearly always produces bad art, as in the case of Feydeau, whom it renders incapable of understanding feminine psychology. One wonders on reading *Fanny* whether bad taste is not another name for that necrosis of the moral sense resulting from too much experience and too little understanding of life. It is bad taste which made Feydeau write the notorious balcony scene, where the hero, crouching on the leads, spies upon husband and wife and sees Fanny break her grotesque promise. It is not, however, merely bad taste but the absence of any sense of proportion which solicits our sympathy for this monomaniac when, after swooning outside his mistress's window, he moans himself off to a solitary seaside resort, another unhappy victim of the social laws.

Excited by the success of this scene, the *clou* of the novel, Feydeau returned to the peeping Tom *motif* in *Daniel* (1859). Here the hero is the cuckold, but not a complacent cuckold, since he publicly exposes his wife's shame in a Paris *salon*. He then goes to Trouville in winter—only a Romantic would do this—and in one of his Byronic meanderings by the wild waves falls in love with an anæmic patrician, Louise. One cannot seriously discuss the actions and thoughts of this uncomfortable maniac who in the evening is to be discovered spying on his beloved as she goes to bed and in the morning posturing as a modern Galahad. As he cannot himself marry Louise Daniel actually offers all his fortune to her fiancé, Georget, if the latter will consent to disappear after the ceremony. Louise dies of heart-failure, caused not by Daniel but by society. So Daniel poisons himself in the family vault beside the corpse of Louise, and his wife elopes to Italy with a new lover. Curiously enough Feydeau was hailed not only as a Realist but as a genius, and, being the vainest of men, warmly agreed that he was both. His later works, however, converted the most fanatical of his admirers and revealed him for what he was — an author of mediocre, Romantic *romans-feuilletons* masquerading as a psychologist and an *impassible*.

The brothers Goncourt, in *Manette Salomon* (1865), explain very clearly what they understood by Realism in art. "Le moderne, tout est là. La sensation, l'intuition du contemporain, du spectacle qui vous coudoie, du présent dans lequel vous sentez frémir vos passions et quelque chose de vous." Like Flaubert, they despised the unæsthetic Realism of the Champfleury-Duranty school, that "caricature du Vrai de notre temps, un épatement de bourgeois." Their ideal was a "Realism to be found outside the stupidity of the daguerrotype and the charlatanism of the Ugly," a Realism necessitating a new mode of expression, "le style contemporain," which should reflect all that was typical of the life of their times. And many years before the arrival of Zola with his theory of Naturalism and of the experimental novel the two brothers laboured by precept and example to transfer to the novel the impassive methods of the scientist.

When we open our newspaper and read that "Mr. X. left Charing Cross this morning for Crete, where he will gather material for his forthcoming novel. He will be back in town next month," it is difficult to be quite fair to the Goncourts. For it was they who began this inhuman business of deliberately setting out to write a novel on a selected theme with selected characters moving in a selected environment. Somehow it would be so much better if the idea of writing the novel came to Mr. X. from having first lived in Crete. There is something rather pathetic in the patient and systematic efforts of the

Goncourt brothers to approach that ideal which they elaborated with so much care and thought. The conception of an absolutely objective novel must have been first suggested to them by Janin, that great admirer of Diderot. The Goncourtian style, the famous *écriture artistique*, they owed partly to Gautier and Flaubert, but chiefly to their own temperament and experience of art. Without ever attaining Flaubert's mystic adoration for the Word as distinct from the Idea, the Goncourts acquired a very pretty flair for the intrinsic beauty of language, for the plastic, picturesque and musical qualities of epithet and phrase. As is well known, they were authorities on the social life of the eighteenth century, and were also justly proud of having introduced France to Japanese art. To the novel, then, they carried over the habits of the dilettante historian and connoisseur: a respect, amounting almost to a mania, for documentation, a talent for the notation of minutiæ and an insatiable curiosity as to abnormalities. They collected human bric-à-brac as they did Japanese prints and Louis XV. pictures, but when they had amassed their material one has the uneasy impression that they did not quite know what to do with it all. To these specialists in human fauna life was a sort of museum full of rare specimens, of deviations from the norm which they invariably mistook for types. As a result, we rarely encounter in their novels any one of those simple incidents or conversations which suddenly illuminate the obscure depths of human nature, No one could give a more vivid impression of a milieu. Think of that exquisite etching of the forest of Fontainebleau in *Manette Salomon*! The same beautiful workmanship is revealed in the creation of atmosphere. There is the authentic hospital odour in *Sœur Philomène*, and the clammy smell of poverty clings to the pages of *Germinie Lacerteux*. But the characters fail to live up to their surroundings. Sœur Philomène is not a typical nursing sister. As Flaubert told the authors, she is an exception and, moreover, as a woman in love she is also abnormal. So the interest inspired by her passion for the *interne* Barnier holds only a local and transitory appeal since we know that never in real life can we witness such a queer plexus of repressions and desires. It is not, of course, necessary that every novel character should be a type: it is, however, essential that the novelist should place his hero or heroine inside the pale of imaginable experience. Sœur Philomène is a clinical study of an abnormal, and all abnormals to be artistically probable should have an abnormal setting. The ghost in *Hamlet* is probable on the battlements of Elsinore: he would not be so on a sunlit village green. One can imagine Philomène in a hospital, but as a patient and not as a nurse. In the same way Coriolis the artist, in *Manette Salomon*, cuts a strange figure as the miserable butt of his Jewish mistress and her haggish relatives. The Goncourts represent his situation as tragic when it is merely irksome and improbable. He is not in love with Manette, and his son is so Judaised that there is no earthly reason why he should sacrifice his artistic soul to the caprices of a mercenary little horror. The dénouement is quite out of keeping with the character of the hero, who in reality would have thrown the whole tribe into the street or else have departed with easels and brushes to a quieter spot.

The Goncourts had a Flaubertian contempt for novels with plots. The invention of a plot implies a dramatisation of life, and this, they feared, would compromise the truth of their interpretation. In theory perhaps they were right, but the fact stands that their two best works, *Renée Mauperin* (1864) and *Germinie Lacerteux* (1865), are cast in dramatic mould. Indeed, the interest of the former is largely that of situation, though the authors intended that it should rest entirely on the "studies" of the modern girl and of the typical modern young man represented by Renée and Henri. Yet Renée is no more typical of her period than M. Paul Margueritte's *garçonne* is of ours. Readers of the Second Empire were properly scandalised at the daring (!) description of the heroine bathing in the Seine with a young man. Yet oddly enough, thanks no doubt to our Mr. Havelock Ellis, it leaves us unperturbed. Nor can we be greatly exercised at Renée's unladylike rejection of one eligible suitor after another. Conventions change so quickly. Renée is merely unconventional, and unconventionality is rarely a sign of character but rather of the lack of it. Now Henri, on the contrary, has a pronounced individuality. He is the Empire version of Julien Sorel, the *homme fort*, the ruthless *arriviste* devoid of all moral sense. M. André Gide would call him an *immoraliste* except that he has sound lungs and is not a sexual pervert. In any case there is power and restraint in the account of Henri's machinations and of his love affair with his fiancée's mother. The narrative of his sudden death at the hands of a complete stranger is a stroke of genius worthy of Stendhal. A second reading of *Renée Mauperin* will discover a tendency to strain coincidence, but that does not seriously detract from the strength of the general conception.

The theme of *Germinie Lacerteux* was borrowed from actual experience. In this story the authors really achieve that "direct vision" of life which was their ideal. In the customary preface they describe their book as "a true, severe and pure" novel, a "social investigation" and a "clinical study of love." A clinical study it certainly is, but hardly of love. Germinie is a servant girl, seduced and bled white by a pimp who cynically deserts the unfortunate girl, leaving her with a mass of debts. Germinie is a nymphomaniac, and now, like an addict deprived of her drug, she discards the last shred of self-respect to satisfy her craving. Strange to say, her mistress only learns of her dual life after the girl's death, when the creditors come croaking on her doorstep. This actually happened in the case of the real Germinie, Rose, who was servant to the Goncourts' aunt: whether it makes probable fiction is another matter.

But the human appeal of this novel does not lie in its apparently accurate description of Germinie's malady, which has no cosmic significance. What is truly moving is the contrast between Germinie's devotion to her mistress and her physical degradation; the eternal conflict between the spirit and the flesh. The real crisis in her life is when she steals a few louis for her loathsome lover. Her drunkenness, her street-walking are merely a natural result of her pathological condition: the theft is a graver and sadder symptom because it marks the commencement of her spiritual *débâcle*. True, she replaces the money, but the realisation that she could have robbed her beloved mistress enlightens her as to the real condition of her soul. As Mme Duras said: "There are certain illusions which are like the light of day. When we lose them everything else disappears." Germinie's illusion was that she could keep her spiritual integrity and at the same time indulge in physical excess, an illusion which accounts for half the sorrow in this world. In *Germinie Lacerteux* the Goncourts drop their silly pretence at insensibility and allow the warmth of natural pity to pervade their work. This ray of the ideal it is which lends reality to their narrative of facts. After all, the doctrine of a completely impassive art is only a form of frustrated Romanticism, because its implication is the monstrous one—that is, it would be monstrous if it were not absurd—that the artist possesses the superhuman power not merely to gaze unmoved at the spectacle of suffering humanity, but to *interpret* that suffering. When Robots take to writing novels it will be time to talk of "impassive" art. However, if we except De Maupassant, the Goncourts carried objectivism in art about as far as it is possible to do so without entirely departing from reality. *Germinie Lacerteux*, together with some of De Maupassant's short stories, represents the best that was produced by the French Naturalists.

Meanwhile, outside the parish of the Realists there were novelists who still believed that idealism and imagination can enter into the novel without detriment to its credibility. Victor Hugo published *Les Misérables* in 1862, *Les Travailleurs de la Mer* in 1866 and three years later *L'Homme qui rit*, all of which belong really to the field of popular literature. Into these immense repositories the veteran Romantic poured all his inchoate and Utopian ideas on the regeneration of society. As a sociologist he is on the level of an Eugène Sue: on the other hand there are passages in *Les Misérables* that do honour to the poet of *Les Châtiments*. Yet despite these intermittent epic and lyric flashes Victor Hugo's novels mark no advance in the development of the genre, save perhaps that the realism of certain descriptive passages undoubtedly inspired Zola in his vast frescoes of contemporary social life. On the whole they are simply glorified *romans-feuilletons*, exaggerating all the tendencies and defects of a Romanticism run to seed.

Of all the novelists who succeeded Balzac only one had his power of imagination and his natural genius for creation. This was Barbey d'Aurevilly, the Hammer of the Realists, the *bête noire* of Sainte-Beuve and Zola. The critics of his time, all save M. Paul Bourget, either affected to dismiss him as a charlatan or, like Brunetière, were sincerely blind to his undoubted originality. Nor has full justice yet been done to D'Aurevilly, though, thanks to Miss Read, his devoted admirer and the companion of his old age, we now possess everything that Barbey wrote. As a critic he forestalled Taine in paying homage to the genius of Balzac and Stendhal, and his *Œuvres et les Hommes* furnish an indispensable corrective to the pronouncements of the "scientific" writers of the nineteenth century. Barbey wrote as he lived, with fire, with colour and with sincerity. A Romantic who detested Romantic morality, a Catholic feared by his more timid co-religionaries, a Realist who loathed Realism, Barbey towers above his generation—a splendid anachronism. He did not so much imitate Balzac as enrich one aspect of Balzac's art. There is a sentence in his *Roman contemporain* that is typical of the man and sums up his whole artistic creed: "Il faut faire, dans les romans, *plus grand que nature*, contrairement aux basses théories d'à présent." For Barbey, the true Realism of Balzac is to be found in his gigantic creations, Vautrin, Goriot, Grandet: the Realists and Naturalists placed it elsewhere—in the accurate transcription of those details which compose the milieu, the character, and the daily life of his men and women. As a rule Barbey used only one background—Normandy, restricting himself to a few characters, all of whom he endows with exceptional passion and energy. It is this procedure (and it is that of the great tragic authors) which has scared and disconcerted critics. Brunetière's "law of probability" for the novel is excellent so long as we remember when to invoke it. It is easy to smile, for instance, at that incident in the *Vieille Maîtresse* (1851) where Vellini, amorous tigress of a woman, gashes her arm and forces her lover to suck her blood, yet nothing could be more completely in harmony with an atmosphere surcharged as in this novel with Romantic passion. Barbey had a godlike worship for Byron, and *La Vieille Maîtresse* is the most Byronic of his works. Yet it remains a convincing study of a man's effort to escape the domination of a frenzied and passionate mistress. After Marigny's marriage to the beautiful and saintly Hermangarde, Vellini follows him, and again he falls under her spell, not because of her sexual appeal but because she is the only woman with whom he can be perfectly frank—a profound psychological truth which no novelist before Barbey had ever exploited in dealing with the eternal triangle.

Barbey adored big passions and exceptional situations. He liked to imagine that he was possessed of a devil and to pretend that he could not distinguish between the infernal and celestial. In this spirit he conceived *L'Ensorcelée* (1854), that tale of a mystic who falls in love with the dæmonic Chouan priest, the abbé de la Croix-Jugan, finally shot dead at the altar by a jealous husband. Told by Barbey, illuminated by his marvellous pictures of Le Cotentin, the novel glows like the windows of a Gothic cathedral at sunset. And in all his novels which are enshrined in the rich setting of the Norman countryside, the dominant note, what Proust would have called the *phrase de Vinteuil* of the D'Aurevilly sonata, is the "light that never was," the reflection of summer evening skies on the still and sinister pools of Le Cotentin.

Barbey is one of the rare novelists for whom powerful situations had no terror. In *Ce qui ne meurt pas*, a youthful work written in 1835 and recast in 1884, he boldly undertakes a theme touched on by De Bernard, Flaubert and the Goncourts, all of whom, however, shirked the reality of the issue. Yseult de Scudemor, a woman of forty, yields through pity to the passionate love of Allen de Cyntry, a Romantic of eighteen who later falls in love with her daughter, whom he marries. Shortly after the wedding, Yseult discovers that she is *enceinte*. In a terrible final scene Barbey confronts the mother with her daughter, a courageous and masterly ending executed with a supreme regard for psychological truth.

A Romantic by his imagination, D'Aurevilly is a Realist in his attitude to ethical and social questions. The Naturalism of Zola not only revolted his æsthetic sense but enraged him by its pretentious and dogmatic scientism. "M. Zola, who would like to drive out human spirituality from literature, is an ape of Balzac in the filth of materialism writing for the apes of M. Littré." It was in defence of idealism that Barbey wrote the *Prêtre marié* (1865), whose hero, Sombreval, is a priest caught up by the prevailing mania for science. Sombreval renounces his faith. His daughter, Calixte, who is a mystic, secretly pledges herself to enter the order of the Carmelites. The tragic conflict between Sombreval's paternal love and his atheistic passion for science evolves in an atmosphere of weird and crepuscular beauty. The renegade, in order to restore his daughter's peace of mind, feigns conversion and is formally received back into the Church, but Calixte learns the truth and is killed by the shock. Sombreval, at the moment when he had almost discovered a cure for her nervous malady, hears the news and commits suicide.

At a time when the novel was in danger of becoming a mere annexe to Science, Barbey d'Aurevilly heroically defended the cause of idealism in art. The brilliance of his style, an incandescent brilliance hot with the fire of a passionate conviction, startled his enemies and alarmed his friends. As a critic he was sometimes magnificently unjust: as a novelist, often flamboyant. Brunetière tried to dismiss him contemptuously as "un vieux paradoxe ambulant." Now Barbey is paradoxical only to the critic who believes, like Brunetière, that there is but one form of reality, much as the writers of the seventeenth century believed that there was a *Beau immuable*, a fixed and unchangeable standard of beauty. In the glow of creation D'Aurevilly, like Balzac, endowed his characters with almost superhuman passion and energy, yet in the main he is a sure and penetrating psychologist. He does not possess Balzac's curiosity as to the ordinary external aspects of daily life, and this is undoubtedly a defect, because the reality of his interpretation is less accessible to the average reader. One often hears it said in praise of a novelist's realism, that his characters would be immediately recognisable if we met them in the street or in a drawing-room. Barbey's characters are too big for that: one cannot imagine them apart from their peculiar environment, but they are none the less real. What disconcerted Brunetière and his "scientific" friends in Barbey's creatures was the violence of their sentiments and the vitality of their imagination.

Obsessed with the idea that the psychological forces governing human conduct are to be discovered only through the study of the average man, they forgot that, on the contrary, it is the actions of what we call abnormally passionate or sensitive people which reveal the inner complexity of the human mind. All the great literary psychologists from Racine to Proust have realised this fact, and Barbey's originality lies in the courage with which he broke away from the narrow and facile conception of Realism held by the Naturalists. Yet, even if we consider his work from the purely historical standpoint, his "documentation," as the Goncourts would call it, in the *Chevalier Destouches* (1864) and in the *Diaboliques* (1874), is above reproach. Did not the historian Albert Sorel tell M. Bourget that the short story called *Le Dîner des Athées* illuminated the Restoration for him just as Balzac's *Une Ténébreuse Affaire* evoked the spirit of the Consulate? At the present moment there are signs that the history of the nineteenth century is being rewritten, and in the process many literary reputations are bound to suffer. Others, like that of D'Aurevilly, will, I think, emerge with a brighter prestige because the critic, in sympathy with the novelist, is beginning to shake off the fallacy that Literature is a by-product of Science. Realism is not the only avenue to reality, and the poet as well as the scientist is seeking to interpret the mystery of life. There is a place for writers like D'Aurevilly, whose art is absolutely subjective, yet who with all his idealism never loses sight of the fundamental theme of all great novels, the relationship between the individual and his social environment.

The idealism of Octave Feuillet, which endeared him to thousands of feminine readers, is an emasculate form of Romanticism. This *Musset des familles*, as he was contemptuously dubbed by the Goncourts, was the official novelist of the Faubourg Saint-Germain and of the château. There is a certain faded charm in Feuillet's pictures of fashionable life under the Second Empire, but his observation never penetrates beneath the surface of his gentlemanly heroes and ladylike heroines. Unfortunately, too, this *cueilleur de muguet*—Barbey's epithet—had the ambition to create powerful characters and tragic situations. *Monsieur de Camors* opens, as *Werther* closed, with a pistol-shot, but ends in the manner of a "Princess Novelette." The pure, well-brought-up young wife converts her Lovelace husband and lures him away from the wicked siren. Everyone is *so* well-bred in Feuillet's novels: the adulteries are so imperceptible as to be almost English, and the passionate love-scenes are conducted in the best country-house manner. Everyone is too civilised to be really attractive, too conventional to possess originality. The world of Feuillet is the best of all possible worlds, where everything comes right in the end, as of course it must when one has been to the right sort of school and has associated with the right sort of people. The eupeptic healthiness of his morality and his naïve snobbery stamp Feuillet as the most Victorian of all the nineteenth-century French novelists.

In *Madame Bovary* Flaubert has left us an almost perfect study of Romantic passion: Fromentin, in his *Dominique* (1863), undertook the more difficult task of analysing Romantic sensibility. Romantic passion expresses itself in action, and in action which is of course anti-social. With these two elements even a mediocre writer can infuse interest into his novel. In *Dominique*, on the other hand, the author deliberately avoids these sources of inspiration so as to devote all his talent to the analysis of his hero's soul. As in the case of Senancour's *Obermann*, therefore, the novel met with a cold reception because to the casual reader it is a book with apparently no dramatic interest. Dominique is brought up in the country. After a lonely childhood he leaves his tutor and goes to college in a little provincial town where he makes a friend, Olivier d'Orsel, who lives with an uncle and two cousins, Julie and Madeleine. Dominique falls in love with the latter but does not tell her. Madeleine marries and goes to Paris, where Olivier and Dominique continue their studies. For a long period the hero's only confidants are his tutor, Augustin, and Olivier, but Madeleine instinctively guesses Dominique's secret. The atmosphere in which these two move is now charged with dangerous currents, and a silent conflict ensues. Madeleine, realising that her only hope of salvation lies in Dominique's sense of honour, precipitates a crisis in order to end an intolerable state of uncertainty. She asks him to help her to fold a shawl and, half by accident, half by design, stumbles into his arms. There is a brief and intensely passionate scene. Madeleine, on the brink of dishonour, utters an agonising cry of despair which awakens in Dominique his one remaining human instinct, that of pity. The dénouement is now obvious. Dominique is filled with horror at the revelation of his own abasement, and the spectacle of Madeleine's remorse fills him with awe. They separate never to meet again, and Dominique retires to his estate, where after many years he marries. A Realist might dismiss this peripeteia as *romanesque*, and he would be quite wrong. Fromentin, a profound observer of the human heart, was careful to avoid the obvious pitfall. Had he attributed Dominique's recoil to the prompting of conscience that would have been ideal and improbable, because the working of conscience implies at least a momentary exercise of the reason. It was conscience which enabled Dominique to refrain so long from expressing his love: in the actual crisis it is not conscience but pity which acts, and pity is instinctive and not rational.

Dominique is a superb study of introversion which may be described as a kind of spiritual narcissism. But the introvert also possesses intellectual powers of a high order, and that is the danger; for, as Augustin warns his pupil: "If the spectacle of a tormented soul is what satisfies you most in emotion; if you surround yourself with converging mirrors to multiply its images to infinity, if you confuse human analysis with divine gifts, if from sensibility you descend to sensuality, there are no limits to such perversities, and I warn you that this is very grave."

Luckily for Madeleine, Dominique's sensibility does not degenerate into that absolute moral debility called sensuality, because at the crucial moment it expresses itself objectively as pity. But Fromentin reveals the dangerous and disintegrating nature of introversion. Like all his kind, Dominique is exquisitely sensitive to the impressions made upon him by his material and human environment. Nature, as interpreted by him, becomes strangely beautiful, since he is endowed with a special kind of vision and memory for the rhythm, colour, perfumes and plastic attitudes of the material world, and all of these he greedily assimilates, fusing them with his ego. Thus Nature ceases to have an individuality: she exists only in order to provide Dominique with sensations. The hours, the season, the weather, the scent of yellow furze, the flash of a swallow's wing, the insect on a blade of grass, become confused with his emotional life, for each sensation, however slight, acquires a special value for Dominique, since it records a state of soul. Sensibility of this type, when it finds an adequate medium of expression, usually produces literature of rare artistic beauty, and it is so in *Dominique*, for Fromentin was an artist in words as well as a painter of great talent. When the introvert falls in love, something very tragic may occur, because inevitably the object of his love shares the fate of everything else that composes his environment. As Olivier tells Dominique: "You treat yourself to all the extreme emotions, from the fear of becoming a dishonest man to the arrogant pleasure of feeling yourself a sort of hero." Proust has expressed much the same truth as follows: "When we are in love with a woman we simply project into her a state of soul: consequently the important thing is not the worth of the woman but the profundity of the state of soul; . . . the emotions which a mediocre girl can give us may allow us to bring to the surface of our consciousness more intimate, more personal, more remote parts of ourselves than would the pleasure we derive from the conversation of a man of superior talent or even the admiring contemplation of his work." Albertine runs away to defend her individuality against the domination of her lover's sensibility: Madeleine, who is of finer temper, gives battle. She takes a tremendous risk, but she wins, because Dominique's sensibility has not developed to the monstrous degree which Proust describes in his hero.

As late as 1870 the new age of industrialism had not found its novelist. In England Mrs. Gaskell, and to some extent Dickens, had seriously attempted to portray the life and character of the labouring masses. In France, Hugo, Sand, and Sue wrote of the people, but in a didactic and doctrinaire fashion; interpreting not the life of the lower classes but their own dream of a future society. The moment was ripe for another Balzac. Technical science had advanced with immense strides, studding all France with mines and factories, casting a network of railways, bridges, and telegraph wires across her fields and rivers. Men and women were herded together in great communities. This and the new conception of time and distance brought a change in human relationships and tended to create a new form of literature. Individual problems could no longer be the exclusive theme of the novelist, for in an atmosphere charged with materialism the melancholy of a René, the passionate despair of a Lélia or the tragedy of a Dominique seemed futile and out of date. In their cold and clinical manner the Goncourts had already, in *Germinie Lacerteux*, opened the way for a social novel of a larger scope. They furnished an example of what could be done by the documentary and impersonal method as applied to the analysis of an individual and exceptional case. Theirs was essentially the naturalistic method which Émile Zola claimed as his own and formulated afresh in his *Roman expérimental* with a plethora of imposing and absurd analogies drawn from Claude Bernard's *Introduction à la Médecine expérimentale*. Zola had two great illusions. The first was that he had an objective and scientific mind: the other, that the art of the novelist was a branch of experimental science. He was convinced that human beings are guinea-pigs, and that if he could catch a pair of thoroughly diseased human guinea-pigs the observation of their progeny would reveal interesting "laws." As he airily explained, the construction of a perfect social state was merely a matter of adjusting individual and milieu so as to conform to these "laws." His hypothetical guinea-pigs he called Rougon and Macquart, a maniac and a drunkard, and it is the imaginary history of their descendants which composes the matter of the twelve novels of the Rougon-Macquart cycle. "Historically," he writes, "the Rougon-Macquarts have their origins in the people: they infiltrate through the whole of contemporary society, they rise to every sort of situation, and thus with the help of their individual dramas they relate the history of the Second Empire."

That this balderdash should have been taken seriously by Zola's thousands of readers is one of the most significant facts in the cultural history of the nineteenth century. A Romantic by temperament, with no humanistic education to offset his natural credulity, Zola was, as M. Léon Daudet describes him, a *primaire*. He accepted without question all the doctrines enunciated by contemporary scientists. A certain Dr. Lucas writes a treatise on heredity and immediately Zola blindly subscribes to every one of his statements. "Heredity," he gravely proclaims, "has its laws, like gravity." Someone advances the curious theory that children of a second bed may reveal characteristic traits of their mother's first husband, and Zola builds a novel on the "law of impregnation." In the same way, and he is excusable because he sinned here in the goodly company of his enemy Brunetière, he worked into the fabric of his writings all the ideas advanced by Darwin in the *Origin of Species*: natural selection, the struggle for life, the survival of the fittest. No mystic of the Middle Ages had such faith in his religion as Zola had in science. His friends, Flaubert, the Goncourts and Tourguenieff, were amazed at his naïveté. He struck them as an ideologist, as indeed he was; a nineteenth-century Rousseau, according to the Russian, who, until he met Zola, had always maintained that Jean-Jacques's peculiarities were attributable to the fact that he was not French. Zola's early letters reveal him as a fanatical idealist and an admirer of George Sand. To his friend Baille he wrote in 1860: "Reality is sad, so let us veil it with flowers —I turn my eyes away from the dunghill and gaze at the roses." But his bitter struggles to support himself and his mother by journalism and the frustration of his poetic ambitions perverted his youthful idealism. "I don't care a fig for Realism . . . unquestionably all artists must be Realists," he wrote in 1860. "They take nature and reproduce it; they reproduce it through their particular temperaments. Only . . . the breeze is favourable to science: despite ourselves we are being carried towards the exact study of facts and things. The movement of the times is certainly realistic or rather positivistic." So Zola trimmed his sails to the breeze and, as it happened, with considerable profit, though to do him justice his motives were not wholly mercenary. His real ambition was to become famous and powerful. Zola was a born reformer. By raising the novel to the position of an exact science he hoped to change the structure of society. Contemporary literature was "rotten" with lyricism and idealism: so, like Jean-Jacques, he preached a return to nature, not, however, by way of sentiment but by way of Science. "I have such a high opinion of the novel as a mode of expression," he wrote in his preface to the *Débâcle*, "I consider it on a par with lyric poetry as the highest form of literary expression, just as last century the drama was the highest form of literary expression, and that is why I have chosen it as the form with which to present to the world what I desire to say about the social, scientific, and psychological problems now occupying the minds of thinking men."

The Rougon-Macquart cycle was to be a realistic historical novel, a documented and psychological study of French society under the Second Empire. With great courage and sincerity Zola addressed himself to the stupendous task of amassing material, but unlike the experimental scientist he set out with certain *a priori* ideas, using his documentation to support them, and where facts were not available he had recourse to his fertile imagination. Judged by Zola's pretensions—and the critic must estimate a writer's achievements by what he claims to do—the Rougon-Macquart cycle is a failure. It is not a scientific document; it is not historically exact and on the whole it is psychologically improbable. Yet on the other hand it includes novels like *L'Assommoir*, *Germinal* and *La Terre*, powerful and convincing studies of the life and *mœurs* of the people. In many others, too, there are descriptions of milieu that glow with lyric fire. Zola was a mighty journalist, a journalist with the synoptic vision and the creative imagination of an epic poet. Like Hugo he was not a psychologist: he could not, like Balzac, trace the effects of passion upon an individual and indirectly upon his social environment. Consequently there are no great characters in the Rougon-Macquart cycle. To this reproach the author would doubtless have retorted that he was interested only in the psychology of the mass. But what does Zola's mass psychology amount to? Is it not simply the notation of what is obvious to the superficial observer; the elementary passions that arise from uncontrolled instincts, the instincts of sex and of self-preservation? Thus Zola can describe graphically what happens when men revert to the brute and abandon themselves to lust, fear and violence. That is interesting but not illuminating. To realise Zola's limitations consider how he handles the question of sex, which plays such a preponderant part in all his work. Consider then what Balzac does with the same theme in one novel, *La Cousine Bette*, and compare his achievement with that of Zola. For the latter the sex instinct manifests itself in only one way. Even in the idealistic *Une Page d'Amour* the intellectual hero, Dr. Deberne, behaves like an animal in rut. For how can one not smile at the spectacle of this pillar of the Faculty following Hélène round a crowded drawing-room breathing hotly on her bare neck? Zola would have interested the psycho-analyst. The sexual act obsessed him to a peculiar degree, and by his vicarious genetic orgies, as for instance in *La Terre*, he reminds one very forcibly of Rétif de la Bretonne or the Flaubert of the *Correspondance*.

Zola is great as the interpreter of energy and movement. The Mine, the City, the Factory, the Machine fascinated him as the Cathedral hallucinated Hugo and Carthage Flaubert. All his vivid scenes are enacted in their shadow. His art is that of the cinematograph producer, enhanced by Rembrandtesque colour effects. A battle, a strike, a street brawl—any display of collective violence appealed to his Romantic imagination, and in such moments he is lyrical and almost epic, as for example in the long account of the strike in *Germinal* or of the collapse of the French army in the *Débâcle*. But the historical picture of the Second Empire is marred by Zola's political prejudices and by his chiliastic or didactic proclivities. His views on priests, financiers, administrators and magistrates are those of the average *concierge*, and are not therefore very significant. The windy tirades of his Marxian ideologists are equally wearisome.

When a novelist, as is the case with Zola, is denied the gift of characterisation he is driven to concentrate upon the description of physical action and material environment. But when he deliberately bases his whole work on an *a priori* idea such as heredity he is still further handicapped. The chief lineaments of character and action are known to the reader from the outset. It may be argued that in a Greek tragedy fate plays a rôle similar to that of Zola's doctrine of heredity, but there is no parallel between the brutish apathy of Zola's heroes and the dæmonic conflict portrayed by classical tragedy. Besides, as we do not to-day as a rule share all Zola's pessimistic opinions on the subject of heredity, the situations which he imagines lose even their melodramatic appeal. That is the weakness of so many Naturalistic works. It is dangerous to compete with medical science and to hang the whole interest of a novel on a pathological state which to-morrow may be divested of all its horror or mystery. Much the same is true of Zola's descriptions of milieu. Factories, mines, and machines, and also, thank Heaven! economic conditions, change with great rapidity. That would not matter very much if these things were but the setting to a Grandet or a Goriot: in the Rougon-Macquart series, however, they never are and that is the fundamental, the fatal defect of all Zola's novels. None of his characters possess the evocative quality which stamps the creations of the great novelists. And this is not entirely because they are not types. Manon Lescaut is not a type, for one cannot visualise a typical courtesan. Yet she evokes a peculiar atmosphere through which move dreams of youth, beauty and feminine mystery. A spiritual ambience surrounds her, and if we try to discover how Prévost generates that atmosphere, we see that it emanates from a definite psychological trait—her passiveness. In the Balzacian types it is easier to detect this centre of irradiation, this focus of the psychological interest. In Grandet it is suspicion; in Vautrin, the creative urge; in Goriot, the craving for love; in the abbé Troubert it is the lust for power. It is in any case not the material environment which lends duration to these characters, though no doubt that gives them an added human interest by rendering them more accessible to our imagination. But without it they would still be great because they symbolise a state of soul. Zola, on the contrary, overloads his novels with superfluous details. His characters, such as they are, never emerge from their background. He reports everything, whereas the true artist selects. Does not life present itself to all of us as a series of impressions rather than as a smooth and uninterrupted stream of causes and effects? And does not the difference between the layman and the artist lie solely in the latter's gift for seizing unerringly upon those things in life which are really significant and which interpret life's direction and meaning? Here Zola failed, partly because he was not a great novelist, partly also because he imagined that he could observe the vast *processus* of human motives, actions and passions as easily as a scientist can examine the progress of a chemical experiment.

Though Alphonse Daudet assiduously frequented the society of Zola, to call him, as did Jules Lemaître, "the most naturalistic of the writers of the new school," is mere amiable juggling with words, for Daudet was never at heart in sympathy with the scientific pretensions of the Naturalists. True, he endeavoured always to achieve impersonality in his art; to enter like Balzac and Flaubert into the mind and soul of his characters; to allow them to evolve freely and naturally without too much interference from the *haïssable moi.* On the other hand, the theory of impassibility seemed to him an exaggeration. "The narrator," he observed, "has the right to display emotion—but discreetly, *in the wings.* Lyricism, Realism, frenzy even—all combine to create power." Alphonse Daudet was a Realist, but in the largest sense of the term. His Realism is closely akin to that of the English nineteenth-century novelists, since it does not exclude sensibility, imagination or idealism. And he has one rare quality almost entirely absent from the writings of his French contemporaries—a sense of humour, that precious ingredient which is the salt of life. The Naturalists did not possess it, and in consequence their novels lack the ultimate savour of reality. A writer without any sense of humour is apt to lack a sense of the true values of life.

The intensely human colour of Daudet's Realism has given currency to the legend that he imitated Dickens. In reality it would be difficult to find a more un-English and more original novelist than the creator of the immortal Tartarin and of those exquisite *Lettres de mon Moulin*, which, like glorious prisms, reflect the radiance and the sadness of the meridional spirit. If Daudet occasionally recalls Dickens it is rather by his defects than by his qualities, by a tendency to force the note of humour or of pathos, as for example in the Passajon episodes of the *Nabab* (1877), or in the maudlin "Little Nell" sentiment of *Fromont jeune et Risler aîné* (1874) and *Le Petit Chose* (1868). But these traits, like his Early Victorian and ghoulish fondness for "the trappings and the suits of woe," were imitated from nobody: they spring from the roots of Daudet's nature and form indeed an essential part of his meridional sensibility.

It is strange to find a keen if sardonic observer of humanity like Abel Hermant gravely asserting that Daudet "saw souls in their complexity and in their intricacies," when, as a matter of fact, all his outstanding characters are of one dimension. Their motives, thoughts and actions are indeed the reverse of complex. Nearly all are naïve egoists eager to gratify an elementary desire—the desire for power, luxury or money. But with the exception of the fanatic Mme Autheman of *L'Évangéliste* and, of course, Sapho, none are really obsessed by a passion.

Again, from first to last, Daudet's characters are static in the sense that they do not essentially develop. In the *Nabab*, the *Évangéliste*, even in the famous *Numa Roumestan*, Jansoulet, Jane Autheman, and Numa appear as the central figures in a series of interesting situations, but the latter possess only an intrinsic and not a relative significance since they do not light up new aspects of the psychology of these men and women. There is almost always in Daudet a lack of fusion between the leading character and the action. Thus Sidonie in *Fromont jeune* attains her object, revenge, thanks to a series of factitious events that do not necessarily arise from the peculiar nature of the heroine. Similarly, in the *Évangéliste* the conversion of Mlle Ebsen comes like a bolt from the blue: it is, we feel, a mere ruse to provide continued employment for Mme Autheman at a moment when she has practically ceased to interest the reader, who by then is quite familiar with her nature. In Daudet, the characters are really completely defined before the action begins: they are not, as in Balzac, dynamic sources of action and of influence.

Daudet is only inspired when he draws upon that famous notebook of his, crammed with meridional memories. His two finest creations, Numa and Tartarin, are not individuals but racial types incarnating the soul of the Midi. In them Daudet dramatises the exuberance, the vitality and optimism of the Southern Frenchman, his childlike mendacity and glorious debauches of imagination. The psychological interest of *Numa Roumestan* lies entirely in the conflict between two races, the North and the South, which is symbolised in the marriage of Numa with a Parisienne. These two characters are not profoundly analysed, but Daudet cleverly blinds the reader to this fact by placing them in a series of swiftly changing settings, all of which throw into relief some fresh aspect of his central theme, the contrast between the rationalism of the North and the romanticism of the Midi.

Daudet has to an acute degree the faculty for evoking atmosphere. One may forget his characters but never their environment. Years after reading *Le Petit Chose* you will recall the musty odours of the *collège de Sarlande*, the terrible *frinc frinc* of of Viot's keys, Daniel's attic filled with the clangour of the bells of Saint-Germain. He is not a colourist, for the memories he evokes are usually of sound and movement and smell, yet always he penetrates into the very essence of things. The *Lettres de mon Moulin* are fragrant with the scent of Alpine flowers, alive with the susurrus of the cicadas, swept by the roar of mistral and tramontane. Thousands have been ushered into the Elysian Fields of French literature through that sunlit portal. Thousands have recaptured their youth in those miraculous pages. Who has not surrendered to the charm and gentle irony of the immortal creator of M. Seguin, of the curé de Cucugnan, of the wicked Tistet Védène? Daudet holds an honourable rank as a Realist, as a sympathetic historian of the joys and sorrows of humble life. He is more sincere than Zola in his hatred of the economic abuses which sadden the life of the poor, more sincere because he was not a demagogue. In all his works there is an undertone of discouragement, a suggestion that truth and courage fight a losing battle against the forces of injustice and brutal instinct. This pessimistic note deepens as he grows older. It emerges in the profound hopelessness of the *Évangéliste* and in the mordant satire of the *Immortel*. No, the true elixir is not to be found in these novels which are Naturalist concoctions. In such *études de mœurs* he acquires a querulous and didactic manner quite foreign to his genius, and they serve only to make us regret the limpid charm, the *brio* and the merciful irony of Daudet the novelist of the *pays d'oc*.

The vogue for Naturalism, as Daudet observed somewhere in his *Souvenirs*, aroused a belated interest in the novels of the Goncourt brothers, and in 1886 M. Bourget devoted one of his *Essais* to a study of their influence on the new movement. In a sense it is true that, as M. Bourget remarks, "they were the masters of the new generation of novelists." As Edmond de Goncourt pointed out, rather plaintively, in his preface to *La Fille Élisa* (1877), he and Jules as early as 1864 had claimed for the novel "les libertés et les franchises" of science. There is no doubt, too, that *Germinie Lacerteux* exercised a directive influence on Zola at a critical point in his development, whilst the latter's theory of the "experimental" novel was largely an extension of the opinions expressed by the brothers in their prefaces as well as in their talks with Flaubert, Taine and Zola. It is, however, an exaggeration to assert as does M. Paul Sabatier that from 1867 to 1890 almost every French novel proceeds more or less directly from the works of the Goncourts. Of course it is easy to discover in the novels of the Naturalists many Goncourtian analogies—a sense of the fatality of life, an attitude of scepticism in regard to the value of human effort at grips with circumstances, a clinical detachment and meticulousness in the notation of details that compose the environment of their characters; but such traits are not peculiar to the Goncourts. They form an essential part of the method of Flaubert, and it would be a difficult if not an idle undertaking, in discussing this problem of influence, to decide precisely what share must go to the Goncourts and what to the author of *Madame Bovary*. Were it a mere matter of comparing texts the critic might risk a dogmatic conclusion, but who knows what fruitful ideas were casually tossed to and fro in the course of those long and fascinating conversations between high priest and neophytes, ideas unrecorded either in the famous *Journal* or in Flaubert's precious *Correspondance*?

After the death of Jules, Edmond added little to the literary reputation of the De Goncourt family. Indeed, *La Fille Élisa* is in every way inferior to *Germinie Lacerteux*. It is a social document of very limited interest, and not a *document humain*, for though the pictures of brothel and of prison life are carefully and even powerfully limned, Élisa herself has little personality and does not stand out from the throng of her sister prostitutes and criminals. Besides, there is a strong humanitarian and propaganda note in this work, which, like *Le Dernier Jour d'un Condamné*, is a "novel with a purpose." But where in Victor Hugo the thesis is discreetly veiled, with Edmond de Goncourt it is painfully obtrusive, and the heroine, one feels, is a mere pretext for a treatise on prison reform. *La Fille Élisa* is the least characteristic of Edmond de Goncourt's novels: it is in fact Zola, and indifferent Zola at that. Except in *La Faustin*, De Goncourt shows himself quite incapable of individualising his characters. *Chérie* (1884), for example, consists of a series of impressions and attitudes with little action to lend unity to the central figure. The heroine is a mannequin, solely designed, one would think, to display the latest modes in Parisian dress and behaviour. She is a rare hot-house bloom, and her neurotic, fantastic personality holds the interest just for a moment but no longer. Chérie does nothing, and her thoughts and sensations are scarcely significant enough to justify the care which the author bestows upon them. *La Faustin*, the least Naturalistic of Edmond de Goncourt's works, is his most successful. Departing from his conception of a novel without action he pours his impressions of theatrical life into the mould of an interesting plot, and if the dénouement is somewhat crude there is great dramatic force in the narrative of this actress's passion for an English *milord*.

Though the younger novelists were in close and constant touch with Edmond de Goncourt, whom they met at Flaubert's, at Daudet's and, more rarely, at his own house, there never was, strictly speaking, a Goncourt coterie. As the father of Naturalism, Edmond de Goncourt may have been the logical leader of the new generation of writers, but it was to Zola that they turned for encouragement. Attracted by the noisy enthusiasm and by the notoriety of the author of the *Assommoir*, Guy de Maupassant, Céard, Hennique, Alexis and Huysmans became regular attenders at Zola's Thursdays in the rue de Boulogne, and in 1876 they can be said to have formed a *chapelle*. This was the famous *queue de Zola*, known later as the *groupe de Médan* since in the summer they accompanied their chief to his villa at that country town. Violently attacked for their scientific pretensions—and to the secret satisfaction of Flaubert, who found them crude and blatant—they loudly advertised their method by which, says the *Revue moderne et naturaliste* (1876), they claimed to show that literary evolution was keeping pace with evolution in science. In 1880 the publication of a collection of war stories, *Les Soirées de Médan*, written by members of the group, brought them more publicity, and incidentally revealed the presence among them of at least one writer of genius, Guy de Maupassant, whose *Boule de Suif* was singled out for special praise by the critics. The other contributions were wholeheartedly damned. Yet, as has been pointed out by M. Léon Hennique, the sole survivor of the Zola clique, there was no real unity of æsthetic opinion in the *groupe de Médan*. All agreed, of course, with Zola's description of the novel as "un coin de la nature vu à travers un tempérament," a definition with which indeed it would have been difficult to quarrel, since it can be interpreted so as to include almost any novel ever penned. In general, also, they sided with Zola's views on the *impassibilité* of the artist, on the necessity for patient and thorough documentation, and shared his hatred of Idealism and Romanticism. To these tenets in fact they adhered with more fidelity than Zola himself. It is, however, fairly clear to-day that their real master was never Zola, but Flaubert, whose *Éducation sentimentale* is indeed a complete illustration of their æsthetic.

We shall refer in a moment to the immense influence exercised on the art of De Maupassant by his *irréprochable maître*. Meanwhile let us glance at the works of the other *Zolistes*. In Alexis's *Madame Meuriot* the heroine Juliette, "tormented by the infinite," is a cross between Mme Bovary and Mme Arnaud, whilst in Gustave the author has fused Léon and Rodolphe. The only Zolaesque incident is the stupid episode of the rape attempted by the aged Dr. Silvy. Henri Céard's *Une belle Journée* is a cynical illustration of Flaubert's favourite dictum: *La vie est bête*. This excellent account of a long wet afternoon and a frustrated seduction is Céard's disillusioned commentary on the futility of any attempt at revolt against what he calls "that law of universal mediocrity which like gravity bends and subjects the world to its commands." Hennique's *L'Accident de Monsieur Hébert* is conceived in the same negative anti-heroic tone. Gabrielle Hébert is a Mme Bovary who does not commit suicide and is left to face a dreadful future between a righteous, wronged husband and a grim, tyrannical mother-in-law. Huysmans's *En Ménage* (1881) is a variant of the *Éducation sentimentale*. It deals, too, with the life of two *ratés*, but

Huysmans lacks Flaubert's genius for the truly significant trait. There is an opening scene, André's discovery of his wife *in flagrante delicto*, which is handled with Stendhalian irony, but, as with all the lesser Naturalists, Huysmans shows no constructive imagination. Properly speaking, the action stops here, and the author is obliged to revert to the stereotyped procedure of his school: the minute and wearisome transcription of obvious phenomena. This is of course the Huysmans of the early manner — before the famous conversion to Catholicism. *Là-Bas* (1891) marks the chrysalis stage, the transition of the Naturalist to religion by way of mysticism. At this period Huysmans is in search of what he describes as spiritual Naturalism, a fusion of Realism and Mysticism which he finds admirably represented in the paintings of the Primitives, notably in Grünewald's "Crucifixion." *Là-Bas* is, however, scarcely a novel at all, and the scabrous love affair of Durtal and Mme Chantelouve is only an excuse for a revolting technical treatise on diabolism. In the *Cathédrale* (1898), there is no action and no characterisation whatever: it is not a novel but an erudite repertory of facts unearthed from medieval history and largely concerned with religious symbolism.

When Flaubert said that the novel of the future would be "scientific" he did not in the least imply that the novelist must slavishly imitate the methods of experimental science. He intended merely to insist on the necessity for accurate and objective observation as a corrective to the uncontrolled imagination and the subjectivism of Romantic fiction. Realism for Flaubert was the attempt not to reconstruct life but to interpret it. The great illusion of the Naturalists on the contrary was that the novelists can reconstruct a human existence as a scientist does a chemical substance, that is to say by reassembling its various ingredients. But the novelist is an artist, and his function is to communicate the illusion of life and not to reproduce life, for never can he hope like the scientist to collect *all* the elements necessary to his synthesis. He can never, therefore, as the Naturalists believed, dispense with imagination. It is this fallacy which is responsible for that final impression of improbability, of incoherence, so noticeable, for instance, in the works of the Goncourts and of all the *groupe de Médan* save De Maupassant, who himself, in the *Revue de l'Exposition universelle* (1889), compared the novels of his colleagues to "mosaïques de faits arrivés en des milieux différents et dont les origines, de nature diverse, enlèvent au volume où ils sont réunis, le caractère de vraisemblance et l'homogénéité que les auteurs devraient poursuivre avant tout." The Naturalists, in their anxiety to avoid the slightest taint of Romanticism, tended eventually to produce not novels but collections of fragmentary observations; albums of snapshots which they wrongly called "human documents." Up to a point this method was excellent, though not very new, for, with all the great Realists from Marivaux onwards, documentation had preceded creation, but it was for them a mere preliminary, a means, and never, as with the Goncourts, an end. The Naturalists failed to achieve that final process whereby the imagination of the genius welds his material into a perfect work of art, that "fusion of illusion and reality" which was Flaubert's ideal. And that is why, despite their careful notation of detail, their laborious *reportage*, the works of these novelists never attain the probability and the homogeneity which De Maupassant rightly considers as the criteria of sound novel-craft. They do not possess the unifying and dynamic force imported by a strong central personage or situation. Here again Flaubert's views have been misunderstood because, though it is true that he attached only a secondary importance to plot, he never maintained, like the Goncourts, that this convenient form could be entirely dispensed with. One must not confuse his philosophy of life with his artistic views. Along with many of his disciples he considered that life was on the whole undramatic, but we have only to look at his two masterpieces to see that he was the last to minimise the value of a clearly defined action sweeping in a vigorous curve from exposition to dénouement. He shows us that life is not spectacular, that it contains very little Romantic tragedy, yet to the meditative observer there is powerful drama in his narrative of the destinies of those *ratés*, Moreau and Deslauriers. There is profound tragic import in this spectacle of mediocrity in the toils of circumstances, in the sober tale of a frustrated dream of happiness.

De Maupassant had even a keener *flair* for the drama that is concealed beneath the common and apparently insignificant happenings of everyday life, and the closing words of that admirable *conte* entitled

Un Soir describe very well this tendency of his mind: "Certain encounters, certain inexplicable combinations of things—without appearing in the slightest degree exceptional—assuredly contain a greater quantity of life's secret quintessence than that dispersed through the ordinary run of events." This "secret quintessence" escaped the scientific eye of the Naturalists, who, in their efforts to reconstruct existence, reproduced much that was of historical interest but missed the suggestive trait that carries with it, like an aura, a fragment of vital reality. A novelist is not a scientist. The effectiveness of his art depends largely on his selective powers, for while it is true that he has more scope than the dramatist, yet he too must exercise economy and submit himself to a discipline. In the conversation, in the actions and thoughts of every human being, there is so much that is not in the least characteristic but purely conventional and common to a whole class. The great novelist does not waste his reader's time or insult his intelligence by laboriously exposing the obvious: on the contrary, his genius discovers language wherewith to interpret the "secret quintessence" which lies glittering beneath the dross of banalities. It is because De Maupassant understood the gulf separating mere photography from artistic interpretation that his work can never be confused with the productions of the other Naturalists.

In this respect De Maupassant is a worthy pupil of his *irréprochable maître*, though admittedly none of his characters are explored so exhaustively as those of Flaubert. Yet his *contes*, those exquisite organisms where nothing is superfluous, have an amazing range of suggestion. If De Maupassant preferred the *conte* to the longer novel it was because he had a more highly developed sense of the dramatic than Flaubert, who could not have composed, let us say, *La Parure* or *En Famille*, superb examples both of suspended interest and of unexpected dénouement. For the older craftsman life was stupid and not usually dramatic. Is not Mme Bovary's tragedy precisely in her failure to accept that fact? De Maupassant would have agreed on the whole that human existence is not dramatic, but would yet have pointed out that the life of every one of us, however uneventful it is on the surface, holds at least one situation which is relatively dramatic, one crisis which calls up hidden reserves of energy, cracks the shell of habit, or else suddenly, as when a smooth, black and shining metal door is slid back, reveals the glare of hidden and unsuspected passions. There is scarcely one of his stories that does not expose and develop such a situation, and in his novels he is happiest when, as in *Bel Ami*, he passes his hero like another Gil Blas through a gauntlet of critical scenes; in a word, when he X-rays his characters by the light of some unusual but highly probable situation. This procedure works excellently in the short story or in the comic novel, where probability is of less account than verve and variety. The serious novel, however, demands a talent for psychological analysis, the ability not merely to explain character by situation but, by a slow process of preparation, to explain the crisis by the help of the characters. In *Notre Cœur*, where the whole action flows from one situation, De Maupassant is obviously ill at ease; in *Pierre et Jean*, which is very short, his embarrassment is not so evident; but *Fort comme la Mort* (1889) reveals his deficiencies as a psychological novelist. Here there are completely irrelevant descriptive passages, and a dénouement which has all the appearance of an afterthought.

Nevertheless, De Maupassant represents a return to the French novel of tradition: he belongs certainly to "that powerful race of observers, psychologists and *véritalistes*," to quote from his own eulogy of l'abbé Prévost, to whose *Manon Lescaut*, he thought, the modern novel owes its present admirable form. And yet if we search the pedigree of the author of *Bel Ami* for an ancestor the name which immediately occurs to the mind is not that of Prévost but of Marivaux; not, however, the subtle analyst who created Marianne, but the author of *Le Paysan parvenu*, that admirable novel of manners whose Jacob is the Bel Ami of the eighteenth century. De Maupassant has added very little to our knowledge of the type so cruelly dissected by Marivaux, though his picture of the hero's environment is incomparably richer than that of his predecessor. Of the two, Jacob is perhaps the more convincing *gigolo*; less ambitious, less energetic, more blandly pleased with himself than Bel Ami, who might justly be labelled a blackleg by the *confrérie* because of the strenuous labour which he puts into a profession whose chief attraction for its adepts is that it dispenses them from doing any work at all. Probably, however, De

Maupassant is historically accurate. If so, it is just another instance of that universal degeneration in the art of living which our traditionalists attribute to the baneful influence of the Third Republic.

Bel Ami is De Maupassant's only memorable creation, though there are others which entitle him to an honourable place in the second rank of the psychological analysts. I refer particularly to his excellent studies of women — Mme Walter, the passionate *dévote*; Mme de Burne, the frigid and selfish coquette; Mme Forestier, the feminine counterpart to Bel-Ami; and that pathetic incarnation of constancy and devotion, the heroine of *Fort comme la Mort*. As a rule De Maupassant's men and women are actuated by greed of money or sexual desire. Love, even in its most ideal form, is always with him fundamentally sensual. Mariolle in *Notre Cœur* is only an apparent exception, for after all what he desires most in his mistress is not some spiritual element above mere physical possession, but merely that greater satisfaction of the senses which comes from the absolute conquest of a woman's soul as well as of her body.

Above everything else, De Maupassant is a painter of manners. To use an out-at-elbows expression, his work does present a *tranche de vie*, a cross-section of French society under the early Third Republic. And the metaphor will be more accurate if one recollects that it is the purple stain—in this case the novelist's imagination—which renders visible the realities contained in the cross-section. Peasants, country gentlemen, doctors, *rentiers*, shopkeepers, *fonction-*

naires, clubmen, cocottes—De Maupassant wrote of them all from first-hand acquaintance. The lives of the peasant and of the Parisian lower middle class interested him perhaps most, probably because they provided so many illustrations of the crass materialism, egotism, and brutishness which for De Maupassant are so characteristically human, though in every class of society he observes a similar spiritual and moral squalor and a similar lack of idealism.

In his universe there is no purpose and no harmony. Society presents a chaotic jumble of warring interests and petty passions. In marriage there is no reciprocity and no sense of honour, since a husband is either a cuckold or a stupid tyrant. A like disaccord exists between man and his natural environment, the disharmony of ugliness and beauty, the contrast between the rapacity of the peasant and the exquisite Norman countryside, between the Philistinism of the Parisian tripper and the sweetness of the Île de France which he periodically defiles by his presence. Yet for all his pessimism De Maupassant is not offensive, because he does not pretend to be impassive. His personality pervades everything he wrote; discreetly it is true, but enough to reveal underneath the irony a sentiment of pity and of confraternity. Sometimes the spectacle of human ineptitude goads him to outbursts of misanthropy, but in reality no one was more interested, and humanly so, in the conduct of his fellows. Few indeed have written with more sympathy and understanding of the sad existence of the lower middle classes and of the horrors of semi-poverty; of the terrible bleakness of a dependent old age and of the loneliness of unmarried women. Two things appalled him always—the mystery of death and the impenetrability of the human soul. That one human being can never really enter into spiritual communion with another seemed to De Maupassant an awful and an intolerable thing. At best, he thought, that brief contact of the spirit and the senses which we call love is but a fleeting lifting of the veil, emphasising as it did for poor Christiane of *Mont-Oriol* the completeness of our isolation. There is in all De Maupassant's work an element not to be found in that of his brother Naturalists, the sombre poetry of a man who was a pagan in his love of the material world, but something very akin to a mystic in his broodings upon life and the hereafter.

CHAPTER IX

RECENT TENDENCIES

It becomes clear as we approach the closing decade of the nineteenth century that Naturalism has lost much of its prestige as a directive influence in the French novel, which, if one may judge from an apparently aimless but intense activity, now seems to enter upon a fresh stage of its development. If we pause to consider its vagaries during the sixty years separating 1830 from 1890 there is one impression which imposes itself with peculiar insistence. It is that reality, for the novelist, is to be found somewhere between the opposite poles of Idealism and Realism. By the reality of a novel I mean its ability to evoke in the mind of the reader the illusion of existence and to offer him a plausible interpretation of human life. The Romantics overshot that reality through overmuch Idealism; the Naturalists by an abuse of Realism. Still, viewed from the standpoint of cultural history, how very illuminating are the artistic errors of these literary schools, revealing, as they always do, the trend of a nation's soul. For despite all that has been argued to the contrary the history of a literary genre is a precious social document, and what form of literature can offer a more eloquent chart of the currents of contemporary ideas and sentiments than the French novel of the period to which we have just alluded?

The Naturalism of the eighties was the extreme expression in literature of an idea dear to the second half of the nineteenth century, the conception of biological science as the gateway to progress in every realm of human thought and action. The determinism which is the inevitable corollary of such a belief was the philosophy of a generation that accepted Taine and Renan as its spiritual doctors; and, as we have seen from its reflection in the novels of the Naturalists, this determinism engendered a fatalistic mood culminating in a pessimism intensified, of course, by the unfortunate events of 1870 and their aftermath. However, after 1880, one can detect the unmistakable signs of a movement in the direction of idealism. The influential critic, Brunetière, though he was the first to apply the theories of Darwin to literary criticism, violently attacked the doctrines of the Naturalists, and by his admirable studies on the nineteenth-century English novelists showed that Realism does not necessarily exclude sensibility, a point of view fortified by E. M. de Voguë's authoritative book on the Russian novel (1886). On all sides the faith in the infallibility of the scientific method received rude buffets, and in literature it became evident to the younger men that the effort to subject Art to Science had resulted in a deadlock. Within the Médan group itself, as we have seen, there was dissension. J.-K. Huysmans tacitly announced his divorce with Naturalism in *A rebours* (1884), which, like Hennique's *Un Caractère* (1889), marks a departure from the Zola formula and a step towards occultism. Céard abandoned the novel altogether for literary criticism, and De Maupassant in his later works began to cultivate the method of psychological analysis which M. Paul Bourget had revived with remarkable success in his *André Cornélis* (1887) and in *Cruelle Énigme* (1885). In 1887 appeared the celebrated manifesto against *La Terre* signed by Bonnetain, Rosny, Descaves, Guiches and Paul Margueritte, who thus publicly disassociated themselves from Zola, whom in violent terms they accused of prostituting his art to a mania for publicity. In one sense the manifesto was a blow at Naturalism, since it repudiated the master of the movement. Its signatories, however, took no immediate part in the idealistic reaction. The Rosny brothers, in particular, still had absolute faith in the regenerative power of science in the domain of art. "Science," they wrote, "is the great source of the imagination and of the intelligence. It is the amplifier of our artistic faculties, of our power to analyse life." And all their novels, whether they deal with prehistoric times or with the civilisation of their own period, illustrate this thesis.

In 1891 it occurred to Jules Huret, an enterprising journalist of the *Écho de Paris*, to investigate the actual literary situation, and his *Enquête*, where are collated the opinions of some sixty well-known men of letters, indicates very clearly the general trend of the novel at the close of the century. On one point nearly all his contributors agreed. Naturalism was no longer an active and governing force. Even Zola admitted this, though he maintained that nothing had yet arisen to take its place or to rival its "immense labeur positiviste." Only one writer, the faithful Alexis, refused to concur in the general view, but his frenzied and heroic telegram to Huret: "Naturalism not dead, letter follows," merely provoked incredulous smiles.

The object of this closing chapter is to trace as far as possible the main tendencies of the French novel from 1890 to the appearance of Marcel Proust's *A la Recherche du Temps perdu*. Such an essay, for several reasons, cannot fail to leave an impression of incompleteness. Most of us like to think that we are living in the excitement of a literary renascence, and the luckless critic who refuses to hail the latest favourite as a Balzac or a Flaubert is apt to meet with a cold and hostile incredulity. Then there is the difficulty of lack of perspective. For whilst it is hard to believe that an objective or "scientific" history of literature will ever be written or indeed is worth writing, yet, as his perspective increases, a writer does tend to become less grossly partial, though still contriving to retain a human contact with his theme. In discussing contemporary literature one cannot of course hope to avoid the reproaches of ignorance and injustice, both of which are nearly always thoroughly deserved. It is, however, possible to elude a more serious charge by disclaiming beforehand, as is done for these pages, the slightest pretence to dogmatism. In what is largely an essay to reveal tendencies and new efforts at expansion in the novel, it will not be possible to do full justice to the artistic gifts of many talented belletrists like Anatole France and Maurice Barrès, who continue to delight us by the limpid qualities of their style and the lucidity and suggestiveness of their ideas. Other very honourable names must perforce be omitted altogether, usually because it is at the moment too early to discern the peculiar trend of their art.

Pierre Loti, to-day somewhat outside the public favour, was already famous before the decline of Naturalism. His very popularity indeed may be interpreted as a sign of the coming change. In *Aziyadé* (1879) there is a passage which contains, I feel, the motif of all his subsequent work, for it strikes the unmistakable Loti note of Romantic pessimism. Describing the extraordinary vividness of his youthful impressions he writes:

> They were pictures come to life, reminders of an anterior existence or else presentiments of a life to come, of future incarnations, of dream countries and, again, promises of wonders of all sorts which the world and life doubtless reserved for me when I should grow up. Well, I have grown up and on my road have found nothing of these things I vaguely glimpsed. On the contrary, everything has gradually shrunk and grown dark around me; the memories have faded, the horizons of the future have slowly closed in and have filled with grey darkness. It will soon be the hour to return to the eternal dust and I shall go away without having understood the mysterious wherefore of all these mirages of my childhood: I shall carry away with me the regret of I know not what countries never found again, of I know not what beings ardently desired and never embraced. . . .

This invincible nostalgia for beauty and romance was the source of Loti's *Wanderlust* and the inspiration of his novels. He travelled widely in the Orient and in the South Seas, full of restless curiosity, a sensitive but not a profound observer, passing all his impressions through the darkly tinted film of his own ego; for he was haunted by the sentiment of his mortality. What appealed to Loti's readers was that element which the Goncourts and their friends were doing their utmost to banish from the novel, *le romanesque*, which we call loosely romance, though to a Frenchman it means something more. It is the expectance of vague delights, the "novelish" aspect of life embracing all that tract of existence which lies outside everyday existence—a country accessible, however, by the magic carpet of the imagination. Loti, in reviving the exotic novel of the eighteenth century and of Chateaubriand, was certain to please a nation which has a passion for Oriental *mœurs*. He was shrewd enough also to understand that the chief attraction of such *turqueries*, as they used to be called, is the piquant contrast between the European and the Oriental conception of the art of love; and, as he did not hesitate to make the public the confidant of his own amorous experiences, it seemed for a time to many that another Chateaubriand had arisen, announcing a renascence of Romanticism. Almost all Loti's work is subjective, and often to an irritating degree, for the constant intrusion of the author's *moi* interrupts the development of character and action. He is not really a novelist but a sensuous and alert impressionist; almost, though never quite, an elegiac poet. His great talent is for vivid and coloured description. Occasionally, too, there are pages tinged with genuine sensibility, and these compensate for Loti's deficiencies as an interpreter of the human heart. *Pêcheur d'Islande* is rich in such passages, for it holds the very tincture of

Breton mysticism. Here Loti may write of death and eternity and yet seem sincere because he is in tune with the pastel atmosphere of Brittany, which conjures up visions of life's fugacity. On the other hand, his exotic novels are tenuous and nerveless things, breathing a spirit of disintegration and of refined sensuality. Were it not for their persistent narcissism they might indeed be charming, but Loti's Romanticism has no passionate ring of conviction: it is an æsthetic and not a spiritual product.

The passing of Naturalism, which was but one phase of the general reaction against Positivism, left the French novel in an interesting if somewhat precarious situation. Though Zola had no doubt overestimated the potentialities of this genre by confusing the rôle of the novelist with that of the man of science, still, as Barrès observed, Naturalism had "enlarged the cadre of the novelist's preoccupations" and, by disciplining his imagination, had taught him the value of accurate observation. There was now a danger lest the younger writers, in revolt against the doctrine of an impassive art, yet believing, as Barrès implies, that the "cadre of the novelist's preoccupations" is capable of unlimited extension, might stretch it to the point where the novel ceases to possess any identity as an individual genre and becomes a mere pretext for social, artistic or political propaganda. What was badly required at this juncture was the directive influence of an original and powerful mind. Yet, as Zola had very correctly remarked, Naturalism, although discredited, had so far no successor.

As usual, however, there was no lack of theorists. Edmond de Goncourt—and he had not a few followers—was convinced that the novel was an effete form of literature which had said all it had to say. To Huret he described it as "un genre dont j'ai tout fait pour tuer le romanesque pour en faire des sortes d'autobiographies, de mémoires de gens qui n'ont pas d'histoire." Others, like Camille de Sainte-Croix and Marcel Prévost, thought that the salvation of the novel lay in a revival of its *romanesque*. However, despite his enormous vogue with the feminine public, there was little in M. Prévost's *marivaudages* to suggest a revolution in fiction. Indeed there is a residue of truth in Sainte-Croix's description of the future author of *Les Demi-Vierges* (1894) as "an industrious young man who economises his own tobacco by smoking the fag-ends left lying about by George Sand; a good bourgeois who, finding that the label *naturaliste* was no longer accepted by publishers and that the label *symboliste* was hard to place, adopted the label *romanesque*. . . ."

It was scarcely likely that the new Balzac would be discovered in the ranks of the Symbolists or in any of the extremist groups now leading the idealistic reaction. With the exception of Huysmans, who drifted from Naturalism by way of satanism into a woolly and mystic Catholicism, the ultras produced no novelists of distinction. The influence of Barbey d'Aurevilly gave rise to a coterie of neo-Catholic writers, the chief of whom, Joséphin Péladan, founded in 1890 the *Rose-Croix catholique* in order to "insufflate into contemporary art, and especially into æsthetic culture, the essence of theocracy." Péladan enjoyed a notable vogue. He was an esoteric who as dramatist, art critic and novelist worked hard to establish the identity of religion and art. Influenced as were so many by the researches of William Crookes, this strange man formed a group of occultists called the *Mages*. One of his most faithful adepts was the novelist, Paul Adam, once prosecuted for the excessive naturalism of his *Chair molle*, but now an enthusiast of *magisme*, the object of which, he told Huret, was to apply the methods of occult science to literature and thus achieve a sort of synthesis of Symbolism and Naturalism. Adam, an original stylist and a novelist of great imagination, later abandoned occultism in order to write novels according to a formula of his own invention. Convinced that the study of the individual had been exhaustively carried out by the great Classics, Adam, in a series of vast historical frescoes, devoted himself to the consideration of man viewed not as an individual but as a "cerebral cell" of the cosmos.

Several fruitless attempts were made to evolve a Symbolist novel. One of the initiators of the movement, Villiers de l'Isle-Adam, has left in his *Ève future* (1886) a queer metaphysical fantasy satirising the pretensions of applied science. His disciple, Remy de Gourmont, the brilliant essayist and the pillar of the *Mercure de France*, the chief organ of Symbolism, tried in his "novel of the cerebral life," *Sixtine* (1890), to illustrate his thesis that the symbol is the "soul rendered visible." This curious work is interesting, not as a novel, because its characters have no reality, but as an example of that intellectual dandyism which we have already noted in the work of Gautier and of Baudelaire. Though none of the Symbolists cultivated the novel with any success several celebrated contemporary novelists have sprung from their ranks, notably M. André Gide and M. Henri Régnier, though the latter, it is true, has shaken off the last vestige of his Symbolistic education. The case of M. Gide is more doubtful, and possibly investigation would show that a direct filiation exists between his early Symbolist tendencies and the *amoralisme* of his present manner.

There is a passage in M. Louis Bertrand's *Idées et Portraits* which not only describes very vividly the spiritual condition of young France in the early nineties but reveals at the same time the important rôle played by M. Bourget in the movement towards idealism. "With the great demagogic stampede of 1880," writes M. Bertrand, "there swept over the land an unprecedented wave of grossness—grossness in thought, in the Press, in books, in public and political morals. The Naturalistic novelists, headed by Zola, strove to demonstrate to us that this grossness was natural, that in every milieu one could discover this base slavery of the instincts. . . . Really the human soul seemed to us abject; the world a battle of obscene and bloody brutes. Action was degrading; Faith one of the forms of eternal illusion; Science harassing, niggard of pleasure and, besides, so limited in her affirmations." The ideas of Schopenhauer now trickling into France served only to increase the gathering darkness, for, as M. Bertrand points out, the young men of his generation saw in the teachings of the German philosopher not the exaltation of the will as the essence of reality but the complete negation of the will to live. Remembering this, one can understand the sensation caused by the appearance in 1885 of M. Bourget's *Cruelle Énigme*, which clove the prevailing gloom like a ray of light. Here instead of impressionism and impassibility his readers rediscovered with delight the logic and humanity of the traditional novel, the rationalism of its psychological analysis tempered by sensibility. With a profound understanding of the contemporary state of mind, M. Bourget in his fiction discreetly reminded his public of the marvellous potentialities of the spirit in its eternal battle with the animal instincts, emphasising once more the fact that the essence of human life is its complexity, and implying that although it may indeed be a *cruelle énigme* it is precisely this enigmatic quality which lends savour and joy to existence.

In *Cruelle Énigme* and in *André Cornélis* it really seemed as if M. Bourget, by reviving the novel of psychological analysis, had inaugurated a new and fruitful period of development in French fiction. *André Cornélis* in particular justified this assumption by its masterly dissection of motives and sentiments, the well-knit texture of its drama, and above all by the author's superb gift for creating that illusion of duration which M. Bourget, acute critic of his own art, has called "the transcription of time." *Le Disciple* (1889), however, revealed him in his true rôle of social reformer and doctrinaire, a rôle which he has never since abdicated, with regrettable consequences to his art. For it must be admitted that, from however admirable motives, he has thus imposed a grave handicap on his undoubted talent. In those excellent *Nouvelles Pages de Critique et de Doctrine* (1895) M. Bourget invokes the name of Balzac to justify his own artistic procedure, and attempts to prove that like Balzac he writes not "thesis" novels but *romans à idées*, since, as he alleges, they are not constructed to demonstrate an *a priori* conviction. Now, with all possible deference to M. Bourget's skill as a craftsman, this is precisely the characteristic defect of nearly all his fictions. For there is an immense difference between having what Balzac calls "a decided attitude towards human affairs, an absolute devotion to principles," and the didactic attitude of M. Bourget himself in *Le Disciple*, *L'Étape*, *L'Émigré* and *Un Divorce*. If we draw a parallel with a novelist whom M. Bourget resembles much more closely than he does Balzac, namely Stendhal, we have only to re-read *Le Rouge et le Noir*, so absolutely free of any didactic intention, to realise the relative inferiority of *Le Disciple*. Robert Greslou is an incredible, Julien Sorel a perfectly credible monster. And if we seek the reason why Julien Sorel, whose conduct if judged by ordinary standards is completely abnormal, should yet strike us as absolutely probable, it is because Stendhal presents him as an individual and not, as does M. Bourget with Greslou, as the living symbol of a philosophic system. After all, in every *roman à thèse* the personages are not so much characters as symbols of ideas, symbols by means of which the author proves infallibly, to his own satisfaction and the reader's irritation, that the future salvation of France depends on a return to monarchism, catholicism or tradition. It is true that M. Bourget is too fine an artist to ignore the value of a dramatic plot, but his dénouements, logical as they appear at first sight to be, are nevertheless essentially artificial because the characters develop, not according to their own nature, but in obedience to an external authority which is the author's thesis. The life that he presents is not life as it is but as M. Bourget thinks it ought to be. Nearly all his works reveal this incessant struggle between the great novelist he might have been and the conscientious social reformer that he is. A striking example of this is to be found in the characterisation of the abbé Fauchon in *Le Démon de Midi* (1914). A scrupulous and clever psychologist, M. Bourget presents a vivid picture of a priest who is led by his study of the gospels to the conviction that the Church is wrong to forbid the marriage of its clergy. Quite suddenly, and with a remarkable absence of logic, the psychologist makes way for the doctrinaire, and the gentle, cultured scholar is transformed into a sexual maniac who brutalises his wife, gnaws his food like an animal, and is only just prevented from committing murder. Fauchon, it is only fair to say, is an extreme example of M. Bourget's didactic manner, yet in a lesser degree the same perversion of reality by the *idée fixe* is evident in all his work after 1890. M. Bourget's ideas may be very sound, but that is not the point: it is rather that he uses the novel as a vehicle for their dissemination. The function of the novelist is not to convert us to his social or political opinions, but to interpret life by offering an imaginary though credible picture of its complexities.

The work of M. Bourget, then, marks no intrinsic progress in the evolution of fiction: on the contrary, rather, it marks a return to the manner of the eighteenth-century *philosophes*. By reviving the public taste for the traditional novel of analysis with its clear-cut dramatic plot he checked, however, the disintegrating influence of impressionism and drew attention to the fact that life is not entirely a procession of physical adventures. For this he deserves unqualified praise. Yet, by making his novels mere pretexts for social and political propaganda, he reverted to the level of works like *Les Lettres de Valmont*, except of course that M. Bourget's theses are presented with much greater skill and plausibility, since this ex-pupil of Taine and Spencer remains scientific even in his attacks on Positivism. Like Zola, M. Bourget regards himself as a writer with a mission, a moral and spiritual surgeon, and that is undoubtedly the source of his weakness, for whilst the novelist in the course of his survey of life must inevitably explore and reveal its social evils, it is hardly his business to propose remedies and solutions.

What revolted Anatole France in the Naturalists even more than their solemn and grotesque scientism was their inveterate Philistinism. Certainly no one can say of the author of *L'Histoire comique*, of *Crainquebille* or of *Les Dieux ont Soif* that he recoils before the realities of life. Yet in all his works he has triumphantly proved in the teeth of Naturalism that one can remain a Realist and still preserve the æsthetic qualities of the French masters, their harmony and chastity of form, temperance of imagination, and, above all, their wise and sure sense of human values. Anatole France is not a great creative novelist. He has not, like Balzac or Flaubert, the dæmonic gift of self-hallucination which hurls a novelist outside his own personality; the divine insanity of imagination which fuses his existence with that of his creations. Rather he belongs to the school of the eighteenth century of which Lesage and Voltaire are the great examples. In an article to the *Revue de l'Exposition universelle* (1889) De Maupassant neatly summarises the characteristics of these writers, and almost every word serves to describe the manner of Anatole France:

> Les hommes de cette école, artistes, aristocrates, ont surtout la préoccupation de nous rendre visibles leur art et leur talent, leur ironie, leur délicatesse, leur sensibilité. Ils les dispersent à profusion autour des personnages fictifs, des automates qu'ils imaginent.

Except for Voltaire it would be hard to find a writer who so flagrantly yet with what charm transforms the novel into a medium for the expression of his casual ideas on art, religion and philosophy. For there is no doubt that Anatole France's most interesting works are those in which the author himself, behind the transparent mask of a Bergeret or a Coignard, holds us spell-bound by the delicious irony of his commentaries on men and things and by the limpid ripple of his beautiful French. After all, provided that Bergeret and Coignard will simply go on talking, does it really matter what happens to them?

We are not interested in their destiny. They are but the reflectors of the author's opinions; spectators and not actors in the drama of life. So if, as it sometimes happens—witness the case of Bergeret—they open the wrong door and are suddenly faced with what might be called a critical situation, we must not be surprised if instead of treating us to the spectacle of a *crime passionnel* they gently close the door again on reality. Events, in Anatole France's world, are not dramatic in themselves but only if we make them so. Life is tense and critical only to the Romantic. Are not those excellent philosophers, Coignard and Bergeret, there to prove the fact? Circumstances which would cause a psychological upheaval in the ordinary man, or at least offer him food for furious meditation, hardly dent the armour of their disillusioned philosophy. There is something not indeed Balzacian, but almost so, in the art with which Anatole France lends the colour of probability to these monsters of equanimity. What preserves them from seeming utterly unreal is their quiet but intense hatred of injustice and their wistful pity for suffering humanity.

The novels of Anatole France, rich as they are in digressions on æsthetic and philosophic matters, cannot be called great examples of the novelist's art. None of his characters display an understanding of the intricacies of the human soul comparable to that evinced by a Stendhal or a Flaubert. Even in the *Histoire contemporaine* (1897–1901), where he follows and at times recalls Balzac, the web is loosely, even carelessly, woven. He cannot, like Balzac, picture the havoc which a passion can produce in the fabric of society. Anatole France is primarily an historical novelist. Few writers have possessed his veneration for the past, his power of resuscitating its spirit. In this he was aided by his amazing erudition, by a peerless faculty of synthesis and an unerring *flair* for the essential, significant trait. His versatility in this respect is incredible, for whether he evokes the soul of ancient Greece as in *Thaïs*, of eighteenth-century France as in *La Rôtisserie de la Reine Pédauque*, or of the Revolution as in *Les Dieux ont Soif*, always he displays the same nonchalant grace and power of persuasion. Perhaps his masterpiece is *La Rôtisserie*, one of the finest historical novels ever written. Here there is complete fusion of the author's personality and the subject. The local colour is perfect down to the minutest detail of language and gesture. The whole social history of eighteenth-century France is crystallised in this marvellous book.

The tendencious quality of his combative novels, of which the most typical is *L'Ile des Pingouins*, detracts from their value as novels, though as polemics they retain a fine savour reminiscent of Voltaire in his happiest vein. One regrets, however, that Anatole France should have erected the *Histoire contemporaine* on the crumbling foundations of a political *cause célèbre*. Already the Dreyfus affair is fading into oblivion, dragging with it inevitably much of the interest of this admirable novel of manners.

Since his death Anatole France has been the subject of much hostile and ill-informed criticism, but, though it may seem premature to say so, he will face the verdict of posterity with smiling imperturbability. It sounds indeed like M. de la Palisse to assert that the *Crime de Sylvestre Bonnard* (1881), the *contes* and *La Rôtisserie* are already classics. So, too, wherever French is loved and taught future generations will inhale the perfume of sensibility and of beauty that cling to *Pierre Nozière* (1899), *Le Petit Pierre* (1918) and *La Vie en Fleur* (1925), for in these is to be found the supreme flowering of the Latin genius.

Le Lys rouge (1894) and the *Histoire comique* (1903), his least subjective novels, have not the same air of perennial freshness. The latter, despite its ironical, maliciously true picture of stage *mœurs*, is tinged with the sort of facile melodrama that spoils Zola's *Thérèse Raquin*. In the *Lys rouge* the interest lies not in the narrative of Mme Martin's amorous dilemma but in the author's exquisite appreciations of Florentine art. One feels here the limitations of Anatole France's psychology of love, which of course he conceives solely as voluptuousness. With rare art, indeed, he shows that sexual love can beget beautiful poetry. For him love "is full of meaning and of images. It is violent and mysterious. It attaches itself to the flesh and soul. The rest is illusion and lies." Yet in *Le Lys rouge* he completely fails to communicate the meaning and the mystery of which he speaks. Is not that perhaps because there is a spiritual element in love of which Anatole France with all his sagacity is wholly ignorant; something that greater novelists like Balzac and Prévost have not found to be "illusion and lies"?

The work of Anatole France and of M. Bourget seemed to foreshadow a return to Classicism. To quote M. Henri Bordeaux, who is one of M. Bourget's most faithful disciples:

> The positivist renascence was bound to lead to a renascence of Classicism by taking us out of individual life and showing us that social, like physical life is subject to laws—invisible laws which we must discover and accept under pain of losing our health and of falling into a decline. The order, the harmony, the measure, and the clarity which good taste half-revealed to us, these are the virtues of our Classic literature—and, in addition, the sense of observation and of social life. There are a few of us who to-day are trying to practise them. For us the social novel towards which our contemporary literature is leading can only be the novel of manners, the equivalent of Classic tragedy. . . . We love life in its manifold forms and yet we are not unaware of a Romantic nostalgia some fragment of which we think we can immobilise in the work of art.

A future generation will define with some degree of assurance what were the main directions followed by the novel of the early years of the twentieth century. Already, however, it seems clear that in style impressionism was going out of favour, having yielded to a general desire for Classic order and harmony. The vogue for impassive art, too, was past, and the profound influence exercised by the English and Russian novelists suggested a type of novel combining both realism and sensibility. Maurice Barrès, discovered and praised by M. Bourget in the last years of the nineteenth century, had stirred the younger generation with his *Jardin de Bérénice*, the third of an ideological trilogy devoted to the cult of the *moi*. For a time it appeared that he was to institute a Romantic revival, though Barrès was careful to point out that by the *culte du moi* he meant, not a return to the anti-social individualism of Sand, but, on the contrary, an effort to "conciliate the necessities of the inner life with the obligations of active existence on the one hand and on the other an act of submission before the Subconscious which may be called the Divine." In his *Roman de l'Énergie nationale*, composed of *Les Déracinés* (1897), *L'Appel au Soldat* (1900) and *Leurs Figures* (1902) Barrès's doctrine reveals itself as race individualism or—to use a word which he invented — nationalism. A fine stylist, if turgidly lyrical on occasion, Barrès in his novels is openly a doctrinaire, so that their interest is largely historical. However, in *Les Déracinés* he has shown that had he chosen to project his creations against a more permanent background than that of local politics we might have been the richer for a vast and strong study of contemporary manners in the vein of *L'Éducation sentimentale*.

At first glance a wide gulf appears to separate Barrès from Paul Adam, who, we observed, was convinced that the *moi* had been analysed in fiction to the point of exhaustion. Adam, it will be recollected, was a Symbolist who strayed for a time in the labyrinth of the Occult. His dream, and he tried to express it in a series of historical frescoes, was to evolve a symbolic or synthetic novel embracing all the contributions made by Romantics, Realists, Naturalists, Symbolists, Psychologists and Neo-Realists. The analysis of the individual was to yield to the study of crowds viewed as collective individuals. Such a novel, he asserted, would produce a new type of emotion, intellectual and æsthetic, in any case vastly superior to that inspired by the old novel of sentimental analysis.

Adam's achievement falls much below his ambition. His style, too, is precious and repellent. Yet his idea of a synthetic novel is full of interest, because it shows the continuation of a movement, commenced by Zola, leading away from the analytic novel. It is curious also to note that Adam and Barrès, starting from different poles, advance towards the conception of a racial novel where, to quote the words of the latter, the individual is most truly himself when he consents to be "un moment de sa patrie et de sa race." Without great surprise, therefore, we find Adam in his later works exalting the rôle played by the Latin genius in world civilisation. Louis Bertrand, in his *Sang des Races* (1899), is inspired by the same idea, which he develops in his highly coloured if somewhat academic studies of Algerian manners and history. This rebirth of the national consciousness, comparable to our Kiplingism, cropped up in various ways. One can discern it in the social and didactic works of M. Henri Bordeaux, who, dogging the footsteps of M. Bourget, emphasises in *La Peur de vivre* (1902) and in *Les Roquevillard* (1906) the need for a French reaction against the disintegrating effect of foreign culture. His favourite theme, and that of M. Bazin's *Les Oberlé* (1901), is the solidarity of the family, regarded by both as the social unit.

To find the genesis of this reflorescence of nationalism in France we must go back to the last years of the nineteenth century. In the name of what they called Naturism, a group of young men, poets and novelists, protested against the mystic and decadent idealism of the Symbolists. In a review entitled the *Documents sur le Naturisme*, which was the precursor of a dozen organs of like tendency, they denounced the excesses of Symbolism — its esoteric and archaistic pretensions and above all its cosmopolitanism, for the Symbolists like nearly all decadents were noisily international. In poetry, for example, they led the revolt against the art of Hugo and of the Parnassians; in painting, all their admiration was for the Pre-Raphaelites; in music for Wagner; in the novel for the Russians and in drama for the Scandinavian theatre. Fundamentally opposed to these were the ideas of the Naturists. "Our elders," wrote one of their leaders, Maurice Leblond, "preached the cult of the unreal, the art of dreams, the search for new sensations. They loved venomous flowers, darkness and phantoms, and they were incoherent spiritualists. The Beyond does not excite *us*: we believe in a gigantic and radiant pantheism. Ah! how insipid and puerile these people seem to us with their little sadisms and their little crises of asceticism. . . . We are going back to Nature. We seek a healthy and divine emotion. What do we care for art for art's sake?" In what directly concerned the novel the Naturists marked a return to tradition. "The great merit of the Naturist generation," again to quote Maurice Leblond, "was to have understood that the individual is nothing if he is not above all a man of his time, attached to his race by strong traditions; and the 'accidents of time or of epoch,' instead of being negligible 'contingencies,' remain on the contrary essentials." In general, then, the Naturists were inspired by a profound love of national art and culture. As novelists they formed no definite school. In the words of Eugène Montfort, each one "tried to see life and to depict it according to his individual temperament or capabilities." Naturism is therefore best described as one of the literary expressions of a new and wide-spread national consciousness. In its last analysis this process of regeneration was an idealistic revolt against the positivism of the nineteenth century. However, as can be seen from the pronouncements of the Naturists, there was no danger of "a return to Nature" in the Rousseauistic sense. Naturism was not Romanticism, but rather an effort to arrive at a compromise between the extremes of Idealism and of Realism: in a word, it was a form of Neo-Classicism. The Naturists were profoundly national. Traditionalists, they wished to restore to the French novel certain qualities that had largely disappeared from it under the naturalistic regime—simplicity and clarity of style, naturalness and sympathy of out-look upon life, sensibility and even lyricism of expression. There was nothing iconoclastic in their ambitions. M. Bourget, Anatole France and Maurice Barrès had reflected a similar spirit in all their works. Even Zola in his interview with Huret had expressed the hope that the novel of the future would reveal "a larger picture of truth, a broader outlook on humanity, a sort of naturalistic Classicism." The Naturists, if one may repeat what has already been said, did not as novelists compose a large or homogeneous group, though as poets they formed a definite school. Subsequent movements, the *École française*, the Humanists led by Fernand Gregh, the *Renaissance classique* headed by M. Bertrand, advocated principles which were fundamentally those of the Naturists. And if at this point the latter bulk rather largely in this discussion, it is simply because their doctrines summarise and reflect somewhat concisely those ideas which in a general way governed the procedure of a great many novelists writing between 1890 and 1914. Few of these followed the original Naturists in all their views, but most of them had a respect for the traditional qualities of the French novel. They strove to achieve purity and lucidity of style and as a rule revealed a keen architectural sense in their construction of plot and character. None, in any case, betrayed the slightest desire to return to the *art impassible* of the Zolaists, though there were several, like Paul Adam and the Tharaud brothers, who were a little alarmed lest Naturism might degenerate into sentimentality. To some extent such fears were not unjustified. In the *Enquête* carried out by MM. Le Cardonnel and Vellay in 1905, one can discern in the replies of a Charles-Louis Philippe, a Delbousquet or a Charles-Henri Hirsch a distinct inclination to glorify the instinct at the expense of the reason, though indeed they are careful to emphasise the necessity for scrupulous observation. Charles-Louis Philippe, the author of *Bubu de Montparnasse* (1901), an admirable and sympathetic study of the relations between a pimp and a prostitute, wrote exclusively of the humble. Yet, in dealing with a corner of life which the Naturalists had so to speak annexed and had certainly explored most exhaustively, Philippe, by his intuitive and "unscientific" method of approach, discovered much that was new and interesting. He was a passionate admirer of Russian art, particularly that of Dostoïeffsky, from whom he acquired the conviction that the novelist, if he will surprise the inner truth of life, must "describe his characters as he would himself." He must, above all, says Philippe, "love his creations, or hate them—which amounts to the same thing." This gifted writer died before attaining maturity, but what he wrote was enough to create a vogue for this type of novel. Henri Bachelin, more objective and indeed somewhat inclined to smile at Philippe's enthusiasm for his subjects, has given us, in *Le Serviteur* (1919) and in *Le Village* (1919), a moving yet faithful picture of peasant life in Le Morvan. Pierre Hamp, the author of *Marée fraîche*, *Vin de Champagne* (1913), which open the cycle called *La Peine des Hommes*, is less concerned with the analysis of individual characters. His aim is rather to offer a synthetic impression of modern industrial life, and by revealing its mechanism to remind us of the toil and suffering involved in the production of the luxuries which the wealthy regard as daily necessities. It would be unjust at this stage not to indicate the debt owed by these writers to the older novelists like Octave Mirbeau and Lucien Descaves, deserters both from the camp of Zola. Lucien Descaves, one of the signatories of the famous manifesto, made his name with *Sous-Offs* (1889), a graphic study of the miseries of life in the ranks in peace time that aroused a storm of indignation. Like Octave Mirbeau, he is a passionate champion of Socialism, as can be seen in *La Colonne* (1901), an historical novel dealing with the events of the Commune. Time has somewhat cooled his ardour, but he is still ready to devote his pen to the cause of justice. Octave Mirbeau, another doughty Socialist, is better remembered for his work as a journalist and dramatist. His *Journal d'une Femme de Chambre* (1900) nevertheless reveals a novelist of great expressive power and accuracy of observation. Up to his death in 1917, Mirbeau's polemical violence and Tolstoian socialism left its mark on a whole school of younger novelists. These, with more objectivity than their master, have continued the manner of Mirbeau and of Philippe. They are not Naturalists, for, though they write of the under-dog, they manage to do so with understanding born of true sensibility, and in language not only convincing but dignified.

The novels of the late René Boylesve illustrate in a very striking fashion what could be achieved by a faithful disciple of Naturism. In *Mademoiselle Cloque* (1899), *La Becquée* (1901) and in *L'Enfant à la Balustrade* (1913) this delightful poet and sure observer demonstrates that Idealism and Realism are but different aspects of reality. There is not a trace of the didacticism of a Bordeaux or a Bazin in these wonderful evocations of Touraine life. And just because of this, he interprets with much more lucidity the tangle of complexities, the backbitings, the thwarted ambitions and unrecorded heroisms that compose provincial life. In mutely splendid contrast to his picture of human pettiness and folly we are conscious always in Boylesve's novels of that supreme loveliness which Nature has bestowed upon lovely Touraine. Some critics have accused René Boylesve of overmuch idealism, but surely this is because they have never tasted that ideal reality, that marvellous elixir made up of light, colour and perfume which for lack of a nobler word one must call the atmosphere of Touraine. Writers like Boylesve are the glory of France, for in them the national spirit finds its most artistic and most sympathetic expression. A Barrès may sometimes alienate us by the exclusiveness of his fervour, but not so a Boylesve, whose love for his native province does not obscure the clearness of his vision. It is thanks in great part to the success of his works that we possess that wealth of regionalist novels with which the twentieth century has so generously enriched the coffers of French literature. The *romanesque* survey map of England, in spite of the admirable achievement of Mr. Arnold Bennett, of Thomas Hardy, and of Miss Sheila Kaye-Smith, is as yet far from complete: in France, on the other hand, it is questionable whether a single square inch of territory has been left unexplored by the novelist. And more surprising still is the high quality of these regionalist novels, very few of which do not bear the double imprint of sincerity and spontaneous talent.

There is another domain of fiction where the French in recent years have challenged our supremacy and possibly outstripped us. The colonial expansion that followed the Franco-Prussian war favoured the development of exoticism in the novel. But where Loti confined himself largely to Japan and Turkey, his successors without moving outside French territory, have discovered a foison of material. Claude Farrère, in *Les Civilisés* (1905), has produced an acrid and unforgettable picture of colonial life in Saigon, and in *La Bataille* (1909), a study of racial contrasts scarcely inferior to his masterpiece. Jean Ajalbert's *São-Van-Di* (1905), *Raffin-Su-Su* (1918), contain unique and interesting commentaries on Indo-Chinese manners. Henri Daguerches contrives to rival Kipling in his *Le Kilomètre* 83 (1913). Kiplingesque, too, is Pierre Mille in the *Barnavaux* series, where he initiates us into the life of the French colonial soldier and incidentally creates an enduring type. M. Nau, in his *Force ennemie* (1903), and other novels of Martinique; the brothers Leblond in their stories of Tunis and Madagascar; Robert Randau, a native Algerian, in his *Colons* (1907), and a hundred other equally able authors, are busily cultivating this attractive type of novel, the vogue for which shows no sign of declining. Here, as in the novel of adventure, which is so often combined with the exotic novel, the influence of Kipling and of Stevenson has been very marked, and a large bibliography would be insufficient to include the names of those who have followed in the wake of Pierre MacOrlan (*Le Chant de l'Équipage*), Alain-Fournier (*Grand Meaulnes*), Pierre Benoît (*Atlantide*) and Philippe Soupault (*A la Dérive*).

This florescence of exotic, colonial and adventure novels is not merely the symptom of an acute attack of nationalism but of something intimately concerned with the art of the novel. As M. Jean Muller has clearly shown in his suggestive *Le Roman* (1913), the work of novelists like Paul Adam, Louis Bertrand and Claude Farrère points the way to a synthetic or epic sort of novel where the intention is to portray characters not as individuals but as the representatives of their race. And after all, does it not almost inevitably follow that the hero of the exotic novel, from the very fact that he is isolated from the men of his own race, will acquire a factitious and even epic stature? It is because of this that the central figure of *Robinson Crusoe*, the prototype of all such works, is such an arresting character. Defoe does not need to analyse the psychology of his hero: it is enough for us that Crusoe is a synthesis of human energy, courage and intelligence. The French "racial" novelists of the twentieth century are therefore but elaborating an idea which Defoe was the first to realise in fiction. Paul Adam expressed it when he maintained that the *moi* had been over-analysed in the novel. In that of course he was wrong, for M. Bergson has shown us that we are just beginning to glimpse the complexities of the human soul. However, there is no reason to suppose that the synthetic novel cannot pursue its evolution without in the least hindering the expansion of the novel of analysis.

J.-H. Rosny in his stories of primitive life, *Vamireh* (1892), *Eyrimah* (1895) and *La Guerre du Feu* (1911), evolved an original variety of synthetic novel where, by situating his heroes in a milieu outside the factors of time and civilisation, he invests them with a new and mysterious personality. It is doubtful, however, whether this prehistoric species of novel, by its very nature essentially imaginative, will hold a durable appeal for a generation like ours, which has been inoculated at birth with a veneration for "documented" fiction. M. Rosny and his imitators, who are well aware of this fact, have always tried therefore to lend their fictions a scientific flavour, and this, one cannot but feel, is an error, since it removes something of that fine romantic bloom which is the distinctive and charming feature of such stories.

To some extent, then, Zola's prophecy that the novel of the future would present "a larger outlook on humanity" has been fulfilled. Certainly in the works of Adam and Bertrand, in the numerous colonial and exotic novels, not to mention M. Rosny's "cosmic" experiments, one can note a distinct effort to enlarge the cadre of the genre. There is a growing tendency to present a synthetic type of hero incarnating the passions and sentiments not merely of an individual but of a race. And there is every indication of new and interesting developments in this direction. After all, no novelist has yet given us an Everyman! Several factors conspire to favour the evolution of such a novel. With the increasing perfection of our means of communication, for example by radio and aeroplane, we are being slowly obliged to readjust our former ideas of time and space and, as a result, our old conception of human nature. Thanks to the world-wide popularity of the cinema it will soon be possible for the average man, both reader and novelist, to take a more intelligent interest in foreign *mœurs* and psychology. The modern cosmopolitan novel indeed marks a notable advance on the old-style fiction, where a foreigner was always an eccentric or a half-wit. Already there are signs that the *Goddam* Englishman with checked cap and enormous brier is out of date in French literature. Nor are there many English novelists who still cling to the fallacy that Frenchmen sport the glossy silk hat, the cloak and imperial of the Second Empire, or address their Fifi as "my little cabbage."

It may be argued on *a priori* grounds that it is impossible to evolve a racial novel, since there is no such person as a typical Englishman, Frenchman or German. In a sense this is doubtless true because, if we view a man in relation to his compatriots, his racial characteristics are invisible since they are submerged in a mass of personal or individual traits. Yet if, like the racial novelist, we project him into a new and larger milieu, isolating him for the moment from the men of his own culture and tradition, undoubtedly he will display another self and one which is predominantly racial and not peculiarly personal. This is what Alphonse Daudet did in *Numa Roumestan*, and his procedure has been successfully imitated by subsequent novelists.

Broadly speaking, there are two categories of racial novel, and for convenience we may call them subjective and objective. In the former, in that cultivated by Kipling, Bertrand and Pierre Mille, the hero incarnates the writer's own nationalism. The second, or objective species of racial novel, is on the contrary quite free from lyricism of this kind, since the author's sole preoccupation here is to penetrate and to interpret the psychology of a foreign race. Such is the attitude of the Tharaud brothers in *Dingley* (1906), in *La Randonnée de Samba Diouf* (1922), in *La Fête arabe* (1912) and in *Le Royaume de Dieu* (1920), excellent studies of English, Negro, Arab and Jewish manners, composed in a cool, pellucid style that perpetuates the authentic spirit of French Classicism.

Whatever name one cares to give such novels—ethnological, racial or cosmopolitan—it is fairly obvious—if we ignore certain surface differences of technique—that all betray a common desire to offer a more spacious interpretation of man's nature and environment. None, however, attempt to break away from the "documentary" method of the Realists since, though their heroes gain in stature by their translation to a larger cadre, and so to speak become more epic, the background against which they are projected is still that of historic fact.

It is precisely this respect for facts of which M. André Gide complains in his *Faux-Monnayeurs* (1926) when he advocates a return to the abstract and universal art of the seventeenth-century dramatists. He writes:

> And I am speaking not merely of the French novel. Just like the English novel, the Russian novel, however free of restraint it may be, is a slave to resemblance. The only progress which it foresees is to approach more closely to the natural. The novel has never known that 'formidable erosion of contours' of which Nietzsche talks, and that deliberate turning away from life which gave style to the works of the Greek dramatists, for example, or to the tragedies of the French seventeenth century. Do you know anything more profoundly human than these works? But precisely, they are human only because they are profound; they do not pride themselves on appearing

human, or at any rate they do not pretend to be real. They remain works of art. . . . Sometimes it seems to me that there is nothing which I admire so much in literature as, for example, in Racine, the discussion between Mithridates and his sons, where we know perfectly well that never could a father and his sons have talked in this way, and where nevertheless all fathers and all sons can recognise themselves. By localising and specifying, one restricts. There is no psychological truth which is not, of course, particular, but there is no art that is not general. The whole problem is there exactly: to express the general by the particular and to make the general express the particular.

Dans les romans il faut peindre plus grand que nature. Barbey D'Aurevilly's phrase gives somewhat more tersely the gist of M. Gide's theory of art, which has the merit of being not very revolutionary if it is not very new. One might pertinently ask M. Gide what Balzac, Stendhal and Barbey D'Aurevilly have done if not to express the general by the particular and the particular by the general. But M. Gide would probably retort that a Grandet, a Julien Sorel or an abbé de Sombreval are still too close to the natural, too localised, to fit his conception of a type. His ideal, if we may judge from his *Porte étroite* (1909), is the *caractère* of French Classic drama stripped of all contingencies like time and space. "Nobody," I can hear M. Gide say, "cares how Phèdre is dressed or what her nationality is. Who is interested in the hundred petty details regarding her social milieu and her daily habits, details which the modern Realist would not fail to emphasise?"

Now, in theory, it seems perfectly simple to transpose a Classical tragedy into the form of a novel: in practice it is extremely difficult. M. Gide forgets that a great deal happens on the stage during the performance of a Racinian tragedy which is not to be found in the author's text. The physical appearance of the actress, her tone, gestures, facial expression, her silences, lend reality to the character and save it from becoming a mere intellectual abstraction. And all these elements, foreseen of course and provided for by the dramatist, who realised that his work is only complete when the curtain falls on its first performance,—these indispensable accessories contributed by the art of the actor, must be translated by the novelist in terms of *his* art, which is not identical with that of the dramatist. So, even if we take what is probably the closest approach ever achieved by a novelist to the method of Racine, *La Princesse de Clèves*, it is clear that Mme de Lafayette, for all her skill, cannot avoid "localising" her drama, which would otherwise seem almost unreal. Racine, too, for that matter used an historical cadre, a conventional one, it is true, for none of his audience really believed in the authenticity of his Greeks and Romans. One can readily sympathise with M. Gide's Symbolistic leanings and his anxiety to be rid of trammels like documentation, local colour and other Realist stock-in-trade, so as to concentrate solely on what he calls the "inner essence" of his characters. But here what concerns us is not so much M. Gide's theory as his achievement. Has he in his novels enabled us to enter more deeply into the penetralia of the human mind?

Some thirty years ago M. Gide caused a great sensation by his *L'Immoraliste*. At that time the vice of sexual inversion, though adumbrated by Balzac in several of his stories, had never been made the leading theme of a novel. *L'Immoraliste* reads indeed like a sort of *Apologia pro pæderastia*, in which the author solicits our sympathy for the sinister catamite whose queer antics and reflections compose the action of the book. It is, however, quite impossible for the most unprejudiced reader to view with any interest, let alone sympathy, the so-called "problem" of Michel's existence, for strictly speaking it contains no problem, and consequently no drama. Starting from the theory that every act, however reprehensible from the point of view of ordinary morality, can be justified by sophists like himself, M. Gide tries to persuade us that there is tragedy in his hero's conflict with the social laws. Sometimes indeed such a conflict can be really tragic, as we have seen in the case of a René or an Obermann. But when he asks us to shed tears because society refuses to allow free play to the individualistic and vicious proclivities of an invert whose "problem" is pathological and not moral, M. Gide is guilty not only of indelicacy but of a rare lack of any sense of reality. And even were we to accept Michel as an objective, analytic study of an Immoralist and not as a modern variant of the Romantic *incompris*, he strikes us as essentially unreal. To take one instance, Michel, apparently for no motive whatever, conspires with his disreputable friends against his own steward to rob his own preserves. M. Gide, one must think, is convinced that he has presented here a significant and dramatic situation. But has he? Molière, it is true, makes Harpagon rob his own stables, and that is really dramatic, since it allows us to penetrate more deeply into the psychology of the miser. Michel's poaching of his own grounds, however, only confirms our already half-formed suspicion that he is a dangerous maniac who ought to be under restraint.

M. Gide imagines that the gravity of the subject elected by a novelist is a guarantee of his excellence as an artist, and the public for a time shared this illusion. The Biblical flavour of his style, less common in French than in English fiction, together with the earnestness with which he insists upon the necessity for raising the novel to a higher "moral plane," is apt to blind us to M. Gide's weakness as an artist. *La Porte étroite*, though, like all his work, it is well written, is very badly composed. Here indeed there is a problem, but it is too esoteric to have a universal appeal. Alissa, the heroine, who renounces her love in order to satisfy her mystic cravings, is an abnormal, interesting to the psycho-analyst but very far removed indeed from the classic types so sincerely admired by M. Gide.

In the *Faux-Monnayeurs* he returns to his favourite theme of inversion, to which, no doubt as an additional attraction, he appends a supplementary thesis on onanism. The *Faux-Monnayeurs* is a string of impressions, *à la Goncourt*, of various forms of juvenile and adult vice. It is rendered still more confusing by the fact that Édouard, the chief character and the author's mouthpiece, treats us to a running commentary on the novel as it proceeds, discusses the various personages and tells us what he proposes to do and never does. "I begin to discern what I might call the *sujet profond* of my book," says Edouard. "It is, it will be, of course, the rivalry between the real world and the image we have of it. The way in which the world of appearances imposes itself on us, the way we try to impose on the external world our peculiar interpretation, composes the drama of our life. The resistance of facts invites us to transport our ideal construction to our dreams, our hopes; to a future life where our belief is nourished by all our disappointments in this." More briefly, and perhaps more coherently expressed, the theme of M. Gide's book is Romanticism, which is precisely the painful awareness of the disparity between our picture of the world and its reality. Yet there is not one character in the *Faux-Monnayeurs* in which this Romantic malady is crystallised and reflected as it is in *Madame Bovary* or in *Le Rouge et le Noir*; and that is simply because M. Gide is not artist enough to penetrate beneath those superficial realities that he mistakes for the "inner essence" of human nature.

M. Gide has made a feeble attempt to apply to the novel the discoveries made by M. Bergson in regard to the rôle of the subconscious—that obscure, mysterious other self lurking beneath our conscious one, and through whose mazy caverns we are sometimes privileged to wander when Sleep has drugged the watchful sentinels, Memory and Intelligence. To Marcel Proust the subconscious is our true self, our authentic ego. It is the hidden treasure house of our real and vital impressions, more real and more vital than those that can so easily and so mechanically be summoned up by the voluntary memory because they have sunk so deeply into the depths of our being. But it is not merely in sleep that these experiences succeed in detaching themselves from the underworld of the subconscious. Frequently a chance sensation, a perfume, a sound, a contact will evoke from what we loosely and wrongly call the Past one of those submerged fragments of brilliantly and intensely lived life. And it is such fragments dug out of the very depths of that rich inner lode—our true self—that constitute for Proust the only true realities of life.

So we must regard his long novel, *A la Recherche du Temps perdu*, as the attempt of a great artist to evolve a new and more powerful instrument by which all of us may look at life in a new way, a magnifying glass thanks to which we may understand that what hitherto we took to be realities were not realities at all. And the literature, the art called "Realistic" is, says Proust, entirely false because it confines itself to the notation of conscious impressions:

> The literature which is content to decimate things, to give only a miserable summary of lines and surfaces, is that which, though it calls itself realistic, is farthest removed from reality, that which impoverishes and saddens us most, for it abruptly cuts off all communication between our present self and the past, of which things have retained the essence, and from the future where they incite us to taste of it anew.

To quote Proust again:

> If reality were this sort of by-product of experience, almost identical for everyone—for when we say, bad weather, a war, a cab-rank, a lighted restaurant, a garden in flower, everybody knows what we mean; if reality were that, of course, a sort of cinematographic film of these things would be sufficient.

But, as he is never weary of repeating, it is hopeless to seek reality in this way. The vital realities lie hidden within us and are evoked by the most trivial things, so trivial indeed that our intelligence often ignores them. Yet we have all experienced, like Proust, the anxious insistence with which certain apparently unimportant things, a group of poplar trees, a chance phrase, the fleeting expression of a face, implore us not to forget them. But if we try to estimate their significance by the intelligence there is no logical reason why they should hold our attention for a moment. Why should the taste of a madeleine, the clank of a hammer on a wheel, the sensation of unevenness in the flagstones in the baptistery of St. Mark's Cathedral, so burrow themselves into Proust's subconscious mind that later, when evoked by an analogous sensation, the taste of another madeleine, the clink of a teaspoon, the act of stepping off the curb outside Mme de Guermantes's, they strike him with all the force of a spiritual revelation? It is because these material impressions are "fragments of existence abstracted from Time"; each one of them carries with it like an aura the self we were when it was first experienced by us. So, in Proust's marvellous but untranslatable words:

A certain name once read in a book contains between its syllables the swift wind that was blowing and the brilliant sun that shone when we read it. In the slightest sensation brought by the humblest article of food, the aroma of coffee, we find that vague hope of fine weather which so often smiled at us when the day was intact and full, in the uncertainty of a morning sky; a flash of light is a vase filled with perfume, with sounds, with moments, with varied humours, with climates. What we call reality is a certain affinity between these sensations and these memories which surround us simultaneously—an affinity suppressed by a mere cinema vision and which by that very fact diverges all the more from the truth because it claims to limit itself to the truth—a unique affinity which the writer must rediscover so as to enchain it for ever in two different terms. You can, in a description, achieve an indefinite succession of the objects which figure in the place described. The truth will only begin at the moment when the writer takes the two different objects, fixes their relationship, analogous in the world of art to what is the unique relationship of the causal law in the world of science, and when he encloses them in the necessary links of a fine style or else, as in life, when, bringing together qualities common to two sensations, he extracts their essence by uniting them both, so as to abstract them from the contingencies of Time, in a metaphor, and ties them together by the indescribable bond of an alliance of words.

This is the supreme achievement of Proustian art. It does not stop at the outward appearance of an impression, but dives deep into it as a bee into the calyx of a flower, sucking out its very essence: the outward impression, the glimpse of the name on a book, for example, or the aroma of coffee, is a mere symbol of a vaster reality.

For Proust the true reality of life is subjective and extra-temporal. We must not think of the past as divorced from the present, since each one of us carries the "past" in his subconscious mind, from which it emerges to the surface of the conscious self, bringing with it, like a water-spider with its crystal bubble of air, a whole milieu rescued from Time and replete with life that was really lived because it was profoundly felt. The true artist, therefore, is he who will find a way of imitating this trick of Nature's and of expressing this rhythmic interweaving of "past" and "present." Thus Proust tells why he knew the beauty of one thing long afterwards in another; why, for instance, he *realised* for the first time what noonday at Combray was in the sound of an electric bell, the mornings at Doncières in the gurglings of the radiator of his Paris flat, the death of his grandmother in the painful act of stooping to button his shoes. The genius of Proust, in order to express these realities, has created a style which, though at first it strike us as complicated, is actually the only skin that will fit the wrinkles of his thought.

Like Bergson, Proust jettisons the old mathematical conception of Time as something divided objectively into years, days, and hours, substituting for it what Bergson calls *durée mobile*. Mobile duration is Time measured from the subjective point of view of our individual consciousness, for which, as we all know, the term "an hour" may be hopelessly inadequate to indicate the duration of a state of soul which in reality may be much longer or much shorter. The whole of Proust's long novel, then, is an extraordinary *tour de force*, an unparalleled effort to see the world of men and things situated not in mathematical Time but in Bergsonian Time or Duration. Viewed thus, existence acquires a new aspect and becomes almost monstrously complex. In Proust's lapidary phrase, which closes the gigantic arch of *A la Recherche du Temps perdu*, he has tried to present "l'homme ayant la longueur non de son corps mais de ses années." There is another passage in *Le Temps retrouvé* where the author, discussing his regret for Albertine, accompanied as it is by a persistent jealousy even after her death, remarks that these sentiments, "which had already by their duration exceeded my most pessimistic anticipations, no doubt would never have changed much if their existence, isolated from the rest of my life, had been subjected only to the play of my memories, to the actions and reactions of a psychology applicable to immobile states, and had not been swept onwards towards a vaster system where souls move in Time as they move in Space." But the vital point for Proust is that these sentiments and passions cannot be isolated or detached from the rest of his *moi*. As the latter evolves in obedience to the law of life, his sentiments in regard to Albertine reflect the changing temperatures and climates of his soul. So Proust feels that to express the reality of his regret or of his jealousy he must resort to what he calls a "sort of psychology in space" different from the "plane psychology" of his predecessors. One must of course read his novel to understand how his psychology differs from that of novelists who see life in terms of conventional Time, and it is very difficult to express in a phrase what that difference implies. Perhaps it will be best illustrated by an analogy suggested by certain passages in Proust's own work. Everyone remembers, I fancy, those marvellous visions of a resurrected Nature where the hero describes the miracle of the steeples of Martinville witnessed from the Balbec train, or the headlong panicky flight, seen from a moving car, of the houses of Montsurvient scuttling madly away, clutching at their vines and roses. For Proust there is a similar *chassé-croisé*, a like changing of perspectives, in our psychological relations with our fellows. That is what he means when, for instance, he writes:

> We cannot narrate our relations with a being, however little we may have known him, without picturing the succession of the most different sites of our lives. Thus each individual—and I was myself one of these individuals—measured duration for me by the revolution he had accomplished not only round himself, but round others, and particularly by the positions he had successively occupied in relation to me.

A la Recherche du Temps perdu is an experiment in a new psychology, and represents therefore an advance in the art of fiction. The novelist, for Proust, is primarily a translator, an interpreter whose function it is "to seek beneath matter, beneath experience, something different." And this is the key to Proust's method of notation, since it explains the fascination of his picture of aristocratic Parisian society from the eighties to the present day. His characters acquire a startling vividness, emerging, as it were, in volume. If we look at a photograph with the naked eye and then through a stereoscope we have a very feeble idea of the difference between a character presented by a novelist of the old school and as revealed by Proust. The complexity of the world appears in a new light, and where a Balzac showed the social interdependence of human beings Proust lays bare the myriad filaments, hitherto invisible, that link our souls. The great fallacy exposed by him is that we can observe life objectively or form an inkling of reality from appearances. Habit, passion, intelligence, amour-propre, erect a constant barrier between reality and our comprehension. Take as an illustration the hero's love for Albertine—one of the master-themes of this novel. To express the reality of that love Marcel (if we may for convenience give him Proust's name) burrows *underneath* the mass of impressions from which the "Realist" would disengage what he would call the life of these two. Yet, as we see from Proust's novel, he would be entirely wrong. To arrive at the true impressions one must, like Marcel, *decode* what we falsely call life, translate the appearances, since language, gestures and acts are nearly always expressed in a purely conventional form that does not at all correspond to reality. Habit disguises our sentiments, giving them a semblance of truth which we are prone to mistake for the truth itself. Like Marcel, we think that we know what people are and what they think, but that is usually, says Proust, because we are indifferent. Let love, or jealousy, which is the inevitable companion of love, fasten on our life and immediately the scales fall from the eyes of our intelligence. Then, like Marcel, we lift the veil of habit and discover to our grief and amazement that the soul of the woman we love is an uncharted sea of mysteries. Then, like him, we listen to the voice of intuition and, plunging deep within ourselves, look for those profounder impressions which are the only true ones.

Obviously, in making Albertine an invert Proust has taken an extreme case the better to reveal the rôle played by jealousy in love, the better to demonstrate that we can never "possess the contact of the loved one's being with every point of Time and Space." For Proust love is entirely subjective and never reciprocal. The woman is the screen on which we project our *moi*, the *negative* of our sensibility. In herself she is of secondary importance, since she is merely the vase which contains the essence of our ideal and not the essence itself. Love is "a sort of creation—of a supplementary person distinct from the one who bears the same name in society and the majority of whose elements are drawn from ourselves." It is an effort to externalise our ego, to find in some other person the reflection which our soul has projected in her. Hence the extraordinary desire of Swann to "know" Odette, a desire which is so strong that he marries this ex-cocotte—a social blunder of the crudest sort. Marriage divests her of that inaccessible element which for Proust is the life of love. Marcel's passion for Albertine derives from the same cause, but in her case the lover never succeeds in surmounting the barrier of ruse and lies that the woman instinctively erects between her secret self and Marcel's insatiable desire to know. And even after her death the enigma remains unsolved. At one juncture it seemed as if Marcel's knowledge of Albertine was complete, but suddenly a chance word, a reference to her relations with Mlle Vinteuil, opens a door through which he glimpses another Albertine. Now for the first time he knows the horrors of jealousy, a jealousy which can never be assuaged because it has for its object a rival with whom no man can compete.

No novelist, it is safe to say, has ever portrayed the passion of jealousy so luridly as has Proust in that triptych consecrated to the folly of Swann and the vices of Charlus and Albertine. By creating the two latter characters Proust has enlarged the contours of the novel, so as to include two new types. Abandoning for a time the exploration of his subconscious self, Proust gives full scope to his *pouvoir réfléchissant*, thanks to which we obtain in the character of Charlus a strange and terrible vision of the invert. The author does not of course enter into the ethical aspect of his subject, nor does he, like M. Gide, solicit our sympathy for a Charlus or represent him as a Romantic *incompris*. He shows us a tragic figure, a great artist afflicted by an incurable malady. One wonders why Proust, whose sense of proportion is so very delicate, should not have confined himself more exclusively to the Charlus who interests us most, the Palamède of the *salons*, where he terrorises all by his stupendous *morgue*, his dæmonic consciousness of superiority. A somewhat similar objection can be raised in regard to Albertine. Proust would reply no doubt that the creation of these two characters was for him a necessity. His study of love, as he conceives this passion, would have been incomplete had it failed to take into account these two abnormal aspects of it. To an expert in the art of analysis, of course, the psychology of the invert must have presented itself as a difficult and therefore a fascinating exercise. But, granting the skill with which Proust isolates the terrible and tragic elements of his theme, it occupies far too large a place in the novel. The result is that when he approaches what he would call the *côté Balzac* of the subject, the reader is left with the final impression that in the Faubourg Saint-Germain every other man or woman is a sexual pervert—which is obviously absurd.

Proust is beyond doubt the greatest literary psychologist whom we have yet encountered in fiction, and though his field of observation is limited to the aristocracy and the higher bourgeoisie, his power of penetration is unsurpassed. This picture of the manners of a social era which opens with the presidency of Macmahon and closes with the Great War is not merely a social document: it is an incomparable vision of the eternal passions and foibles of humanity. It was Diderot, was it not? who said that the great literary types should be revised every fifty years. After Molière, after Balzac and Flaubert, Proust has something new to tell us, something which affords us new food for meditation on the queerness of the animal, man. The profound truth that emerges from his characterisation is that in every man there is an arrant fool. Thus a Cottard can be a marvellous clinician but, outside his specialty, a complete *primaire* with the sense of humour of a child of ten; a Brichot—profound well of learning—is as ignorant of humanity as a cart-horse; Norpois, a magnificent diplomat of the old school, passes critical judgments on literature which would shame an undergraduate; Bergotte, an artistic genius of the first rank, tamely submits to the bullying of a Mme Verdurin, the supreme type of charlatan and *bas bleu*. A recent critic of Proust has uttered the amazing statement that his novel has no "philosophic background." How is it possible to follow the destinies of a Charlus, a Saint-Loup, a Mme Verdurin or a Morel; to attend a reception at the Guermantes'; to talk for an hour with Charles Swann or to listen to the conversation of the *clan* at La Raspelière, and not realise that we are witnessing a modern version of the eternal human comedy in the company of one of the greatest sceptics of our age. A more childish and, if anything, more inept reproach levelled at Proust is that he is a snob; that he has failed to explore the psychology of the lower classes. The author would reply that the subject of a novel is of little importance. The great artist, to borrow his phrase, "can make as precious discoveries in an advertisement for soap as in the *Pensées de Pascal*." And, as Proust turned away from the spectacle of human vanity and selfishness, racked with spiritual and physical suffering, he made what for him was his supreme discovery. It is that happiness is to be found only in Art, in the pursuit of that essential truth and beauty which all of us unconsciously extract from life and secrete in the cells within us. Most men, slaves of habit, seek the reality and the beauty of life in surface impressions, in the outward appearance of things. At times they are naïvely sad when these afford no lasting joy. The true philosopher, in Proust's eyes, is the artist who, like Elstir of the *Recherche du Temps perdu*, looks for the roses in that *jardin intérieur* which is in all of us if, like him, we will only cultivate it.

The world unfolded by Proust staggers us by its complexity as it astounds us by its beauty. Is not that because, half emerged from the age of rationalism, we have grown accustomed to expect simple and material explanations of life's deepest problems and lost to some extent the sense of wonder? As a corrective to this attitude of mind, as a reminder of the profounder and more richly coloured spiritual existence which underlies our rational one, the work of Proust has an enduring value. In *A la Recherche du Temps perdu* the great forces of Idealism and Realism meet and coalesce in a blinding flash through which the dazzled eye of the reader seems to behold the image of a living reality. One thing, however, is certain. It is that Proust's work signalises the complete overthrow of an old dogma; for never again, surely, can the novelist return to the nineteenth-century conception of a purely objective art, of a Realism which confines itself solely to the "scientific" notation of unidealised life.

INDEX

The principal references are indexed in black figures